HOW LEADERS CAN INSPIRE ACCOUNTABILITY

Three Habits That
Make or Break Leaders and
Elevate Organizational Performance

MICHAEL TIMMS

◆ FriesenPress

Suite 300 - 990 Fort St
Victoria, BC, V8V 3K2
Canada

www.friesenpress.com

Copyright © 2021 by Michael Timms
First Edition — 2021

All rights reserved.

The details in many of the stories shared in this book have been altered to preserve the anonymity of the persons involved

No part of this publication may be reproduced in any form, or by any means, electronic or mechanical, including photocopying, recording, or any information browsing, storage, or retrieval system, without permission in writing from FriesenPress.

ISBN
978-1-03-910229-3 (Hardcover)
978-1-03-910228-6 (Paperback)
978-1-03-910230-9 (eBook)

1. BUSINESS & ECONOMICS, LEADERSHIP
2. BUSINESS & ECONOMICS, DECISION-MAKING & PROBLEM SOLVING
3. BUSINESS & ECONOMICS, MANAGEMENT

Distributed to the trade by The Ingram Book Company

Praise for
How Leaders Can Inspire Accountability

"The ultimate guide for embracing accountability as a leader! Learn to create a culture for your team and company that inspires humble accountability and improves the trust and collaboration of all!"
– Marshall Goldsmith is the New York Times #1 bestselling author of Triggers, Mojo, and What Got You Here Won't Get You There.

"Accountability is a vital and rare differentiator of great leadership, which is why Michael Timms has written this important and timely book. I thoroughly recommend this book to every leader."
– Ed Sims, CEO, WestJet

"There is a gap in developing great leaders and Michael Timms has clearly found the bridge. The three habits of personal accountability will help anyone and everyone as it has certainly done with our leaders."
– Lawrence Eade, President, Purdys Chocolatier

"I have read many leadership books and this one for me is ground-breaking and has already changed my approach to leadership. I highly recommend this read not only to further develop your leadership acumen but to strengthen your relationships in all areas of your life."
– Patricia Jones, President and CEO, Calgary Homeless Foundation

"Michael Timms has created 3 simple success habits of personal accountability which is an invaluable resource for business leaders around the world."
– Nancy MacKay, CEO, MacKay CEO Forums

"The message of How Leaders Can Inspire Accountability elevates what people at Purdys are being asked to do: produce results, which is very different from completing tasks. It also shifts the communication from a competitive tone, focused on achieving department goals, to a cooperative tone, focused on achieving common goals. This principles in this book are as applicable to leadership as they are to our personal lives."

– Karen Flavelle, Owner & Chair, Purdys Chocolatier

"I could not put down Michael Timm's book 'How Leaders Can Inspire Accountability.' Michael challenges each of us as leaders to dig deeper in identifying what drives people to be accountable. From self reflection and feedback to engaging our employees to coming up with solutions; we can all inspire and influence accountability within our organizations."

– Lyn Krutzfeldt, President, Asura Health Services & AdvantAGE Assist Group

"If you're serious about increasing your organization's effectiveness, then you must read Michael Timms' 'How Leaders Can Inspire Accountability'. Michael distills his formula for leadership success into a practical approach based on three habits that will help to elevate organizational performance. The book is full of simple, practical tools and techniques that can encourage accountability and help ensure we set employees up for success. This should be required reading for new and experienced managers alike."

– Rob Miller, CEO, PRT Growing Services Ltd

"*How Leaders Can Inspire Accountability* is an effective business book that suggests means of developing work cultures focused on cultivating accountability. With its memorable mix of personal anecdotes and scholarly research, this is a grounded text. Easy to use and understand, this is a book marked by fun language that amplifies its points. It is confident in addressing the nuances of its difficult topic, ably imparting the notion that accountability is worth achieving, even if it takes hard work to do so."

– *Foreword* Clarion Reviews

"A lean, sharp, and readable leadership enhancement program."

– *Kirkus Reviews*

TABLE OF CONTENTS

    1. A Leader's First and Most Important Duty   1

Principles of Leadership 13
    2. What Is Accountability?   15
    3. Developing the Superpower of Systems Thinking   33
    4. Unraveling the Mystery of Leadership   45

Habit 1 – Don't Blame 55
    5. Blame Spawns Three Deadly Cycles   57
    6. Do You Have a Culture of Accountability
        or a Culture of Blame?   67
    7. Why Do We Blame?   75
    8. Wired to Blame, Not Explain   85
    9. How to Stop Blaming   91

Habit 2 – Look in the Mirror 99
    10. The Power to Overcome Our Problems   101
    11. We Aren't Very Self-Aware   115
    12. How to Look in the Mirror   129
    13. Heroes Look for Explanations, Not Excuses   149
    14. Accurately Diagnose Before You Prescribe   155

Habit 3 – Engineer the Solution 157
    15. Engineer Solutions to System Problems   159
    16. Strategy 1 – Make Reality Transparent   167
    17. Strategy 2 – Clarify the Critical Steps   181
    18. Strategy 3 – Automate the Right Behaviors   197
    19. Strategy 4 – Design the Environment   213
    20. Engineer the Solution to Set Others up for Success   223

    21. Putting the Three Habits Into Action   227

    Endnotes   241

Dedicated to the brilliant minds of Stephen R. Covey and Simon Sinek, who greatly influenced my thinking on leadership, and to the many other authors and researchers whose work laid the foundation for this book.

1. A Leader's First and Most Important Duty

Where have all the great leaders gone?

Abraham Lincoln is one of my favorite historical characters. While he was certainly not a perfect leader, the characteristics he possessed that enabled him to end slavery, win the Civil War, and endear himself to all who knew him are hard to find among the people who occupy some of the most prestigious leadership positions in business and government today.

Mahatma Gandhi, Martin Luther King Jr., Mother Teresa, and Nelson Mandela also come to mind as examples of great leaders. None of them were irreproachable, but they were all able to take an insult without responding in kind. They all demonstrated humility. Each of them put their mission and the needs of those they led above their own interests. They all tried to bring out the best in others while they accomplished their goals and achieved great things. Each of them strove to take a higher moral path than their detractors. Most importantly, each of these leadership exemplars worked on changing themselves first and improving their own character before they instructed anyone else on how to behave.

We all intuitively know these time-tested attributes of leadership are true. Why then are we able to point to so few examples of people in leadership positions who consistently behave this way? Where, indeed, have all the great leaders gone?

I have a theory about that. It is born out of the unique work I do with my clients.

I work primarily with senior management teams to help them create a culture that produces better leaders. One of the first things I do with my clients is help them establish a standard of leadership that becomes their "North Star," guiding them to a clear understanding of what good leadership looks like in their organization. Then we make this leadership standard the primary criteria for promotion to leadership positions.

Most organizations promote people to leadership positions based on technical ability, tenure, or the hiring manager's "gut feel." These are all poor predictors of leadership success. Instead, my clients have identified the few learnable behaviors that *they know* produce a disproportionately positive impact on people and results within their organization.

Now, before I continue, I need to clarify something. I don't help organizations come up with a laundry list of all the behaviors that characterize the perfect leader. That's what most organizations refer to as their "leadership competency model." Every leadership competency model I've ever seen reads like Dr. Frankenstein's instruction manual for assembling the perfect leader. Nobody, including the incumbent executives, could ever live up to the description of leadership that they use to evaluate others.

Instead, my clients ask their employees to be themselves and embrace their unique talents and non-talents that make them who they are. They just ask their employees to work on developing a few habits that, when added to their existing collection of unique strengths, will help them become exceptional leaders.

Not all good leadership behaviors produce an equally positive impact. Some leadership behaviors are more potent than others. I facilitate focus groups within client organizations to discover the highest-impact behaviors that consistently lead to successful outcomes. To accomplish this, we reverse engineer their organization's success stories to identify patterns of behavior that enabled or facilitated their successes.

Although similar themes inevitably emerge across various companies and industries, some leadership behaviors are more impactful in certain organizations depending on the nature of the work and the organization's culture. For instance, the highest-impact leadership behaviors at a high-tech company will likely be somewhat different from the highest-impact leadership behaviors at a social services non-profit organization. However, one leadership competency comes up *every single time* I work with focus groups regardless of the organization's size or industry: accountability.

This finding in itself is worthy of further investigation, but what's really interesting about this is that the idea of accountability as a key leadership competency tends to be discussed among focus groups in three distinctly different contexts.

1. Demonstrating personal accountability

2. Holding others accountable in a positive and uplifting way

3. Creating the conditions of organizational accountability

I regularly speak to CEO peer groups across the country. When I talk to them about accountability, I do a little experiment with them. I tell them that we only have time to discuss one of these three aspects of accountability and that I'd like to know which aspect they would prefer to learn about. What I *don't* tell them is that their responses will have no bearing on what I'm actually going to share with them. Then I ask them to select which aspect of accountability they want to learn about using a live polling app. The results are displayed on a monitor behind me.

You know which one they most often ask to learn about? It doesn't really matter because that's not the point. Before I ask them to vote, I already know which one they *won't* choose: demonstrating personal accountability. This is the last thing CEOs want to learn about when discussing accountability. Why do you think that is?

This brings me back to my original question: where have all the great leaders gone?

I am not suggesting that the thousands of CEOs to whom I have presented lack personal accountability. What I'm saying is that most leaders fail to realize that before they can instil accountability in others, they must become the supreme example of accountability within their organization. This is a leader's first and most important duty. No one will take ownership of results to a higher degree than their leader does. The behavior of those in leadership positions sets the standard of accountability for their organization, and most people in leadership positions can set a much higher standard; they just don't realize it. As Nobel Peace Prize winner Albert Schweitzer once said, "Example is not the main thing in influencing others. It is the only thing."

> No one will take ownership of results to a higher degree than their leader does.

Why Accountability Matters

A couple of years ago, I was working with a top-notch client organization that continually impressed me. The client was a group of car dealerships. Now, a group of car dealerships doesn't usually spring to mind as the type of company that's going to change the world, but you wouldn't know it from their mission statement. Selling cars is what they do, but their mission is to *make a meaningful difference in the lives of everyone they interact with*. That's a pretty lofty ambition for a bunch of car salespeople, but that's precisely what they believe they are doing. In fact, every employee I met could recite their mission statement by heart. Better yet, each one could tell me a story of how an employee recently fulfilled their company's mission.

For example, one employee saw a broken-down car on a bridge and noticed the dealership's logo on the licence plate holder. This employee immediately pulled over and arranged to have the car towed to the dealership at no charge. The employee fully understood the company's mission and took the initiative to fulfill it, even when he wasn't on the clock.

When working with this client, I also heard a story about how the VW dealership came together to fulfill a special request. A potential customer wanted a special edition Volkswagen Beetle, except the customer was a vegan, and she didn't want any leather in it. The problem was, special edition Beetles all come with a leather interior. Every other VW dealership in the country turned her down because, well, how in the world do you get the leather off a steering wheel and replace it with rubber? Nobody would have blamed them if they told her they couldn't do it, but this dealership's mission was to make a meaningful difference in the lives of others. So, a handful of employees took on the challenge to fulfill this client's wish, removed all the leather, and replaced it with cloth upholstery and synthetic trim.

It was evident that the CEO and the CFO were thoughtful, driven, caring people who made employee engagement a top strategic priority. This client is a great example of what I call a "purpose-driven and people-first" company.

However, one day when I was meeting with the whole senior management team, the CEO said something that really struck me. He said that although employee engagement scores were consistently high, he felt they were not translating that positive energy into achieving the results the organization was trying to achieve.

Then the CEO asked his senior managers to estimate how often they got the results they wanted. The room went silent. Finally, one senior manager spoke up. "I'd say we're about fifty-fifty." Most heads around the table nodded in agreement.

I'm not sure if my jaw actually dropped, but I was lost for words as I tried to reconcile how such an impressive organization in all other respects had such an abysmal goal-achievement rate.

Having a highly engaged workforce that understands the organization's mission and is committed to achieving it is generally regarded as the holy grail of leadership. And yet, this company of highly engaged, purpose-driven employees was missing their goals just as often as they were hitting them! How could this be?

Before you begin to suppose that this story is an anomaly, much research has confirmed that it is not. Numerous studies have shown that organizations only fully achieve their goals about 30–50 percent of the time. This is not because they are using bad strategies but because of their failure to consistently execute their strategies.[1, 2, 3, 4]

You may be wondering if this is also the case in organizations with a highly engaged workforce. Apparently so. The story about my dealership group client is similar to what I hear repeatedly in my consulting work (and I work with some great organizations). Organizations with highly engaged employees (according to their employee engagement scores) often fail to focus that positive energy into consistently achieving the organization's goals.

It's hard to believe, but organizations that report having high employee engagement still struggle with some of the following problems.

- Employees who say, "That's not my problem."
- Employees who bring most problems to their managers to solve.
- Employees who think providing excuses for poor results absolves them of accountability.
- Pointing fingers and passing the buck anytime something goes wrong.
- Lack of cooperation and teamwork within work groups.
- An "us versus them" mentality between departments and between corporate and field locations.
- Managers who don't address poor performance.
- Defensiveness when poor behavior or results are addressed.
- A constant feeling of being in firefighting mode and never having time to work on strategic work that will improve longer-term results.
- An unimpressive track record of achieving individual and organizational goals.

High employee engagement is an important factor that substantially increases an organization's odds of getting the right results, but employee engagement alone is not enough.[5] It is not enough simply to be a motivating leader; you also need to know how to create a culture of accountability that focuses people's positive energy on consistently producing the right results.

The reason we care about accountability is not so we can blame and shame people when they make mistakes. We care about accountability because we want to get the right results in the first place, and if we don't, we want to fix things to make sure we get the right results next time.

That is why we care about accountability. Accountability is the mechanism by which goals are consistently translated into desired results. Accountability is personal and organizational leverage.

> Accountability is the mechanism by which goals are consistently translated into desired results.

Three Problems of Creating a Culture of Accountability

Nathaniel is an electrical engineer who works for a large telecommunications company. He was hired right out of university and has been with the company for five years. Once or twice a year, Nathaniel and his work group are invited to a meeting ostensibly to talk about the company's values. Having seen this production several times before, he knows that the last value to be discussed at the meeting will be "accountability."

Management likes to leave accountability to the end so they can butter people up in the beginning with nice stuff like "integrity" and "respect" and then come down hard with the "accountability" hammer to drive the message home.

Nathaniel, and everybody else at the meeting who is not standing behind the podium, knows that this whole management song and dance is really just a theatrical way to present the "You're not doing enough to help the bottom line" show.

The director of customer service kicks things off with a speech about going the extra mile for customers and for the company. Doing so, he says, will help "strengthen our culture of accountability." Nathaniel misses the last couple of minutes of the director's monologue as the question "Did he just imply that we already have a culture of accountability?" rattles around in his brain.

When Nathaniel tunes back in, he realizes it's now the VP of HR speaking into the mic. She rails on and on about "acting like a team" and "helping out your teammates." With every inflection in her voice, Nathaniel feels as though she's poking him in the chest. Regardless of all her high-minded words, all Nathaniel hears is "You need to do better" over and over again.

Do better at what? Nathaniel wonders. *Besides, if it's a choice between helping my teammates and achieving my own goals, I'm going to choose achieving my goals every time to avoid the blame and punishment that's sure to follow if I don't.*

Next, the VP of operations gives a lifeless tribute to "taking initiative."

"Wait a minute," Nathaniel whispers to his neighbor, "are we still talking about accountability, or is this a different value?"

This is the first major problem with creating a culture of accountability: *there is no clear and generally accepted definition of accountability*.

Finally, the division president takes to the stage to rally the troops with a speech about "making personal sacrifices for the good of the company."

OK, that's the final straw. Nathaniel broods. *Isn't this the same guy who flies first class wherever he goes and who forced out the last director of operations who publicly criticized him for paying himself and the rest of the executive team a bonus the same year they laid off employees?*

This is the second major problem of creating a culture of accountability: *executives routinely behave in ways that directly contradict their message of accountability.*

When the meeting is over, Nathaniel and his workmates somberly shuffle back to their workspaces feeling unmistakably beaten with the accountability stick. As Nathaniel sits back down at his desk, he can't help but feel like he's done something wrong, but he doesn't know what. Despite having just endured a thirty-minute lecture about accountability, Nathaniel realizes he is no clearer about what specific things management wants him to do differently to be more accountable.

This is the third major problem organizations have with creating a culture of accountability: *nobody knows precisely what they must do differently to demonstrate accountability.*

Variations of Nathaniel's story have played out countless times in workplaces throughout the world. Management knows they want something more from their employees, but they can't articulate it, and they clearly aren't modeling it. If they were, there would be little need for the speeches.

Why This Book?

Leadership is becoming an empty promise—a quaint idea that has no bearing on our present reality. We've been told for decades about the incredibly positive influence that leaders can have on individuals and organizations, but most of us aren't seeing it. Sure, we occasionally hear stories in the media of great leadership; but then again, we also occasionally hear stories about UFO sightings. We'd like to believe that great leaders exist, but most of us, tragically, don't have any firsthand evidence that they do.

For years, those in leadership positions have been demanding more accountability from their followers. However, in their quest to get others to take ownership of results, most people in authority are oblivious to how they routinely set the opposite example when they: a) blame employees or circumstances for their problems, b) fail to acknowledge how they themselves are contributing to the organization's problems, and c) try to "fix" or fire people instead of fixing the systems within which their people work. These behaviors produce a predictable outcome: people who are more concerned with passing the buck than solving problems. The individuals who occupy the most important positions in our corporations, governments, and non-profit organizations are missing something fundamental about leadership: leadership begins with modeling personal accountability.

After researching, writing, and teaching about accountability for many years, I have discovered critical and timeless principles that govern accountability in three distinct domains.

1. Developing personal accountability

2. Building accountable relationships

3. Creating the conditions of organizational accountability

Each of these three domains of accountability can be influenced by applying different practices. Influence over each of these domains is dependent on how well one masters the previous domain. Put another way, you can't create organizational accountability until you know how to build accountable relationships, and you can't build accountable relationships until you, yourself, are exhibiting a high standard of personal accountability.

This is the first of three books that explores each of the three domains of accountability in detail. Developing personal accountability comes before all other principles of accountability. Why? Because, as stated earlier, you can't inspire accountability in others until you exemplify it yourself.

> **You can't inspire accountability in others until you exemplify it yourself.**

In addition to striving to be a great husband and father, my personal mission is to demystify leadership to make it easier for just about anyone to become a great leader. I wrote this book primarily for people in leadership positions to illustrate that great leadership is demonstrated through certain learnable behaviors, not personality traits. As people in leadership positions develop the habits of personal accountability, their examples will inspire others to want to emulate them, creating an immensely positive ripple effect throughout their organization.

Developing personal accountability will help you do three things at once.

1. Solve or prevent many of your problems

2. Strengthen your character

3. Become the kind of person other people want to follow

Yes, I know this sounds like a panacea, but developing personal accountability is just that: a remedy for most of the problems you and your organization are facing. Personal accountability is the starting point of great leadership. It is a fundamental element of character that turns ordinary people into heroes.

The principles contained in this book are applicable to anyone who wants to achieve greater success in life and greater assurance that they are on the high road. Imagine feeling that whatever situation you are in, you can always respond to your critics in a way that puts you on the moral high ground. Suppose you knew how to increase other people's respect for you instantly. Consider what it would feel like if you knew that no matter what life threw at you, you had a simple formula for increasing your odds of successfully handling your challenges.

That is the promise of this book.

Many of these principles will be familiar to you. I haven't invented any of them. My goal is to share the essential framework that governs accountability so you can: a) see how all the principles of accountability work together and b) learn to harness these principles in your life to become a better person, a great leader, and achieve greater success.

Warning: This Book Is Not for the Faint of Heart!

In this book I share the three habits of personal accountability—three key behaviors to exercise personal accountability. Although these habits are remarkably simple to understand, they all go against our basic nature, and sometimes it really hurts to exercise personal accountability.

One of the underlying themes of personal accountability is that we don't know as much as we think we do. Our beliefs about how to get the best results in life may, in fact, be wrong. This means we must be willing to have an open mind.

When you boil it right down, this book is about how to become more open minded about solutions to problems and how to become a better human being—a better leader, a better employee, and a better member of society. But that's not all. A fortuitous by-product of exercising personal accountability is that it has the tendency to inspire others to follow your example, thereby elevating their performance.

Now, if you are willing to have your mind changed about the way you think about problems, and if you are willing to bear a little psychological discomfort as you practice what I teach, then let's begin.

Go to AvailLeadership.com/inspire-accountability-resources to access a free Personal Accountability Assessment.

PRINCIPLES OF LEADERSHIP

2. What Is Accountability?

Contrary to popular belief, accountability is not a frightening word—or at least it shouldn't be. Regrettably, as Nathaniel learned in the earlier example, when management uses the word "accountability," they are usually using it as a stick with which to beat people. Consequently, many people in leadership positions are teaching those they lead to fear the very thing that will make them and the organization successful.

This is a serious problem because when you look at virtually every personal or organizational success story, you will find accountability at the heart of it. Accountability is the root of every positive outcome that leadership and business authors have been writing about since the dawn of time. Here is a sample of some common themes in leadership and business literature.

- Teamwork
- Servant leadership
- Culture change
- Employee engagement
- Measuring the right things
- Operational excellence
- Personal effectiveness
- Goal setting
- Feedback
- Execution
- Emotional intelligence
- Focusing on strengths
- Innovation
- Purpose
- Motivation
- Strategy
- Success

Accountability is at the center of what virtually every leadership and management book is trying to produce, which is *people who get the right results more often*. Compared to the mountain of literature printed annually that is full of ideas and strategies designed to get the right results, relatively little of it targets the heart of what we're after: more accountability.

Accountability is the common denominator of every behavior that brings about positive results. Accountability is the foundation upon which all great individuals, teams, and organizations are built.

Accountability Defined

Accountability is about striving to achieve the right results, nothing more and nothing less. It is not about blame or punishment. It is not a word that should strike fear into the hearts of those who hear it. If you want to be successful, embracing accountability is the surest way to achieve it.

To get the right results, you must focus on the *results* rather than on merely completing *tasks*. Getting my children to clean up the kitchen after meals provides a perfect example of this. My wife and I want to teach our three daughters the value of work and the importance of cleaning up their own mess. So, we created an after-meal task chart consisting of three jobs.

- "Clear Table" (put condiments back in the fridge, pack up leftovers and put them in the fridge, bring pots and common dishes to the dishwasher)
- "Load Dishwasher" (load and unload the dishwasher)
- "Wipe Counters & Vacuum" (wipe the kitchen table and counters and vacuum the kitchen floor)

Each child was assigned one job that they would be responsible to complete for the whole week. Each week the jobs would be rotated to a different child. Shortly after implementing the job chart, we noticed several problems.

1. Individual tasks were often done poorly.

For example, the child responsible for "Wipe Counters & Vacuum" would, in fact, wipe the table and counters, but since that's all we asked them to do, they felt that one wipe would do. They moved the cloth over the table one time. Done. The table was still sticky from dried syrup and milk spills, but as far as they were concerned, their job was done.

2. Even when individual tasks were done adequately, the kitchen was still a mess.

How close to the dishwasher, exactly, did the child responsible for "Clear Table" have to place the dirty dishes? If the counter closest to the dishwasher was too full of dirty dishes, and the dirty dishes had to be placed on a different counter, then the "Load Dishwasher" child felt that it was not her job to go to the other counter to retrieve the overflow of dirty dishes.

What if "Wipe Counters & Vacuum" was done before all the dirty dishes were loaded in the dishwasher? Was this child supposed to come back and clean up the mess left on the counter after the dishes were loaded?

Dealing with these kinds of issues every single day drove my wife and me to the brink of insanity. We felt like we needed to specify every possible scenario and explain in great detail what their responsibilities were in each situation. Realizing this would probably push us over the brink, we took a different approach. We decided to focus our children on the results we were after (a clean kitchen) instead of the individual jobs required to achieve the results.

"When I said wipe the counter," I told my daughters, "what I meant was make sure the table and the counters are clean. That may mean wiping them several times or using a scrub brush to get the really grungy parts. You decide. The table and the countertops just need to be clean when you're done."

Now after completing their assigned tasks, each child must get the permission of the remaining children before they can leave. This means they must all look up from their individual tasks to assess the results and decide if the results meet the cleanliness standards. Often, the child who thought her job was done is helped by the other children to see what else needs to be done to achieve the ultimate goal, which is a clean kitchen.

Although my daughters continue to find creative ways to complicate this simple goal of a clean kitchen, the system is working much better now. They now view each other as partners rather than enemies in their quest for freedom from chores (in part because they know Dad will call them all back to the kitchen if it isn't totally clean). When people care about the results they produce, we call them owners. By focusing on the desired results, my daughters became joint owners of making sure the kitchen is clean after every meal.

In addition to taking ownership of results, accountability is about working to improve future results. When people care about the results they produce, they naturally ask themselves questions such as,

- How can I increase my chances of getting the right results in the future?
- What could possibly happen to prevent me from getting the right results? What can I do to ensure that doesn't happen?

Taking ownership of results means working to get the right results now and in the future. Therefore, the definition of accountability is this:

> Accountability is taking ownership of results and working to improve future results.

The essence of taking ownership of results is focusing on what you *can do* to bring about better outcomes instead of focusing on what you *can't do*. The world will throw a lot of unpleasant and even cruel curveballs at us. That's a given. Expect it. Nothing good ever comes from bellyaching about how unfortunate and unfair those curveballs are. The past won't help us except to illuminate what we could have done differently to avoid or reduce the impact of those curveballs. Once you've mined the past for insights about how to improve your future, move forward. Accountability is focused on the future, not the past. Although we cannot choose the form of adversity we will face in life, we can choose how we plan for it and how we respond to it.[1]

Also implicit in the above definition of accountability is initiative. Focusing on the desired results, instead of simply focusing on completing the tasks required to achieve the desired results, generates motivation to act. When we focus on achieving a certain outcome, a natural tension develops in our minds that pulls us from our current state to the desired state. The motivation generated by this tension will drive us to figure out the steps to achieve the goal. Without this motivation, the odds of achieving the desired outcome are drastically reduced. Tasks may get done but not to the degree or with sufficient coordination to accomplish the end goal. Initiative, therefore, is a natural outcome of focusing on the desired results.

Initiative alone, however, is not accountability. As I will discuss later, when leaders don't demonstrate the three habits of personal accountability, they unwittingly kill the initiative in others.

Accountability may best be understood by examining what it produces—the fruits of accountability, so to speak. To illustrate, I have compared some of the fruits of high accountability in the workplace with the examples of low accountability mentioned earlier.

FRUITS OF LOW ACCOUNTABILITY	FRUITS OF HIGH ACCOUNTABILITY
People who say "That's not my problem."	Doing whatever it takes to achieve the desired results
Offering excuses and abandoning problems	Suggesting solutions they intend to carry out themselves
Finger pointing	Admitting mistakes
Lack of trust and cooperation	Going out of their way to assist colleagues
An "Us" vs. "Them" mentality	Treating other departments like customers
Managers who don't address poor performance	Managers who provide improvement feedback and far more reaffirming feedback

Defensiveness to feedback	Requesting feedback
Constant firefighting mode	Integrating lessons learned into SOPs to continually improve outcomes
Missed deadlines and unachieved goals	Regularly reporting progress and mitigating obstacles to ensure goals are met
Zero consequences for results	Everyone feels the impact of success and failure

Now that we have a good idea of what accountability is and what it looks like, let's explore some common misconceptions about accountability and clarify what it is not.

THE DIFFERENCE BETWEEN RESPONSIBILITY AND ACCOUNTABILITY

Responsibility is taking ownership of activities. A person who keeps their commitments and completes the tasks listed on their job description is responsible.

Accountability is taking ownership of results. A person is accountable if he or she: a) focuses on the results he or she is trying to achieve, b) does what it takes to produce those results, and c) owns the consequences of those results.

The distinction between responsibility and accountability was made clear to me when I worked with a payroll supervisor named Susan. Susan was one of the most responsible people in the company. She documented every instruction she was given to make sure she executed those instructions to the letter. In fact, she wouldn't take any action unless she had written authorization to do so. However, when something went wrong—when we didn't get the results we wanted—Susan was the first to say, "I only did what I was told to do."

Susan wanted nothing to do with the outcomes of her work because there was always a chance that the outcomes could be bad. To insulate herself from any potential negative consequences, Susan would never make any decisions; she would only carry out other people's decisions. She would only take ownership of tasks, not results.

Susan wasn't as concerned about the outcome as she was concerned about staying out of trouble. She was responsible but not accountable. Accountability, therefore, is caring more about achieving the right results than about completing tasks.

Accountability is caring more about achieving the right results than about completing tasks.

We want people to be responsible, but it is more important to be accountable. You can do everything on your job description and still not get the right results. Completing your tasks is all for naught if they don't achieve the desired results.

ACCOUNTABILITY IS NOT BLAME AND PUNISHMENT

The word "accountability" has been weaponized in popular culture and has become synonymous with "blame and punishment." When people say, "That politician must be held accountable for his actions," what they're really saying is, "That politician is to blame and must be punished for his actions." However, accountability is not the same as blame and/or punishment. To be accountable means to take ownership of results, good or bad. It means finding solutions to problems to produce better results now and in the future.

To be blamed, on the other hand, is to be accused of culpable actions. The problem is that culpability is not as obvious as we think it is. Blame is often assigned before all the facts are known. Blame assumes that people, not the systems they operate in, are the problem. It is focused on the past and on punishing offenders. The rationale behind assigning blame is that identifying offenders and punishing them will correct the poor behavior. *If I just rub their nose in it*, the thinking goes, *they'll learn better*. The reality is that the only thing people learn from being blamed is to become better at hiding their mistakes.

We live in a society that has blurred the lines between the words "accountability," "blame," and "punishment." In fact, many people use those words interchangeably. The truth is that blame has no place within the concept of accountability. Blame is what people do when they *don't* want to accept accountability themselves. Nothing good comes from blame. In fact, blame spawns a host of counterproductive behaviors that we'll explore later.

ACCOUNTABILITY IS NOT ROI

After reading one of my articles on accountability, a CEO wrote to tell me that she found my ideas around accountability extremely helpful. So helpful, in fact, that she said she was going to start calculating a ROI (return on investment) for every employee in her company. She said she planned to use it as a metric for performance discussions with them.

Let me be clear that accountability is not the same thing as return on investment. Accountability is taking ownership of results and working to improve future results. Measurable individual contributions to the bottom line tell part of the story of individual performance, but there is real danger in focusing on it.

Although this CEO did not plan to publish each person's ROI, management will presumably share it with employees on a case-by-case basis. The first time they do, it won't take long before the question "Did you know that management calculates a ROI for each of us?" goes viral throughout the company. This will send a clear and unambiguous message that, regardless of anything else employees may do for the company, all management really cares about is how much money each employee makes or saves the company.

When employees believe the company is primarily concerned about individual financial performance, they will begin to treat their work as a financial transaction and nothing more. "Treat me like a number" one Millennial wrote, "I'll return the favor. This job will quickly become nothing more than my rent payment."[2] Say goodbye to discretionary effort.

One of the hallmarks of accountability is the willingness to put the success of the team above personal interests or convenience. In fact, the people who have the greatest positive impact on organizational results are often *not* the greatest individual contributors. A study by the National Bureau of Economic Research revealed that the better an employee was at sales, the worse he or she was at managing others.[3] The study also revealed that the inverse was true. Sales actually increased under managers who produced lackluster results in their previous sales roles.

Possibly even more enlightening than the study's surprising discovery is the explanation. Star individual performers tend to collaborate less with their sales colleagues. When more collaborative but less successful salespeople were promoted to manager, their teams achieved 30 percent more sales than teams led by less collaborative managers who were previously more successful salespeople.[4]

Employees who have the greatest positive impact on people and results can fly under the radar because they prioritize team success over their own glory. This phenomenon is as true in sports as it is in business. Star baseball players, for example, might be able to hit home runs and sell admission tickets, but they don't necessarily win games. The movie *Moneyball* tells the story of how Billy Beane, the general manager of the Oakland Athletics, forever changed the game of baseball in 2002 by exploiting this fact.[5] After assembling a team of low-profile players who played more for their team's success and less for their own personal glory, Beane's club went on one of the longest winning streaks in baseball history and was able to compete with baseball teams that had more than three times as much money to spend on players. Beane himself was a baseball player who didn't live up to expectations but who flourished as a general manager.

Making a connection between individual ROI and accountability is not only based on a weakly correlated premise, it will also demotivate and demoralize most of the workforce who get the message that management only views employees as an input into their money-making machine. Making people aware of objective measures of their performance is a good practice provided those measures take into consideration all aspects of performance and do not prioritize profits over people or purpose.

"That's Not My Problem" – The Antithesis of Accountability

Sure glad the hole isn't at our end.

Seventeenth-century poet John Donne famously wrote that "no man is an island," arguing that we are all interconnected. If there was any doubt in your mind that we are all connected, the global COVID-19 pandemic should serve as striking evidence that our actions unavoidably impact others. The world was negatively impacted by China's initially slow response to the COVID-19 outbreak in their country, but we also benefited from their efforts and the efforts of other countries who ramped up their response when the magnitude of the threat became apparent.

If you believe that a falling domino is someone else's problem, just wait until the trail of dominos circles back around and hits you in the back of the head. We all breathe the same air. Our safety at work is dependent on us and others noticing and reporting hazards. Our mood influences and is influenced by the moods of those around us. A problem in operations will become a problem for sales when they don't have enough of the right product to sell. A problem in sales will become a problem in operations when they must lay off workers because there isn't enough work. Blaming others for problems that we think are their responsibility to solve will not insulate us from the long-term repercussions of those problems.

> Blaming others for problems that we expect them to solve will not insulate us from the long-term repercussions of those problems.

The following clever story about four people named Everybody, Somebody, Anybody, and Nobody illustrates how the "It's not my problem" attitude destroys teamwork and sabotages organizational success.

> There was an important job to be done, and Everybody was asked to do it. Everybody was sure Somebody would do it. Anybody could have done it, but Nobody did it. Somebody got angry about that because it was Everybody's job. Everybody thought Anybody could do it, but Nobody realized that Everybody wouldn't do it. It ended up that Everybody blamed Somebody when Nobody did what Anybody could have done.[6]

Many people are under the misguided belief that they were hired to perform a particular job. That is not accurate. People are hired to help their organization succeed, period. To be clear, "their organization" doesn't refer to their team or their department; it refers to the organization that gives them their paycheck. A problem for one team within an organization will eventually become a problem for everyone if people are standing around with their hands in their pockets saying, "It's not my problem," or worse, pointing fingers and saying, "It's your problem."

Regrettably, many managers and human resource departments have unwittingly propagated the "It's not my problem" attitude and its inbred cousin, "It's not my job." They have done this by writing job descriptions in terms of activities instead of desired results, being inflexible and uncreative about who performs what work, and rewarding individual contributions at the expense of cooperation. Managers also reinforce a subtle twist on the "It's not my job" mindset when they get defensive anytime someone from a different department offers them advice. "Don't tell me how to do my job!" the miffed manager snorts. Such comments and attitudes keep people firmly entrenched in their silos. When things go wrong, people with the "It's not my problem" mentality lob blame bombs across enemy lines in the form of emails CC'd to half the company.

Atul Gawande, a surgeon and author, observed that the most common obstacle to effective teamwork is not the high-performing prima donna jerks who are occasionally allowed to terrorize workplaces. "No," he writes, "the more familiar and widely dangerous issue is a kind of silent disengagement, the consequence of specialized technicians sticking narrowly to their domains. 'That's not my problem' is possibly the worst thing people can think, whether they are starting an operation, taxiing an airplane full of passengers down a runway, or building a thousand-foot-tall skyscraper."[7] Although some professions carry higher consequences than others for eschewing problems, every unresolved problem leads to consequences that someone will eventually have to bear.

People who have an "It's not my problem" mentality have been trained that this is the safest approach to deal with their problems. They have learned how to hide behind their activity-based job descriptions to shield themselves from accountability for results. What people who play the "It's not my problem" game don't recognize is that persisting at this game holds them back at work and in life. For example, they never seem to get the promotions for which they keep applying. To soothe their egos, they tell themselves (and anyone else who will listen) that management is out to get them. The people close to them may believe that explanation for a while, but over time, that excuse wears thin, and they know it. The "It's not my problem" attitude sets in motion a dark spiral of low performance and low confidence, with the two outcomes reinforcing each other over time.

It can be frustrating and even infuriating to have someone with the "It's not my problem" mentality on your team. But guess what? They are frustrated too. Life is not working out very well for them. Not only do they likely have nearly constant turmoil at work, but their family relationships are also probably a mess too. Imagine what it would feel like to constantly be on the defensive and feel like you must always keep your guard up to protect your self-esteem at work and at home. These people need to learn a better way to deal with life. They need to see what demonstrating personal accountability actually looks like and the benefits of doing so. They need a model. You can be that model.

Accountability Is Personal and Leadership Power

Greatness in individuals and in organizations begins with being accountable. People who think and say things like "It's not my problem" or "It's not my fault, so I shouldn't have to deal with it" rarely get ahead in life. Even if they do, they will never reach their potential because if they don't take ownership of their current situation, they can't effectively influence their future results. If people don't acknowledge how their actions brought them to where they are now, they won't have a clue how to get themselves to a better place.

If you look closely at widely respected people and organizations, you will find that they consistently model high levels of accountability. They don't blame others for their problems; they focus on improving themselves, and they establish processes that consistently help them get better results.

If you are serious about getting better results for you and for your team, the first and most powerful thing you can do is demonstrate the three habits of personal accountability. These habits constitute the three primary sections of this book:

Habit 1: Don't Blame – Blame kills accountability.

Habit 2: Look in the Mirror – Acknowledge your part in the problem.

Habit 3: Engineer the Solution – Fix processes, not people.

These three habits may appear deceptively simple, but they are the antidote for low accountability and the formula for consistently achieving better results. When I introduce these three habits to CEOs, they often excitedly say, "Yes, that's exactly what I want my employees to do!" However, as we know, leaders set the standard of accountability for their organizations. People won't demonstrate a higher level of accountability than their leader for very long. If employees see those in leadership positions pass the buck when things go badly, they will too. If the CEO gets defensive when someone suggests the CEO's way isn't the best way, guess how employees will respond to feedback? And executives who try to improve results by simply increasing numeric targets each year and saying "do more with less" had better get used to disappointment. Those in leadership positions set the upper limit on accountability for their organizations. It is up to them to make sure it's an extremely high limit.

As I discuss throughout this book, exercising personal accountability is a source of personal power that increases your capacity to get the right results more often and helps you remain on the moral high ground. However, improving your own outcomes is not the only benefit of personal accountability. Personal accountability is also a source of leadership power. The more you apply the three habits of personal accountability, the more you will elevate the people around you. For instance, the more you restrain your impulse to blame, the more confidence the people around you will gain in their abilities. The more you look in the mirror, the more you will notice the things you are doing that hamstring the efforts of the people who work for you. The more you engineer the solutions to your problems, the more the people you lead will focus on the things they can change to get better results instead of focusing on beating up themselves or their teammates for setbacks. Exercising personal accountability is one of the greatest ways to strengthen your leadership influence and elevate the people around you.

Archimedes, the ancient Greek mathematician, physicist, and engineer, explained the power of leverage in this famous quote attributed to him: "Give me a lever long enough and a fulcrum on which to place it, and I shall move the world." Leadership is the ultimate lever because nothing else has the equivalent potential to change the world for good. However, leadership applied by someone with weak character who does not take accountability for results usually produces undesirable outcomes.

Take, for instance, former Wells Fargo CEO, John Stumpf. In September 2016, Wells Fargo was fined $185 million for opening over two million checking and credit card accounts without the consent of its customers in what became known as the Wells Fargo Account Fraud Scandal.[8] In what was described as a "pressure-cooker sales culture," employees were driven to sell products that customers didn't need or request in order to meet unreachable sales targets. Employees described frequent crying, vomiting, and panic attacks brought on by the stress from management.[9] Some employees reported that their calls to the company's ethics hotline were met with either no reaction or resulted in the termination of the employee making the call.[10]

In an appalling display of a lack of accountability, Stumpf insisted that management didn't do anything wrong and refused to admit that the culture he created had anything to do with the scandal. Instead, he blamed the scandal on the 5,300 frontline employees who were caught creating fraudulent accounts, whom he fired. In some cases, management even took the extra measure to ensure some of those former employees could never work in the banking industry again.

After Stumpf repeatedly denied accountability for any wrongdoing, Sen. Elizabeth Warren, who led the Senate Banking Committee investigation, said, "Come on . . . this went on for years and they didn't smell anything in the air about fake accounts?" In fact, the Wells Fargo sales culture and its impact on customers was documented as early as 2011 by the *Wall Street Journal,* and the scandal was blown open in a 2013 *Los Angeles Times* story.[11, 12] Stumpf knew full well what was going on, but he chose to look the other way. As a result, the bank was required to pay out almost three billion dollars in settlements, which led to it having to close four hundred branches.[13, 14] In 2020, the Department of Justice and the Securities and Exchange Commission (SEC) fined the bank an additional three billion dollars. As for Stumpf, he reluctantly resigned, agreed to forfeit forty-one million dollars in stock options, was fined 17.5 million dollars, and in a sweet twist of irony, was banned from working in the banking industry like the employees whose careers he ruined.[15] In November 2020, the SEC filed civil charges against Stumpf.[16] Unfortunately, the consequences Stumpf received offered an infinitesimal measure of comfort to the 5,300 employees who were fired and the employees who were laid off when their branch was closed because of his weak character and poor leadership.

When the *Los Angeles Times* article was published in 2013, Stumpf was given an opportunity to take a serious look at how his actions and the actions of the executive team were creating a culture that encouraged thousands of employees to commit fraud. He didn't. He refused to acknowledge how he contributed to the problem and was therefore unable to fix it.

Organizations that are led by people who display low accountability usually suffer as a result. If you doubt that, just watch people who a) blame everybody but themselves for problems, b) believe they never do anything wrong, and c) try to solve their problems by fixing or firing people, and then look for the trail of devastation they leave in their wake. These people inevitably create more problems than they can ever solve because accountability is an essential prerequisite to finding sustainable solutions.

Accountability is the fulcrum upon which leadership is placed and which gives leadership its power. If the fulcrum is placed in the wrong position as a result of low accountability, leadership has little power.

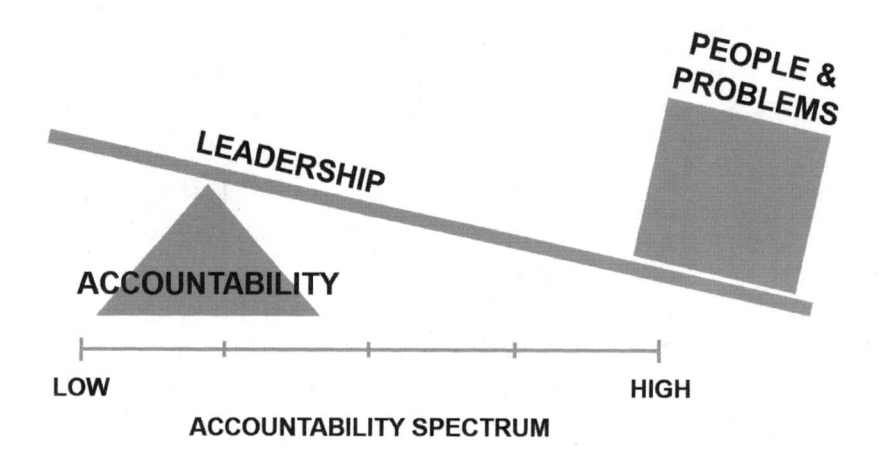

PEOPLE & PROBLEMS

LEADERSHIP

ACCOUNTABILITY

LOW — **HIGH**

ACCOUNTABILITY SPECTRUM

As leaders exercise personal accountability and apply the other principles of accountability that I will share in future books, they harness the mechanical advantage produced by working within natural laws, effectively moving the fulcrum to give them greater leverage. Leaders use this advantage to find sustainable solutions to their toughest problems and to elevate those they lead.

Principles of Leadership

PEOPLE & PROBLEMS

LEADERSHIP

ACCOUNTABILITY

LOW — HIGH

ACCOUNTABILITY SPECTRUM

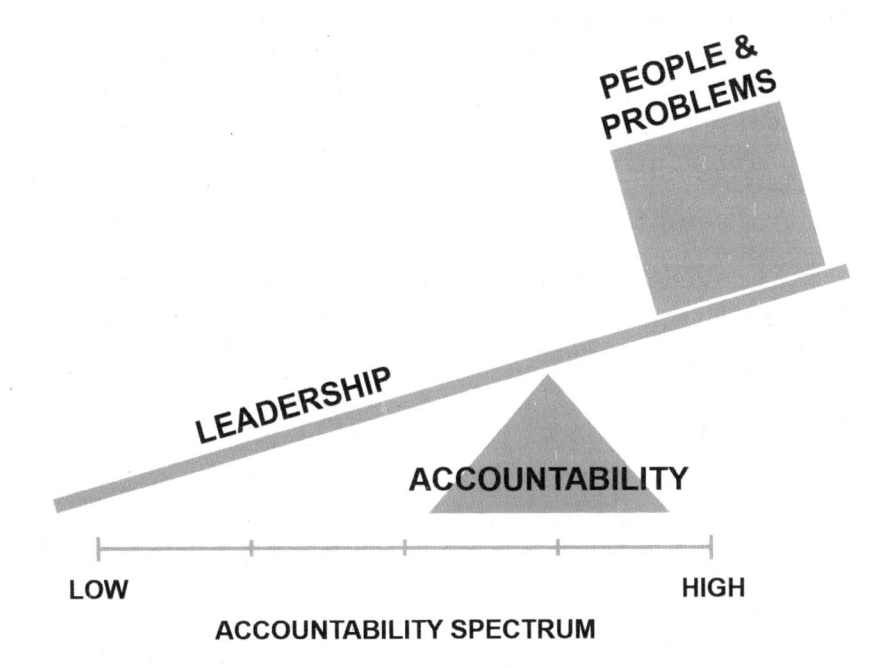

Contrary to popular belief, leadership is not a mystical art. In fact, leadership is fairly straightforward. Certain behaviors have a disproportionately positive impact on people and results. Exercising personal accountability uses natural laws to make leadership easier. It is one of the simplest, most powerful ways those in leadership positions can become stronger leaders.

3. Developing the Superpower of Systems Thinking

Wouldn't it be great to possess a superpower? Perhaps when you were a child you wished you could fly, have super strength, or be invisible. Throughout this book, you're going to discover that you can develop the superpower to see things that other people can't. This superpower is called systems thinking.

Distinguishing the Forest from the Trees

Most people standing in a forest can see the trees that surround them, but often they don't notice the decayed trees they are standing on that constitute the forest floor. Nor do they think much about the glacier that created the river and the aquifer that provide life to the forest.

I have hiked through forests and past lakes and rivers right up to the top of mountain peaks where I could see such glaciers. I remember the first time I noticed a small pool of water forming under a melting glacier as I stood perched above it on a rocky summit. My eyes followed the movement of the small stream that flowed from that glacier all the way down one side of the mountain. Once it reached the bottom, the stream banked around the base of the mountain and down a valley. Around the corner and partway down the valley, the small stream met another stream that was formed by a glacier I could see across the valley. It dawned on me that these two small streams flowing from the two glaciers formed the river that fed the large lake that channeled the water down the raging river I had hiked along for three hours that morning.

That was a beautiful "Aha!" moment for me. It thrilled and amazed me that within this epic, sprawling view laid out before my eyes, I was witnessing the birth of a river! The water melting from the glacier appeared to be flowing at a pace and volume not much greater than the water running from a bathtub faucet, but by the time it got to where I began my hike, the water had become a raging river strong enough to pulverize a log into toothpicks. When I began my hike that morning, I simply noticed the raging river I was hiking beside and hadn't given a second thought about where it came from.

This is what being a systems thinker is like. You begin to notice the relationship between things that you previously only saw as discrete events.

We tend to notice the relationship between things only when they are physically located close to each other and when the interaction between them happens within a short period of time. In other words, cause and effect are often obscured by distance and time.

The river I was walking beside all morning was physically located beyond my view of its source, the lake, and beyond the source of the lake, the glacier. This is the "distance" part of the equation. The water within that river had come from the glacier several days before I walked beside it. This is the "time" part of the equation. Only when I walked past each part of the river-making process in a single day and then elevated my vantage point so I could see several parts of the process in a single glance was I able to piece it all together in my mind.

Of course, I knew the theory of where rivers come from, but it didn't snap into place in my mind until I moved myself to a higher vantage point. That vantage point eliminated the obstruction of the distance between all those interrelated parts and the time it took for them all to connect.

This is the essence of systems thinking. To see how the individual components of our lives and the world around us interact with one another, we must elevate our thinking to see past the obstructions of distance and time. Until we do, many of the solutions to our problems will remain obscured. Systems thinking, therefore, is elevating our thinking to see the relationship between things that are separated by distance and time.

This is why developing the superpower of systems thinking is so essential to developing personal accountability. How can you expect to solve your most difficult problems if you can't see what's causing them?

As mentioned earlier, accountability leads us to get the right results more often. The primary reason you don't get the right results as often as you'd like is not because you don't have the capacity to solve your problems; it's because quite often you can't actually see what's causing your problems in the first place!

Before you can solve your problems and get the right results, you must first clearly see what's causing your problems.

Systems thinking is simply a more enlightened way of looking at problems to discover insights that would otherwise remain undetected.

Systems Create Their Own Behavior

Peter Senge is a management theorist who popularized the term "systems thinking" in the 1990s. Senge defines systems thinking as the discipline of "seeing patterns where others see only events and forces to react to."[1]

Senge's classic example of a negative, reinforcing system (also known as a vicious cycle) is the nuclear arms race between the United States and the USSR. The Americans saw the Soviet buildup of nuclear arms as a threat. So, the US added more nukes to their arsenal. The Soviets saw the nukes the American's were adding to their arsenal and concluded that this represented a threat to the USSR. So, the Soviets, in turn, added more nukes to their arsenal, and so on.

This perpetual cycle of aggression led to the creation of almost 64,500 nuclear warheads at the height of the arms race in 1986, even though one hundred nuclear weapons is the most any nation could deploy without causing significant damage to their own country.[2,3]

In hindsight, you might be tempted to say, "How could any rational person let it come to that?" but the people making the decisions at the time would reply, "What rational person would not respond in kind to my enemy's armament buildup?"

The real problem was not necessarily the people involved but the system they had created that dictated their decisions. "The system," writes environmental scientist, Donella Meadows, "to a large extent, causes its own behavior!"[4]

How could the USA and the USSR not see the system that was pulling their strings? Because of the delay built into the system. Senge notes that it could take up to five years for one side to gather intelligence on the other side's weaponry and design and deploy new weapons. It was the "temporary perceived advantage," Senge writes, that kept the escalation process going. "If each side were able to respond instantly to buildups of its adversary, incentives to keep building would be nil."[5]

As this example illustrates, we find it exceedingly difficult to see the relationship between things that are separated by distance and time. Systems that produce their own behavior play out all the time around us, often without us noticing. In fact, we often unwittingly create systems that produce behaviors in others that we don't like.

For example, a simple but all too common system in the workplace is managers who unwittingly encourage their staff to bring all problems to them to solve instead of empowering employees to solve their own problems.

Virtually every manager on the planet wishes his or her people would solve their own problems more often, or at the very least offer some possible solutions to the problems they bring to their boss. But here's the issue: most managers are good problem solvers, and they know it! That's what got them promoted to manager in the first place. So, when employees bring problems to their managers, most managers simply can't help themselves from blurting out a solution. It's as though most managers think their job is to play whack-a-mole all day. See a problem over here? Whack it with a solution. See a problem over there? Whack it with a solution. Since managers keep solving employees' problems for them, employees don't learn how to solve their own problems or even how to come up with possible solutions.

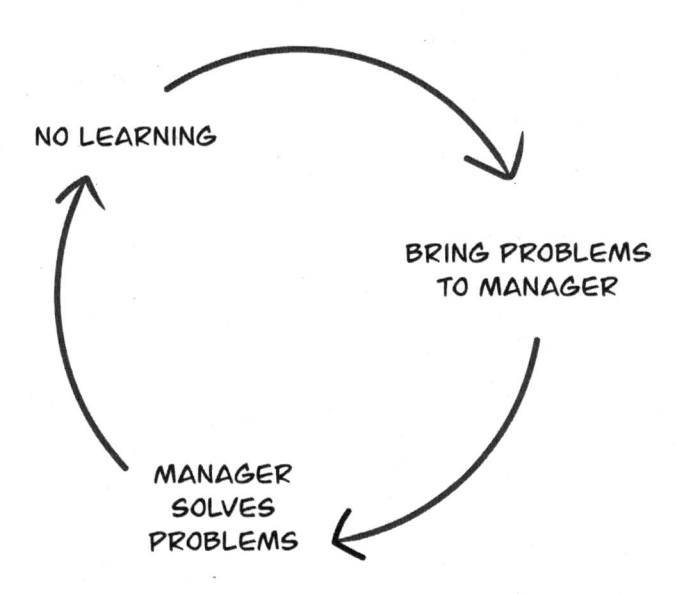

```
        NO LEARNING
              ↑
              |              BRING PROBLEMS
              |               TO MANAGER
              |
         MANAGER
         SOLVES
         PROBLEMS  ←
```

Solving problems might be what gets someone promoted to manager, but most managers fail to notice that by solving their people's problems, they are training people to bring their problems to the manager *without* first searching for a solution. What rational person would do all the extra legwork required to solve their problems when the fastest way to solve the problem, and the surest way to solve the problem exactly the way the boss wants it solved, is to ask the boss?

Systems create their own behavior. Now here's a systems solution to that problem. Once someone becomes promoted to manager, his or her job should change from being a problem solver to being a teacher of problem-solving skills. Many managers must have missed that memo when they were promoted into management. Managers are responsible to build the capacity of those they lead. Rather than providing solutions when their staff bring them problems, managers who understand and accept this responsibility ask questions of their staff that empower them to think and solve problems for themselves.

Here are some questions that good leaders ask people who come to them to solve their problems:

- How do you think we should fix this? What are some possible options?
- What similar challenges have you faced in the past? How did you solve that problem?
- Where can you get the information you need to solve this problem?
- Who or what will your solution affect? Who should you talk to before you implement your solution?
- What is your plan B if the solution you implement doesn't work?

Managers who become frustrated that their employees only come to them with problems should take a close look at the system they have created that may be reinforcing this undesirable behavior. On the other hand, managers who embrace their role as teachers of problem-solving skills create a virtuous cycle of learning and capacity building within those they lead.

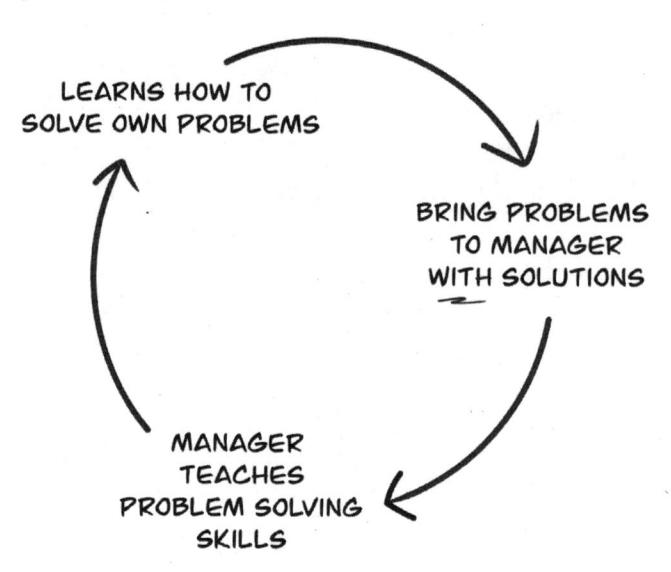

LEARNS HOW TO SOLVE OWN PROBLEMS → **BRING PROBLEMS TO MANAGER WITH SOLUTIONS** → **MANAGER TEACHES PROBLEM SOLVING SKILLS** →

As management consultant Edwards Deming discovered, "Every system is perfectly designed to get the results it gets."[6] In other words, if you are getting undesirable results, there is likely a system at work producing those results, and quite often, managers unwittingly created that system!

Deming is credited with helping Japan's manufacturing industry emerge from the ashes following WWII to become a beacon to the world when it comes to quality manufacturing. Deming later brought Total Quality Management (TQM) techniques to America and the rest of the world in the 1980s and 1990s and became known as the father of the quality movement.[7]

After all his work with large Japanese and American manufacturers, Deming estimated that over 90 percent of problems in business are systems driven and that management is directly responsible for most mistakes, not the people who appear to make them.[8] Keep that in mind the next time you discover a problem at work.

Management is directly responsible for most mistakes, not the people who appear to make them.

Most People Don't Notice the Systems That Are Pulling Their Strings

As noted earlier, we have a tough time seeing the connection between cause and effect when these elements are separated by distance and time. Let me give you another example with which I am quite familiar.

A big part of my work is helping organizations establish an ongoing leadership development process to help them become less dependent on recruiting to fill management positions. In a very real sense, many organizations' dependence on recruiting has turned into a full-fledged addiction. My job is to help organizations kick their addiction to recruiting.

Virtually every time these recruiting addicts have a vacancy, they are forced to look outside the organization to find top talent because they don't have qualified employees who can step up. Why not? Because employees have witnessed time and again that the best positions go to outsiders, so they have learned that "If you want to advance your career, you need to go somewhere else." So, many of the most ambitious employees do go elsewhere. Those who stay tend to check out mentally and resign themselves to the likelihood that they will never move up in the organization, so they don't even try to develop themselves.

Subsequently, when such organizations need to fill a key position, they have so few internal candidates to choose from that they feel compelled to look outside the organization again, which perpetuates the vicious cycle.

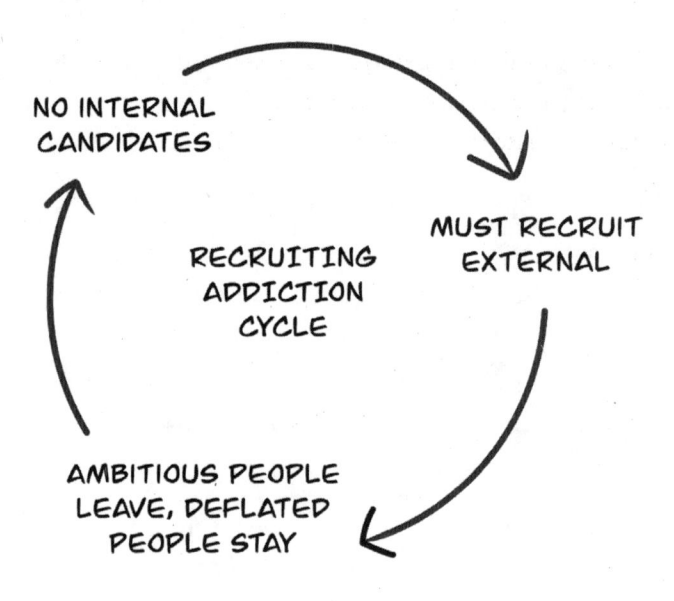

RECRUITING ADDICTION CYCLE

NO INTERNAL CANDIDATES → MUST RECRUIT EXTERNAL → AMBITIOUS PEOPLE LEAVE, DEFLATED PEOPLE STAY → (back to NO INTERNAL CANDIDATES)

On the contrary, organizations that invest in developing their employees are flush with talent. Not only do they create their own internal pipeline of leaders, they also get far more stellar external applicants because a) word gets out in the labor market that "if you want to fast-track your career, get a job with _____" and b) since most management positions are filled internally, the organization can focus its recruiting on entry-level positions, and it is far easier to recruit entry-level candidates than experienced candidates.

The first time that managers experience the lightning-fast fill time resulting from qualified internal promotions, they say, "I think we need to do more development," which perpetuates this virtuous cycle.

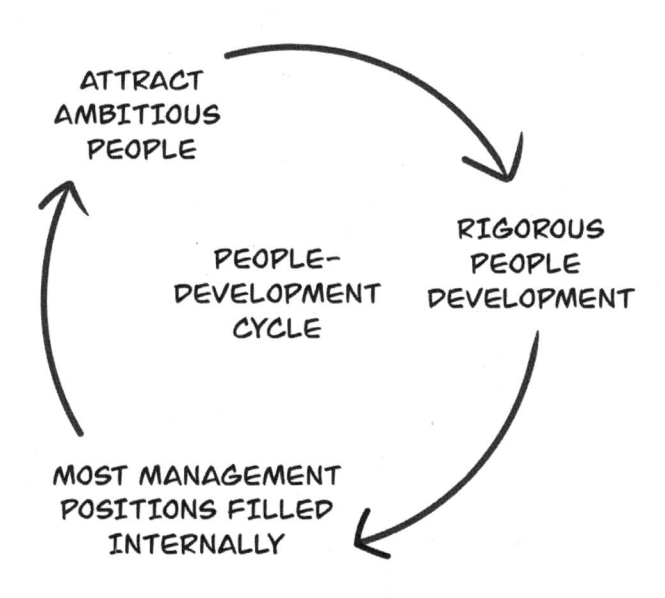

```
        ATTRACT
       AMBITIOUS
        PEOPLE
                              RIGOROUS
           PEOPLE-            PEOPLE
         DEVELOPMENT        DEVELOPMENT
            CYCLE

       MOST MANAGEMENT
       POSITIONS FILLED
          INTERNALLY
```

Organizations that are addicted to recruiting can't see any way out of their addition. They only see what's right in front of their noses: the short-term problem (a vacancy) and a short-term solution (recruit a replacement). They can't see the system they created that got them into this mess because the cause is separated by distance and time.

Cause: Deciding not to invest seriously in employee development.

Distance: The problem of not having enough qualified candidates to fill job openings didn't originate in the recruiting department; it originated in the executive boardroom. Senior managers made employee development a low priority.

Time: This decision was made a long time ago, but the vacancy needs to be filled now.

I'll say it again: we have a tough time seeing the connection between cause and effect when cause and effect are separated by distance and time. This is the essential problem that systems thinking addresses. You must elevate your thinking beyond the here and now, so you can see the big picture to solve your most difficult problems.

Systems thinking is elevating your thinking beyond the here and now, so you can see the big picture to solve your most difficult problems.

Change the System, Influence Your Outcomes

Systems are all around us, but usually we are blissfully unaware of these systems, how we influence them, and how they influence us.

There are many types of systems. The examples provided above are "reinforcing systems," which are commonly referred to as "vicious cycles" or "virtuous cycles," depending on the outcome they produce. But really, a system is any type of structure through which results are produced. "Structures" can include habits, processes, or the physical layout of your environment.

You make decisions every day about how to structure your workspace, your living space, your routines, and your habits to get the results you want. If you believe drinking eight cups of water a day is good for you, you will likely put a water bottle on your desk to make it easier for you to accomplish that goal. If you believe that walking for thirty minutes a day will help you maintain a healthy body weight, then you might purchase a watch that can count your steps. These are examples of simple systems that we consciously design to help us get the desired results.

Have you considered the structures you live and work within that you haven't consciously designed? Probably not. Whether you know it or not, whatever outcomes you receive, whether good or bad, there's a good chance they are the result of a system. Here's the good news: you can usually influence the systems that are producing your outcomes!

Many of your problems that you think are beyond your control because you believe they are caused by other people or circumstances are actually within your influence. For instance, you cannot control whether you get a chronic physical ailment, but you can reduce your chances of getting one by the diet and exercise regime you establish. I know many people who complain, with good cause, about their disabling physical ailments, without ever acknowledging how their eating habits and lack of proper stretching and exercise for the past thirty years increased the likelihood of acquiring such ailments. Likewise, I know people whose healthy habits have either prevented the same ailments that disabled their family members or helped manage those same ailments so they have not become disabling.

The same scenario plays out all the time in the workplace. I constantly hear heads of human resources departments complain about the poor leadership skills of the managers and executives within their organization. When I ask them why they think that is, some of these HR professionals astutely acknowledge that the root cause of this chronic and pervasive lack of leadership skills is that people are generally promoted to leadership positions based on technical ability or tenure, not leadership ability. They say this with their hands on their hips and a shake of their head as if to say there is nothing they can do about it.

One time when I spoke at the California HR Conference, I asked a room of two hundred heads of HR the following question: "How many of you have a consistent criteria for promotion that management all agrees to and applies when making promotion decisions?" Zero hands went up.

The system that is producing an overabundance of managers with poor leadership skills is a terrible or non-existent promotion criteria. Working with management to implement a better promotion criteria is squarely within these HR professionals' scope of influence. This is a key principle of accountability: you can influence the systems that are producing your results!

Your environment and the processes you unknowingly follow are usually not designed to produce optimal results. You need to elevate your thinking to see how various events are connected to and influence one another, so you can design a better system that produces better results.

The gateway to solving your chronic problems is to ask this question: "Is it possible that other, less obvious, factors are causing my problems?" Asking this question will allow you to rise to a higher level of thinking, so you can begin to notice the true cause of your problems that are separated by distance and time. Once you enter the path of systems thinking and begin noticing the subtle factors that are causing your problems, the next question you must ask is "How can I influence these factors to produce better outcomes?"

As you develop this superpower of systems thinking, you will increase your capacity to take ownership of results and improve future results. In other words, systems thinking helps increase personal accountability.

4. Unraveling the Mystery of Leadership

Leadership is not the mysterious cosmic force that it's been made out to be. It isn't an art and it has little to do with charisma. Leadership is simple cause and effect. Certain behaviors have a greater positive impact on people and results than other behaviors. It's that simple.

With all that's been written about leadership, it's surprising how much misinformation exists on the subject. So, it is important to clear up some misconceptions about leadership before I explain what leadership really is.

The False Dichotomy of Management Versus Leadership

Social media posts are full of tables and infographics like the one below contrasting management with leadership.

MANAGERS	LEADERS
• Do things right	• Do the right things
• Organize work and resources	• Set the vision and strategy
• Are concerned about efficiency	• Are concerned about effectiveness
• Focus on the short-term	• Focus on the long-term
• Ensure positions are staffed	• Ensure people are aligned
• Seek for control and order	• Seek to empower
• Push	• Pull

Definitions that pit management against leadership like this are garbage. Like soda pop for the brain, this simple way of differentiating managers and leaders might taste good to consume, but in the end, it's just empty calories.

This soda pop definition of managers versus leaders simply separates the strategic activities of management from the operational activities of management. At worst these caricatures demonize the term "manager," making it synonymous with "bad leader." Consequently, the word "manager" has become something of a repugnant term in modern business literature.

The soda pop definition of management and leadership promotes three false notions.

1. **Managers and leaders are on opposite ends of the same spectrum.** They're not. Managers, directors, vice presidents, and executives are all management positions. Every level of manager makes decisions that direct the affairs of an organization. They are all responsible to organize people, tasks, and resources to achieve the desired results. Leadership, on the other hand, is not a position. Leadership is a method of influencing people.

2. **Senior managers are excused from being disciplined, organized, and aware of the details.** Good leaders are also good managers. Did Martin Luther King Jr., who most regard as an excellent example of a leader, simply give the famous "I have a dream" speech and let his "lower-level" managers figure out how to organize the civil rights movement? Of course not! Both senior managers and lower-level managers must be tactical and strategic. They simply apply their management skills in a different context and with a different scope. While it is true that some people in senior management positions are more skilled at big-picture thinking, and others are more skilled at organizing and executing, both types of individuals can be effective

leaders if they hire people who complement their strengths and compensate for their weaknesses.

3. **Being an executive means you're a leader.** I get an involuntary twitch in my neck when I hear senior management teams refer to themselves as "senior leadership teams." When I hear this, I picture Napoleon crowning himself emperor. You can't designate yourself a leader. Your position in the hierarchy has nothing to do with leadership. You are only a leader when others willingly follow you because they trust and respect you, not because they fear the consequences of not doing so. When organizations use the terms "executive" and "leader" interchangeably, people begin to believe that leadership is a position reserved for only a few. This notion is categorically false.

You are only a leader when others willingly follow you because they trust and respect you, not because they fear the consequences of not doing so.

Management is a position. Leadership is how one chooses to influence others. They are apples and oranges, so let's stop comparing them. The question isn't about the difference between management and leadership. What we're really talking about is the difference between how people choose to influence others to achieve the desired results.

What Is Leadership?

TWO WAYS TO INFLUENCE PEOPLE

People can apply two basic types of influence within organizations.

1. **Coercion:** This occurs when someone in authority uses positional power to obtain the compliance of others by controlling their outcomes, such as determining their compensation,

benefits, work assignments, and working conditions. People do what those in authority want them to do because they are incentivized to do so.

2. **Leadership:** This occurs when people voluntarily choose to follow someone else. People do what leaders want them to do because they trust and respect their leader.

A manager, a sports coach, and a parent all occupy leadership positions because their responsibility for other people gives them greater opportunity to exercise leadership influence. However, occupying a leadership position does not make one a leader. Many people in leadership positions *are not* leaders because they rely primarily on their formal authority to influence others (i.e., coercion).

Managers who use coercion to influence people teach employees that employment is a contract and nothing more. "If you do what I want, things will work out well for you. If you don't do what I want, all bets are off." As one executive put it, managers who rely on coercion to motivate employees are simply attempting to "tickle their greed and fear in the right combination."[1] Naturally, people who are trained to view work as a transaction tend to focus on extracting the most value for themselves out of the deal. Consequently, managers who rely on their positional power to influence others turn employees into mercenaries. Mercenaries don't care about achieving the organization's mission; they only care about looking out for their own interests. Mercenaries know that trust has nothing to do with work. It's all about the implied contract. Quid pro quo. If no incentive is provided for a mercenary to do something, it will not get done.

The more managers can align individual interests with team goals and with achieving the organization's mission, the more coercion can work. However, individual interests will never be perfectly aligned with team and organizational goals. People will always be faced with situations where there is no incentive to cooperate with others or go out of their way to do the right thing. This is where coercion fails. Coercion also fails because people can only stand to be coerced for so long. As soon as mercenaries think they can get a better deal elsewhere, they will leave. This is why coercion can work for a while, but organizations led by those who rely on their positional power to get results rarely achieve enduring success.

LEADERS CARE ABOUT PEOPLE AND RESULTS

People in leadership positions who are primarily concerned with getting results tend to rely on coercion to get those results. Leaders, on the other hand, care as much about the people they lead as they do about achieving the desired results. Leaders demonstrate that employment is a contract *and* a relationship.[2] The contract is the exchange of value. The relationship is about how employees feel about their work, their boss, and the organization that employs them.

People don't decide how hard to work or when to quit based on the stated or implied employment contract. Human beings make decisions based on their feelings and simply refer to facts to justify their decisions. This is why the relationship portion of employment is as important, if not more important, than the details of the stated or implied employment contract.

> Leaders care as much about the people they lead as they do about achieving results.

PEOPLE COME FIRST

Because leaders care deeply about the people over whom they have stewardship, leaders give them a noble cause to strive for instead of focusing them on increasing quarterly earnings so everybody can get a bigger bonus. Leaders respect those they lead by asking for their input on important decisions. Leaders err on the side of transparency rather than secrecy. They allow others to make decisions that enable them to develop and gain confidence in their own abilities. Leaders encourage others to take on responsibilities outside their comfort zone and then meet with them regularly to provide coaching to ensure they don't fail. Leaders do all this knowing full well that the people they lead may leave at any time, but they do it anyway because leaders believe the development and fulfillment of those they lead is just as important as achieving the organization's mission.

Human beings cannot be optimally effective until their own needs are met. This is why leaders and successful organizations put their people first. Let me be clear, employees' needs are not more important than the organization's mission. A company's mission, for instance, won't be achieved unless the company retains its customers and attains a steady revenue stream. However, in every organization, employees' needs must be met first. It is a natural sequence of events. We are reminded of this principle every time we hear (or more likely, ignore) the safety demonstration on airline flights. The flight attendants instruct us to put our own oxygen mask on before attempting to assist others. Likewise, true leaders know that the surest way to achieve organizational goals is first to meet the emotional needs of those they lead. Only when employees know that their leaders care about them as much as their leaders care about results will employees feel safe enough to innovate and be engaged enough to engage customers.

Leadership's dual focus on people and results—the relationship and the contract—requires far more time and energy than coercion. Allowing others to make decisions and try new things means they'll make mistakes. As well, when you are concerned about people's development and emotional well-being, a greater investment of time and effort is required to achieve results. It is simply more efficient in the short term to coerce people than to lead them. However, as Stephen Covey once wrote, "With people, slow is fast and fast is slow."[3] In other words, if you want quick, unsustainable results, then treat people like resources, grind value out of them, manipulate them to get them to do what you want, and then fire them when their performance dips. If you want sustainable results and hope to achieve your mission, demonstrate that you care about your people as much as you care about achieving results.

TRUE LEADERSHIP REQUIRES CONSISTENT PRACTICE

Leadership requires conscious thought and effort. Coercion, on the other hand, occurs any time someone in authority isn't consciously trying to lead. Any time there is a power imbalance between two people, coercion is the default method of influence. It happens unintentionally all the time. Why? Because people generally do what those in authority want them to do. People aren't stupid. They know who determines their pay and who can promote or fire them. We are all naturally inclined to cater to those who have more power and authority than we do. Most of us unconsciously try to curry favor with those who have more authority than we do in the hopes that being in their good graces will someday benefit us. This is not a cynical view of human nature; it is the result of thousands of years of learning the same lesson: be nicer to people who can help or hurt you. Consequently, unless those in leadership positions deliberately choose to lead when they interact with those they have stewardship over, they are, by default, coercing.

Take meetings, for example. All it takes to slip into coercion mode is for the person with the most authority in the room to disregard the power imbalance between him or her and everybody else. When this person fails to elevate other people's voices above their own, they are, by default, coercing. The entire direction of the discussion changes the moment the person with the most authority speaks.

Demonstrating leadership in meetings requires conscious thought and effort. As a leader, it takes discipline to hold your opinion until everyone else has spoken to allow the discussion to unfold without your undue interference. It takes mental energy to remember who hasn't spoken and invite them to do so. It takes self-mastery to thank people for sharing perspectives that you disagree with to make it safe for everyone to speak up. It takes humility to sincerely reassess your preferred course of action when many on your team disagree with you.

Leadership is harder than coercion and it requires your constant attention, but it's worth it. Influencing people through leadership instead of unconsciously coercing them produces more sustainable results while simultaneously elevating the lives of those you lead.

LEADERSHIP DEFINED

Leadership is about helping individuals reach their potential while also ensuring that the team achieves its goals. If we distill this observation down to its simplest form, we are left with the following definition of leadership.

> Leaders elevate others to achieve a common goal.

Based on this definition, who can be a leader? Is the title of "leader" reserved only for the heads of companies or other organizations? Must one be an executive to be a leader? The beautiful truth of leadership is that anyone can be a leader if they want to. Leadership begins with caring about people *and* results. The rest, as I will discuss, is learnable.

Both coercion and leadership provide us with leverage to accomplish our goals. Coercion, as I have discussed, is not a sustainable advantage. Its utility is diminished the moment individual interests and incentives are not perfectly aligned with team and organizational goals, and coercion is rendered completely useless the moment incentives stop. Leadership, on the other hand, is not only sustainable, it is also ennobling. All you need to access the mechanical advantage of coercion is formal authority. The key to access the greater advantage of leadership is personal accountability. No amount of charisma or other admirable leadership attributes can compensate for weak character. Leadership begins with exercising personal accountability.

The Litmus Test of Leadership

How can you know if you are truly a leader as opposed to someone who simply occupies a leadership position? The answer to this question can be found in the analysis of the definition of leadership. Let's take a closer look at the key elements of leadership.

- **Elevate others**. Leaders elevate others by helping them discover and enhance their strengths, encouraging them to exercise their agency, and by building their confidence in their abilities. Like parents, leaders make personal sacrifices to help others reach their potential. This includes sacrificing their time, ego, and status, restraining their impulses, and inconveniencing themselves to make a difference in someone else's life.

- **Positive change**. True leaders bring out the best in people and inspire positive change. Terrible leaders bring out the worst in people and inspire negative change. Positive change is motivated by a desire to build a better future without causing harm to others. In contrast, negative change is motivated by fear, revenge, greed, and selfishness and usually ends up benefiting some and hurting others.

- **Achieve a common goal**. Inspiring people to act is only half of the equation. Leaders mobilize others to realize a worthy goal that one person alone cannot achieve. Followers are willing to do what it takes to achieve the common goal primarily because they are inspired by: a) the goal itself, b) their leader's character (not to be confused with charisma), and c) their leader's care for them.

These three elements of leadership—elevate others, positive change, and achieve a common goal—combine to produce willing followers. Therefore, the litmus test of leadership is the answer to this question:

Would anybody willingly follow me if they weren't being paid to do so?

Based on this test, how many people in positions of authority are really leaders?

The above definition and test of leadership may sound like the ideal because it is so far from the norm, but this is how true leadership works, and it is possible. Maya Angelou famously wrote, "I've learned that people will forget what you said, people will forget what you did, but people will never forget how you made them feel." How did she learn this? Angelou worked with Martin Luther King Jr. as a civil rights activist and fundraiser. King inspired Angelou to adopt and achieve his dream because, in her words, "He was a prince of peace" and dispensed "a comfort of courtesies while trying to make wrong right."[4] On another occasion she said of King, "He had no arrogance at all. He had a humility that comes from deep inside."[5] King's influence undoubtedly elevated Angelou to reach a potential she likely wouldn't have dared imagine before meeting him.

Abraham Lincoln's biographer wrote that "The powerful competitors who had originally disdained Lincoln became colleagues who helped him steer the country through its darkest days." Edward Bates was one of Lincoln's rivals for the presidency. Lincoln eventually appointed him as attorney general. Even Bates, who initially viewed Lincoln as a well-meaning but incompetent administrator, eventually concluded that Lincoln was an unmatched leader, "very near being a perfect man."[6]

Fortunately, you don't have to be perfect to be a leader. You simply need to care deeply about people and results. As I will discuss, demonstrating the three habits of personal accountability is the most fundamental evidence that you care about both people and results. Practicing these habits builds the type of character that inspires others to follow. The three habits of personal accountability also provide a formula to help you achieve the right results more often and with more consistency. Exercising personal accountability is the key to unlocking the mechanical advantage of leadership to elevate others to achieve better results.

Now that we have a shared understanding of what leadership is, how accountability gives leadership its power, and how systems thinking can help us achieve better results, we are ready to learn about the three habits of personal accountability. The remainder of this book explores each of the three habits of personal accountability in detail: don't blame, look in the mirror, and engineer the solution.

HABIT 1 – DON'T BLAME

Blame kills accountability

5. Blame Spawns Three Deadly Cycles

Blame is like a virus. Its effect on organizations is similar to how a virus affects the human body. When blame infects an organization, it spreads quickly. For instance, a CEO may blame the Research and Development (R&D) team for not coming up with any innovative new products in the last eighteen months. If the CEO keeps his resentment to himself, it only impacts his perspective. However, when the CEO shares with the VP of sales his conclusion that R&D is inept, like a behavioral sneeze, he releases the blame virus into the organization.

While the CFO reviews the lower-than-expected sales figures at the following executive meeting, the VP of sales half-jokingly says, "Well if R&D would give us something new to sell, we wouldn't be in this mess." The head of R&D detects that the VP's remark drew a subtle smirk from the CEO. Feeling betrayed, the head of R&D launches into a rehearsed tirade of all the ways the organization has hamstrung R&D, such as insufficient budget and lack of support for proposed new products. This, of course, provokes defensive responses from the indicted executives who then attempt to extricate themselves from any association with the poor sales results. Subsequently, the meeting devolves into an unproductive debate where sharp words and not-so-subtle digs leave wounds that linger and divide the organization. Blame is like a virus because it multiplies and spreads quickly, harming the host and others who become infected by it.

Blame is perpetual negative energy that creates its own inertia because it causes a chain reaction. Our natural tendency is to try to distance ourselves from problems that might make us look bad. When our egos are threatened, our brains tend to grasp for any reasons why the debacle might not be our fault. Quite often, those reasons just so happen to incriminate someone else, so we feel justified deflecting blame elsewhere. Here's the problem though: once the blame virus has infected an organization, it circulates like a slippery projectile. Since we are all naturally gifted at deflecting blame, blame tends to stay in perpetual motion, inflicting harm every time it bounces from one defendant to the next. The issues may change over time, giving the illusion of closure; however, once we've been blamed, the bruise remains tender long after impact, leaving us more sensitive the next time something goes wrong. This steadily increases our inclination to defend ourselves the next time we sense we might be blamed for something, and so the cycle of blame continues.

Blame kills accountability because nobody will dare take accountability for poor results if they think they will be blamed for doing so. Blame harms the organization because people's energy becomes focused on defending themselves rather than moving the organization forward—like a sick body that must mobilize white blood cells to fight a virus. Healthy organizations can focus their energy on working together to improve results. A sick organization, like a sick person, becomes weak and ineffective until it can expel the virus that is diverting its attention away from making progress.

**No one will take accountability
if they think they will be blamed for doing so.**

Countless dollars are thrown out the window (think stacks of hundred dollar bills) from three self-destructive cycles that are put into motion as soon as the blame virus is unleashed. These three cycles are the Cycle of Inaction, the Cycle of Ignorance, and the Cycle of Infighting.

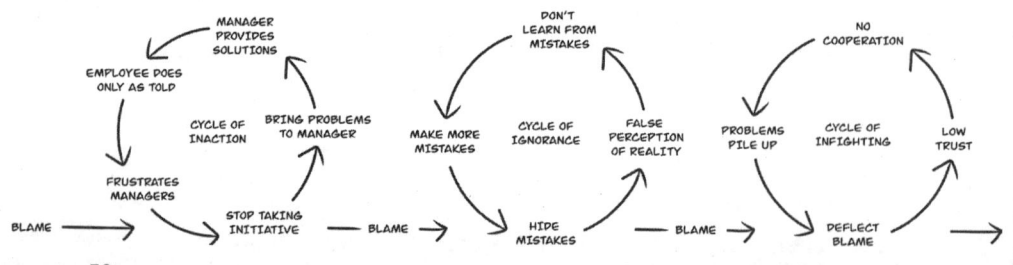

The Cycle of Inaction

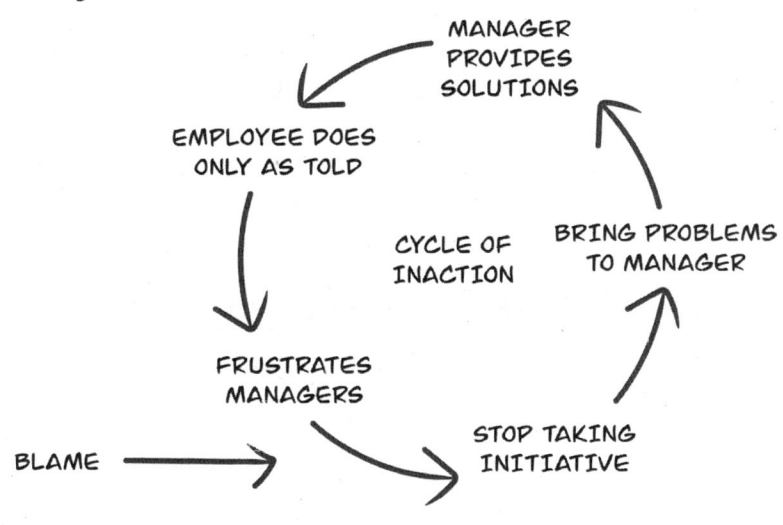

```
        MANAGER
        PROVIDES
        SOLUTIONS
EMPLOYEE DOES
ONLY AS TOLD
                CYCLE OF    BRING PROBLEMS
                INACTION    TO MANAGER

        FRUSTRATES
        MANAGERS
BLAME ──→            STOP TAKING
                     INITIATIVE
```

While blaming colleagues may spread the blame virus throughout an organization, blame incites a far more insidious and counterproductive effect when a power imbalance exists between the combatants. The very act of blaming someone is a form of punishment. Its primary intent is to protect oneself and to shame the accused. People tend to fear punishment and shaming, and fear is generally paralyzing.

When a manager blames an employee for making a mistake, the employee tends to recoil into the safety of thinking, *From now on, I'll wait until I'm told exactly what to do*. Almost overnight, this employee stops taking the initiative and instead brings all problems to their manager to await instructions on how the boss wants the problems to be solved. Of course, this lack of initiative frustrates the manager. The employee senses their boss's frustration but isn't sure of the reasons for it. This state of uneasiness can cause a confident, competent employee to turn into a mumbling, bumbling, mindless servant paralyzed by fear. *Better to do nothing than try something and get in trouble again,* they reason.

Stephen Covey aptly named this cycle of behavior "Gofer Delegation" (go for this, go for that) because the boss ends up doing all the thinking, and employees simply carry out the boss's orders. Managers unintentionally train their staff to be gofers far more often than they know. When someone takes the initiative to solve a problem, but their solution doesn't work out, managers who beat them up for their mistake are communicating the following message loud and clear: "Don't do *anything* unless I tell you it's okay to do it!"

Managers who find that their employees bring all problems to them to solve should ask themselves this question: "Have I blamed or otherwise expressed frustration at my staff at some point when they took the initiative and made a mistake?" If the answer is yes, the manager needs to do some damage control that includes admitting that blaming was the wrong thing to do, apologizing, and coming up with a plan to prevent it from happening again. This plan might include providing guidelines within which the staff may exercise their initiative and treating mistakes as learning opportunities rather than punishing initiative.

If the answer is no, the manager hasn't blamed his or her staff for taking the initiative, then perhaps the staff member has been trained by previous managers to be a gofer. Susan, the highly responsible but totally unaccountable payroll supervisor I discussed earlier, was certainly trained by her boss to be a gofer, so she didn't do anything unless explicitly asked.

People who have been trained to be gofers have effectively been in an abusive relationship with their boss. It will take no less than a direct intervention to address the gofer behavior and identify where it's coming from. After assuring the person that he or she will not be blamed for taking the initiative in the future, it will take lots of time and evidence for the employee to believe it's safe to venture out of his or her "gofer hole" again.

The irony of the Cycle of Inaction is that managers frequently blame their staff for not taking initiative when it's often the managers themselves who have paralyzed their employees.

The Cycle of Ignorance

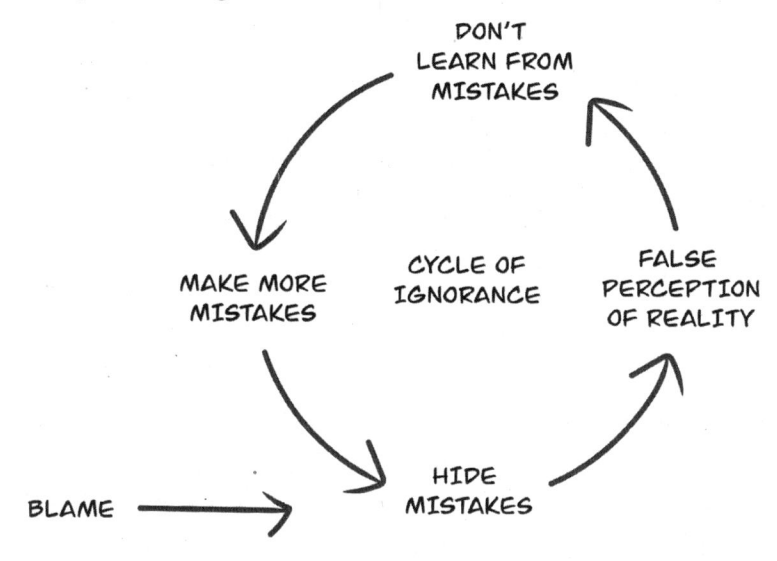

```
            DON'T
         LEARN FROM
          MISTAKES

  MAKE MORE      CYCLE OF       FALSE
  MISTAKES      IGNORANCE     PERCEPTION
                              OF REALITY

                    HIDE
  BLAME  ──→      MISTAKES
```

The ostensive rationale for blaming someone is that if you sufficiently rub their nose in their mistake, the offender will think twice before making the same mistake again. Studies (and common sense) have proven otherwise.[1] Instead of making fewer mistakes, people in blame-and-shame cultures simply get better at hiding their mistakes.

In a business environment, hiding mistakes results in lower productivity, poorer quality, and ultimately, lower profitability. However, in some industries, hiding errors costs lives. A report from the Institute of Medicine in 2000 estimated that forty-four thousand to ninety-eight thousand people die each year in US hospitals due to medical errors.[2] Since nurses are the final point of delivery in the medication administration process, they are often the ones who get blamed for mistakes.

In a 1996 landmark study out of Harvard University, researcher Amy Edmondson revealed just how harmful the fear of blame is on organizational culture and performance.[3] Edmondson designed her study to determine if some work groups were better than others at catching and preventing mistakes. To do so she followed eight hospital teams in two hospitals over the course of six months. Edmondson expected to find that poorer-performing teams would report more mistakes, but to her surprise, the opposite was true. The better the team performed in terms of quality of care, collaboration, efficiency, and leadership, the more errors were reported. The explanation for this puzzling result became apparent when her research team interviewed the medical team members. It turned out that the highest-performing teams were typically led by managers and doctors who did not blame team members for making mistakes. "There is no punishment; you just let the doctor know and fill out an incident report," reported one nurse. Edmondson noted that errors were discovered and remedied more often "in units in which members are less concerned about being caught making a mistake." In contrast, the worst-performing teams were led by "authoritarian" managers who regularly blamed employees for mistakes. "People don't advertise errors here," one nurse said. "If there's no adverse event, then don't report it." Edmondson's study provides unequivocal evidence that blame inhibits learning and improvement.

When people successfully hide their problems and mistakes, management remains oblivious to what is really going on in the trenches. They aren't getting the results they want, but they don't know why. So, management aimlessly introduces new incentives or quality-control programs hoping this will change things, but the real reasons for the poor results remain obscured because the root causes are not being exposed. As a result, no learning occurs.

A more recent study, also investigating medical errors made by nurses, supported Edmondson's conclusions but added additional insights.[4] Consistent with Edmondson's findings, researcher Peggy Hewitt found that 74 percent of nurses in her study reported that some errors are not reported to management because they feared their managers' reaction. In Edmondson's study, nurses reported not reporting mistakes if there were no adverse effects. However, Hewitt found that nurses were also reluctant to report errors if they believed the problem wasn't *their* mistake. For example, if a patient missed a scheduled antibiotic injection because he or she was away from the unit for three hours, the nurse on duty thought, *It's not my fault the patient isn't here, so I'm not going to report it.* Or if patients received their antibiotics forty-five to sixty minutes late on a busy surgical unit, the nurse thought, *It's not my fault we're busy and understaffed, so I'm not going to report it.*

These are not cases of nurses not understanding that a problem exists. The nurses understand the potential risk if patients miss their antibiotics or receive them late. The nurses are simply highly motivated not to report these problems because they don't want to deal with their manager's reaction. They know there is a good chance they will be blamed for the error. When they are blamed, they will have to prepare a defense to explain why it wasn't their fault, knowing that this explanation may or may not keep them out of trouble. Understandably, the nurses think, *Why would I put myself through that when I didn't do anything wrong?*

Management can't address problems that they don't know exist or if the true cause remains a mystery. They will never be able to identify and solve the problems that are occurring right under their noses if employees are afraid to bring the problems to their manager's attention.

Further exacerbating the Cycle of Ignorance is the fact that when problems come to light, the employees' energy is not focused on solving problems; it's focused on protecting their backsides. When people operate within a culture of blame, they shift their energy away from solving problems and focus instead on hiding or deflecting blame.

The destructive power of blame is amplified by our primal instincts. Cognitive function essentially shuts down when the knives come out.[5] Our brains interpret blame the same way they interpret a physical attack.[6,7] When we feel the stress of having to defend ourselves, our brains transfer control over thoughts and emotions from the prefrontal cortex, which is where complex problem-solving originates, to the amygdala, one of the most primitive parts of the brain.[8] Unfortunately, the amygdala can only offer one of three suggestions for how to deal with our problems: fight, flight, or freeze. Consequently, people become less creative and less able to think rationally when their backs are up against a wall. So, even when employees aren't hiding problems from their boss, they won't be willing or able to solve those problems if they feel they are being blamed for them. Blame triggers the "fight or flight" response, which inhibits people's ability to solve the very problems for which they are being blamed.

Blame triggers the "fight or flight" response, which inhibits people's ability to solve the very problems for which they are being blamed.

The Cycle of Ignorance is like a black hole. Once organizations become caught in its grasp, organizational learning doesn't just stop, it regresses. Fewer and fewer issues surface because people are afraid of the consequences. Even when issues do come to light, people's energy is not focused on learning from them. Ignorance is not bliss. Rather, it's fatal to organizational performance.

The Cycle of Infighting

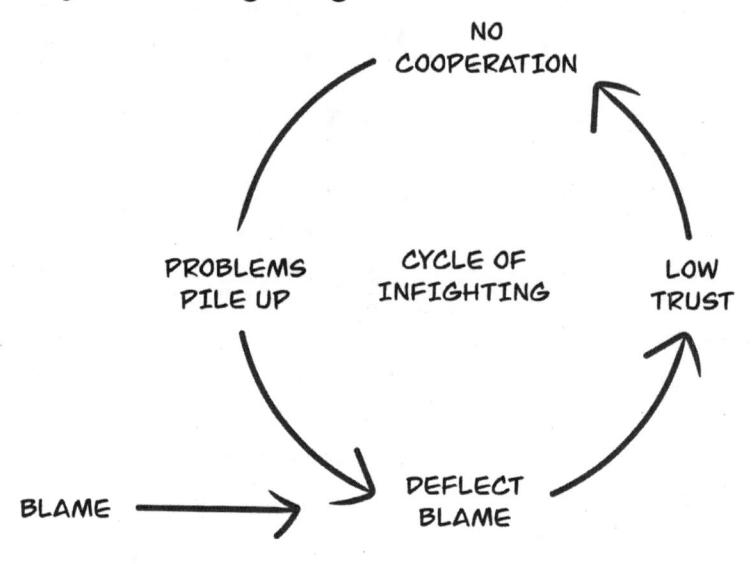

Diagram: Cycle of Infighting — NO COOPERATION → LOW TRUST → DEFLECT BLAME → PROBLEMS PILE UP → NO COOPERATION; BLAME → DEFLECT BLAME

When people within an organization fear their leaders and one another, they expend a tremendous amount of energy trying to protect themselves. Simon Sinek taught this vitally important leadership principle in his book, *Leaders Eat Last*.[9] According to Maslow's hierarchy of needs, once human beings have sufficient food, water, and shelter, their next

Habit 1 – Don't Blame

most powerful need is to feel safe. When people inside an organization don't feel safe, they will engage in all sorts of unproductive behaviors to protect themselves. This subtle war that is being waged inside organizations has become known as "office politics."

The primary goal of office politics is to deflect blame and defend one's "turf." Trust and cooperation cannot exist in such an environment. Organizations embroiled in turf wars become less effective for three reasons.

1. **Wasted time.** The first casualty of office politics is time. The more time people spend crafting meticulous emails designed to deflect blame and protect their position, the less time they have to do their job. These email wars consume enormous amounts of time and accomplish nothing except to further entrench hard feelings.

2. **Fewer allies.** When someone first joins an organization, everybody in that organization is their potential ally in their quest to fulfill the organization's mission. These are people who they can rely on and go to for help, colleagues who will willingly share their knowledge and resources with them to help reach their shared goals. When people feel blamed by colleagues, potential allies become enemies. Employees lose access to their colleagues' knowledge, skills, networks, and other resources that would help them do their job well and move the organization forward.

3. **Problems aren't getting solved.** Lasting solutions are usually the result of a joint effort. Engaging in the blame game doesn't just delay finding solutions to joint problems; it drives solutions further away. For instance, when product managers and engineers blame each other for late product releases, they end up clogging up the product-development process, which inevitably delays future product releases. When sales representatives and customer-support teams blame each other for declining

customer retention, this will drive away more customers who are being told, "Your issue is a different department's problem to solve." The more that people engage in blame wars, the more unresolved problems will pile up. These new problems provide even more reasons for people to defend their performance while also supplying them with fresh ammunition with which to fight their next battle. And so the Cycle of Infighting goes 'round and round.'

Edmondson's study, described above, highlights how contagious the blame virus can be. In one of the high-performing teams with a no-blame culture, one nurse reported that "there is an unspoken rule here to help each other and check each other." On the other hand, Edmondson observed that blame tended to spill over into other work groups. In fact, blame in one work group led to "resentment and blame across group boundaries." Those interviewed described "backstabbing" and "cliques." While observing one such unit, a researcher even overheard one nurse make "a mean-spirited comment behind the back of another nurse while explaining why she refused to help the other nurse."

Spreading the blame virus around the organization creates an "us versus them" mentality that erodes trust and cooperation. When trust and cooperation go out the window, so do performance, quality, and bottom-line results.

6. Do You Have a Culture of Accountability or a Culture of Blame?

Some refer to culture as "the way we do things around here." More accurately, culture is the patterns of behavior that form within an organization. Why do people in an organization begin behaving in similar ways? Did they all get together and have a secret meeting where they agreed to behave a certain way? No, they didn't. The invisible force that influences people to behave in similar patterns is power, or formal authority. Evolutionary forces have hardwired human beings to pay close attention to people or things that affect their livelihood and survival. Today, we are not concerned about fending off a saber-toothed tiger or stalking our prey. Instead, we are paying close attention to what our boss says and does so we can behave in a way that might improve our odds of getting a raise or a promotion. We're also paying close attention to our boss's body language and tone of voice to estimate our chances of getting that raise or promotion. In a hierarchy, everybody looks up the food chain for cues on how to behave to improve their odds of achieving favorable outcomes. This isn't a Machiavellian scheme; it's prudence. The result is groups of people who behave in similar patterns.

Employees don't create culture, and culture doesn't "just happen." Those in positions of authority create the culture—intentionally or unwittingly—by how and what they indicate is important to them. Patterns of behavior emerge when employees come to the same conclusion about what their managers' true priorities really are. For instance, earlier in my career I worked for a company led by a president and executive vice president (EVP) who made it clear that EBITDA (earnings before interest, taxes, depreciation, and amortization) was their top priority. This priority was so clearly understood by us, the senior managers, that we created a new way to greet each other. Instead of saying "Hey, Steve," when we saw each other in the office, we'd point to each other and say, "It's all about the EBITDA!" I kid you not. That was the corporate culture. It was all about the EBITDA. Consequently, any discussion about employee engagement was quickly squelched, and morale plummeted. We knew that the top two executives viewed employees as simply a "resource" to grind money out of.

Within that broader corporate culture, a strong subculture began to emerge under my boss, the EVP. The EVP was a workaholic. He did not have any children, and his wife was also a busy professional. The EVP would come into work at 7 a.m. and often leave after 6:30 p.m. He would then work from home, sending us emails until late at night. The EVP would derisively refer to employees who arrived and left work on time as "nine to fivers." We learned very quickly that to have any chance of getting a good performance rating from him, we too needed to come in early, leave late, and respond to emails at night.

Working silly hours wasn't written in any policy manual or employment contract. The EVP never explicitly said that's what he expected. Not surprisingly though, we all, in unison, began working longer and longer hours. How managers behave reveals their priorities far more than what is declared in policies or value statements. Behavior is contagious, especially the behavior of those in positions of authority.

The same is true of cultures of blame and cultures of accountability. If your boss communicates that being right is important to them and blames "those idiots in accounting for making our lives unnecessarily difficult," the odds are that you will blame too. However, if your boss communicates that collaboration is important, when the boss says, "I've set up a meeting with the controller to see if we can improve the expense reimbursement process. Want to come?" you're more likely to attempt to resolve your problems in a similar fashion. It's the behavior of the people in charge, not their stated intentions, that creates culture. Those in leadership positions either provide an example of accountability that others want to emulate, or they spread the blame virus.

Cultures of accountability and cultures of blame are on opposite ends of the corporate cultural spectrum. The groundwork for a culture of blame is laid when those in authority view other people as the primary source of problems. True leaders, on the other hand, see people as problem solvers. When problems arise, those who preside over cultures of blame focus on finding the offender(s) and making an example of them. When problems are brought to the attention of effective leaders, they focus on finding and fixing the faults in the processes that contributed to the problem instead of assuming that one or more people were entirely the cause of the problem.

Cultures of blame and cultures of accountability create entirely different outcomes because of the way the people in those cultures respond to problems. People in cultures of blame are afraid to confront problems. People in cultures of accountability take ownership of problems and their solutions, no matter who or what caused them.

Perhaps you have seen the difference between blame and accountability in the organizations for which you have worked. The following table illustrates the difference between cultures that tolerate blame versus those that foster accountability.

How Leaders Can Inspire Accountability

	CULTURE OF BLAME	CULTURE OF ACCOUNTABILITY
BELIEVES	People are the problem	People are problem solvers
	Problems are headaches	Problems are learning opportunities
	Admitting mistakes is a sign of weakness	We are all still learning
FOCUSED ON	Who is wrong	What is wrong
	The individual	The process
	Fault finding	Fact finding
	The past	The future
	Assigning punishment	Improving future results
RESULTS IN	Making assumptions	Considering alternatives
	Hoarding decision-making authority	Delegating decision-making authority
	Hiding problems	Surfacing problems and solutions
	Finger pointing and CYA behavior	Learning from mistakes
	Distrust	Trust
	Turf wars	Cross-functional cooperation
	Risk averse	Calculated risk taking
	Waiting until told	Taking initiative
	Lack of innovation	Innovation

Most organizations are somewhere in the middle of the blame/accountability spectrum. That is, most workplaces have a culture that is somewhere between one that promotes blame and one where everyone acts with accountability 100 percent of the time. However, cultures of mostly blame and cultures of mostly accountability do exist, as illustrated in the studies mentioned earlier. Perhaps you can think of an organization you worked for or a team you were on that was led by someone who consistently modeled accountability. More likely, you can think of a boss who blamed. Think of the climate those managers created and the outcomes they produced. Odds are, you preferred working on the team with the manager who modeled accountability, and you probably performed better as a result. This link between leader accountability, workplace culture, and results has been proven numerous times.[1] One study in particular provides deep insight into this link between accountability, culture, and results.

A Tale of Two Cultures

Researchers Teresa Amabile and Steven Kramer studied 238 professionals in twenty-six project teams within seven companies to determine how positive and negative work environments arise. They studied the effects of both types of environments on the individuals who worked there as well as the effects of both types of environments on the success of the enterprises themselves.[2] Their unique study collected copious amounts of data from all 238 professionals, including nearly twelve thousand individual journal entries. While all seven companies faced similar business challenges, certain companies and work groups managed their challenges in starkly different ways with drastically different results.

A CULTURE OF FEAR AND BLAME

One of the worst companies profiled in the study, a consumer products company with products in almost 80 percent of American homes, was referred to as the "Karpenter Corporation" (a pseudonym). It's executives and managers relied heavily on coercion to motivate employees and engaged in blame wars. This climate was established by the top brass. During a division-wide meeting with the COO, someone asked what was being done about the morale problem. "There is no morale problem in this company," the COO replied. "And for anybody who thinks there is, we have a nice big bus waiting outside to take you wherever you want to look for work." The COO was communicating loudly and clearly, "Those who bring up problems will be sorry they did," so employees learned not to speak up.

A typical example of this reluctance to speak up surfaced when a packaging engineer discovered that a new product handle kept breaking during routine testing. When the team discussed options for how to address it, they agreed that the product was poorly designed but that it was too late to redesign it. Instead, they decided to find a solution to the breakage through packaging. Now here's the kicker: someone on the team had noted the weakness in the product handle a month earlier but was afraid to mention it. If that person had felt safe to speak up, the team may have had time to fix the handle properly. This case was far from unique. When problems with a product arose at this company, they were usually ignored or patched over. Employees knew their leaders didn't want to hear bad news, so no time was allocated to learn from problems.

Another instance of this culture of blame within the Karpenter Corporation played out in a battle between R&D and manufacturing. The R&D team was working overtime to get a new product into production to fill a huge order within a tight deadline. The R&D team breathed a collective sigh of relief when they managed to get their new product into production in time to meet the deadline. To their shock and horror, the following day, they learned that manufacturing had shut down production for their product because the packaging hadn't arrived. However, the packaging was due to arrive that day, and manufacturing could have easily stored the newly manufactured products in an empty warehouse until the packaging arrived. Manufacturing did not need to shut down production, so why did they? Because the VP of R&D and the VP of manufacturing were engaged in a turf war, and the VP of manufacturing saw this unnecessary delay as an opportunity to get even with his rival.

This toxic culture of blame and low accountability infected nearly everything that happened at that company. The once-proud company with a historic past went bankrupt only four years after it was named one of the ten most innovative and successful companies in America. It didn't go bust because of an accounting scandal or because of poor market conditions. It died because, four years before its collapse, the company brought in a new top executive team who relied on coercion instead of leadership to influence those they presided over. Moreover, this executive team carried the blame virus.

A CULTURE OF ACCOUNTABILITY

On the other end of the accountability spectrum, the researchers discovered a team leader in a different company who knew precisely how to model personal accountability and inspire others to do the same. Graham, the team leader, was a chemical engineer at Kruger-Bern Chemicals (also a pseudonym). Graham's team was tasked with the responsibility of developing a safe, biodegradable polymer to replace petrochemicals in cosmetics.

In contrast to Karpenter's management, Graham was known for his non-judgmental openness to discussing problems with his team. On one occasion a team member named Brady couldn't get the parameters right on the equipment and had to abort a trial of a new material that caused a significant weeklong delay. Without hesitation, Brady told his manager about the bad news. Although disappointed by the setback, not only did Graham not blame Brady, he took accountability for the problem by reporting that *"Our* trial . . . had to be aborted."

On another occasion, Graham demonstrated all three habits of personal accountability when a bad product review almost derailed the team's biggest sale. When the infuriated VP of marketing contacted Graham about the unsatisfactory product, Graham promised her a quick solution. Graham called an emergency team meeting to explain the situation and request ideas on how to solve the problem.

Watch how Graham demonstrated the three habits of personal accountability to address the problem.

Habit 1 – Don't Blame. Graham focused everyone on the facts and didn't blame anyone for the product failure. Furthermore, he did not allow anyone else to make any personal accusations.

Habit 2 – Look in the Mirror. When offering his assessment of the situation, Graham began by noting the mistakes he had made on the project. Following their leader's example, everyone else began pointing out how they too had contributed to the problem when creating the sample or communicating with the customer.

Habit 3 – Engineer the Solution. After accurately diagnosing the problem, Graham's team was able to come up with a solution and communicate their plan to the client, which the client accepted. Within days, Graham called another team meeting to debrief about the crisis, identify lessons learned, and change the process to ensure the mistakes they made on the project were never repeated.

Because of the way Graham responded to problems, his team members frequently updated him on their progress and setbacks without being asked. Graham's team acted like a team and was able to perform well under pressure.

It is interesting to note that the senior managers at Kruger-Bern were not effective leaders. They regularly gave Graham conflicting orders and left him severely understaffed. It would have been easy (and understandable) for Graham to blame upper management any time his team encountered problems, but he consistently modeled the behavior he wanted from his team. Not surprisingly, his team followed his inspiring lead.

This example highlights that different subcultures can exist within the same work environment. Once again, culture is a reflection of the priorities and behaviors of those in authority. Cultures of accountability are a reflection of accountable leadership.

7. Why Do We Blame?

If blame causes so many problems, and if we hate being blamed ourselves, why do we do it? Before we can effectively cure ourselves and our workplaces of blame, we need to understand the answer to this question.

There are a few key reasons and one big reason why blaming others seems to be an involuntary human response when things go wrong.

1. IT FEELS GOOD

When things go wrong, it usually makes us mad. When we think we've found an outside reason for our problems, something or someone to blame, punishment feels satisfying.

In one of the most-viewed TED talks of all time, Brené Brown defines blame as "A way to discharge pain and discomfort."[1]

Brown's definition of blame reminds me of a scene in the movie *Office Space*. Throughout the movie, the frequent printer jams become a symbol of the inhumane office environment created by the organization's idiot boss. When the employees finally come up with a plan to get revenge on the company, they take the printer to an open field and give it a gangster-style beating to vent their frustrations (it's both vicious and hilarious at the same time). Obviously, the printer wasn't the cause of all their frustrations, but that's not the point. Smashing it served as an outlet for their pent-up feelings. Blaming people or circumstances when things go wrong is an outlet.

2. WE THINK BLAMING WILL MOTIVATE OTHERS TO CHANGE

Many of us believe that if we get mad at someone for something, they will feel badly for their mistake, apologize, and immediately correct the undesirable behavior. You know, the same way we respond when people blame us. Yeah, right!

Why, then, would we expect others to respond differently than we would? If you are in a position of authority over the people you are blaming, they may feel the need to appear contrite to appease their boss. This may give you the impression that blaming your subordinates when things go wrong is an effective solution. Instead, more than likely, the people you are blaming have just learned to hide the behavior that got them in trouble and often go on to plot their revenge.

3. TO PRESERVE OUR SELF-ESTEEM

As one psychologist wrote, "It's easier to blame someone else than to accept responsibility."[2] For insecure people, their self-worth comes from being right. "I am right, you are wrong, which means I am better than you, and I have value." Blaming others is a way to make them feel superior to others. It's an ego boost.

Accountable people, on the other hand, don't get their self-esteem from being right. They get it from the belief that they are capable of overcoming their challenges.

Only confident people have the capacity to be accountable because, unlike insecure people, they are able to acknowledge their role in problems without it shattering their self-esteem, and they take the initiative to solve them.

4. TO EXPLAIN WHY THINGS HAPPEN (THIS IS THE BIG REASON)

Human beings have a deep need to explain the world around us. We feel that if we can explain what is happening and why, we can have some control over it. Unfortunately, this deep need, combined with other psychological forces, causes us to come to a lot of incorrect conclusions.

The following section explains the psychological forces at play that encourage us to conclude that other people are the cause of our problems and why that conclusion is usually wrong.

It's Often the System, Not the Person

There are basically two ways of explaining human-related problems: the person approach and the systems approach.

The person approach views human errors as "arising primarily from aberrant mental processes such as forgetfulness, inattention, poor motivation, carelessness, negligence, and recklessness," writes systems expert James Reason.[3] Naturally enough, managers steeped in the person approach tend to focus their solutions on "fixing" people through training, poster campaigns that appeal to people's sense of fear, threats of discipline, naming, blaming, and shaming. In other words, the person approach assumes that human error is the *cause* of most problems.

The premise of the systems approach is that human error is the *consequence* of bad systems. The systems approach acknowledges that human beings make mistakes and will always make mistakes. That is a given. With this in mind, who's the dummy when someone makes a mistake, the person who made the mistake or the person who designed a process that assumed people wouldn't make mistakes?

Although we can't "change the human condition," Reason explains, "we can change the conditions under which humans work."

As far as we can tell, the systems approach to human-related problems emerged toward the end of World War II.[4] The US Air Force (USAF) became concerned about the number of pilot errors that resulted in unforced aircraft crashes. So, the USAF hired human factors pioneers Fitts and Jones to investigate the problem and advise the US military on how to select less error-prone fighter pilots. Instead, Fitts and Jones discovered it was not the pilots who were broken; it was the design of the cockpits.

"For example, pilots confused the flap and gear handles because these typically looked and felt the same and were co-located. Or they mixed up the locations of throttle, mixture and propeller controls because these kept changing across different cockpits."[5]

Fitts and Jones's findings were profound: the world is not unchangeable. To produce better outcomes, it's easier to change the environment than to try to fix the human condition. "We can re-tool, re-build, re-design, and thus influence the way in which people perform," one researcher concluded.

The new system-centered view is credited with having saved countless lives and dollars during World War II and the Korean War.

Since Fitts and Jones published their research in 1947, governments, the aerospace industry, healthcare, and the business world have all radically changed the way they view problems. Managers in these industries no longer blame people when things go wrong. Instead, they look for environmental factors that contribute to problems and then engineer solutions rather than trying to train human fallibility out of people.

Actually, none of that really happened.

High-consequence industries such as aerospace and health care have just recently got the "systems approach" memo, and they still have a lot of work to do. The business world is mostly unaware that a memo was issued. And governments aren't sure if their union agreements permit them to read such memos.

As I will explain shortly, several factors prevent our brains from accepting the systems approach. Human beings are essentially programmed to default to the person approach upon discovering a mistake. This is why most workplace problems and accidents continue to be blamed on human error (the person approach) when, in fact, other factors (systems) play a much larger role.

For example, in 2006, California doctors at a children's hospital accidentally removed the wrong side of a patient's skull during brain surgery.[6] An investigative report by the California Department of Health services determined that the cause of the accident was "failing to follow proper procedures." In other words, the investigators blamed the surgeon. Consequently, new procedures were mandated to prevent future errors.

However, a Rhode Island hospital that implemented those very procedures had three highly publicized wrong-side brain surgeries in less than a year. Wait a minute, why did surgeons keep making the same mistake?

Researchers investigating wrong-site surgeries such as these concluded that the protocols hospitals implement to prevent mistakes are often overly complex, making errors more likely.[7] Simply put, the very procedures people design to prevent errors can actually increase the risk of errors when they don't take into consideration the human condition. This is like offering a cure that is worse than the illness.

The old adage "To err is human" is more accurately stated as "To blame is human." The next time you watch a news report about a tragic accident, notice how often the reporter and witnesses default to the person approach as they try to explain the cause of the accident. The explanation usually comes down to one or more of these three common culprits: someone was either lazy, careless, or incompetent.

Here's one such example of our propensity to blame people instead of systems.

On July 25, 2013, a speeding train in Santiago de Compostela, Spain, took a corner too fast and derailed. Seventy-nine people died. It was Spain's worst rail accident in forty years.[8] Here are the facts:[9]

- The train's black boxes showed that the train was travelling at 192 km/h moments before the crash. The speed limit on the curve was 80 km/h.

- Spanish media reported that a year before the crash, the train driver made a Facebook post stating, "It would be amazing to go alongside police and overtake them and trigger off the speed camera." The driver posted a photo of a train's speedometer at 200 km/h (124 mph).

- Initial investigations ruled out mechanical or technical failure, sabotage, and terrorism.

- The driver confessed: "I ****** up, I want to die. So many people dead, so many people dead."

Conclusion? There are only two possible explanations: human error, recklessness, or both. Most people would be inclined to think, "Let's put this guy in jail, throw away the key, and be done with it."

However, there were other facts that the media and the public weren't very interested in considering because this was a slam-dunk case of negligence, right? Not so fast.

- A few minutes before the derailment, the driver received a call on his work phone. It was the ticket inspector asking the driver to instruct him on how to enter an upcoming station to facilitate the exit of a family with children. The call lasted almost two minutes, which is a long time when you are travelling at 192 km/h. Railroad employees are not allowed to use phones except in case of emergency, but ticket inspectors do not have access to the driver's cab. The driver told the court he lost sense of where the train was during the call and thought he was on a different section of the track.

- Shortly before the train crashed, the train had passed from a computer-controlled area of the track to a zone that requires the driver to take manual control of braking and deceleration. The curve in question did not have an automatic braking system, as did other high-risk sections of the track. According to a Spanish journalist, "There were arguments for having that section of the route remade completely, but the city's land tenure regime makes expropriations an administrative nightmare. So the bend was left as it was, and speed was limited there to 80 km/h."

- The driver previously warned the company about that curve: "I already told those guys at safety that it was very dangerous. We are human and this can happen to us. This curve is inhuman."

- Regarding the Facebook post, speeds of 200 km/h are normal and fully permitted on high-speed line sections. The social media post was irresponsible and unwise under any circumstances, but it appears more like a smoking gun in the aftermath of such an accident.

Ultimately, the Spanish courts found the driver at least partially responsible and sentenced him to four years in jail. However, should the rail company have foreseen the communication problem between drivers and other employees and designed a safer way to communicate? Probably.

Could the rail company have engineered the track to prevent this foreseeable accident from occurring? Absolutely. And that's the rub: the people closest to accidents and problems usually get blamed when things go wrong when really, they are often at the tail end of a bad system.

Everybody makes mistakes. When the likelihood or severity of mistakes is high, the primary responsibility for ensuring that mistakes don't happen rests with system designers, not the operators.

The people closest to problems usually get blamed when things go wrong when really, they are often at the tail end of a bad system.

The two Boeing 737 Max 8 crashes provide another example of people's propensity to blame the operators instead of the designers. On October 29, 2018, Indonesian-based Lion Air Flight 610 crashed after takeoff from Jakarta, killing all 189 people on board. Not even five months later, Ethiopian Airlines Flight 302 crashed on March 10, 2019, again shortly after takeoff, killing all 157 people on board. Both crashes were linked to the Max 8's Maneuvering Characteristics Augmentation System (MCAS), which automatically pushed the airplane nose down if the airplane's sensors detected a risk of a stall. In both crashes the pilots unsuccessfully fought the automated MCAS system while the plane repeatedly and relentlessly forced the plane's nose toward the ground.

Why did the planes crash? According to Republican Congressman Sam Graves, who testified at the House Aviation Subcommittee hearing on May 13, 2019, "pilots trained in the US would have been successful" in handling the emergencies on both jets. He and many others blamed the crashes on inadequate training of the Indonesian and Ethiopian pilots. In other words, the pilots of the crashed planes were accused of being incompetent.

So, what really happened? Here are the facts.

- Boeing designed the Max 8 to rely on only one "angle-of-attack" (AOA) sensor to inform the MCAS system when to engage.[10] In both Max 8 crashes, the AOA sensor failed, erroneously activating the MCAS system. The aviation industry was well aware that AOA sensors are liable to fail.

- When the malfunction of an airplane component could have catastrophic consequences (the potential to cause a crash), airline manufactures are supposed to build in redundant components as fail-safes. For instance, Boeing's rival, Airbus, typically uses three such AOA sensors on their equivalent aircrafts.[11]

- Over the last decade or more, Boeing began emphasizing speed of production and cost reduction, described as an "all-consuming focus on shareholder value."[12] The sales team was directed to sell planes for delivery four years out at prices the company didn't yet have the capability to meet. To meet these cost-reduction targets, engineers' performance evaluations were based in part on how much their designs ended up costing. These and other measures introduced by senior management created tremendous pressure throughout the organization to cut costs.

- To rush the Max 8 into production, Boeing's senior managers issued a mandate to engineers that any design changes must be small enough not to require pilots to undergo new simulator training.[13, 14] If the Max 8 added an additional AOA sensor as a fail-safe,

Habit 1 – Don't Blame

Boeing would have presumably had to install an alert in the cockpit as well. The addition of a cockpit alert would have likely triggered the need for new simulator training, thereby causing a delay.[15]

- To help Boeing catch up to its rival, Airbus, the Federal Aviation Administration (FAA) allowed Boeing to conduct its own safety assessments, and FAA managers pushed the agency's safety engineers to speedily approve the resulting analysis.[16] This is about the most egregious case of the fox guarding the henhouse that one can imagine.

The pressure that Boeing put on its employees to get the Max 8 into customers' hands as quickly as possible was symbolized by "countdown clocks" on the walls of conference rooms. When you put enough pressure on people, they will eventually make poor choices to appease their boss and save their jobs, even if it means cutting corners on safety.[17]

The best-trained pilots on the planet cannot compensate for a system that allows a single sensor failure to awaken a sadistic machine with its hand on the yoke that is intent on forcing the plane down. This was confirmed in two separate flight simulations when highly trained pilots failed to save the plane under similar conditions faced by the Indonesian and Ethiopian pilots.[18] Furthermore, when things began to go sideways during the two doomed flights, the pilots were bombarded by a barrage of alerts, flashing lights, and loud clacking noises. "Who knows what any of us would have done [in that type of situation]?" a veteran US airline captain said. "The manufacturer isn't supposed to give us airplanes that depend on superhuman pilots," he added.

Blaming those closest to the mess may be the easiest and most satisfying way to deal with our problems but doing so is overly simplistic and leads to institutionalized ignorance. The closer we look at mistakes and how they happen, the more we learn that the primary causes of many workplace problems are not people but the systems in which they operate.

83

8. Wired to Blame, Not Explain

Psychological Wiring

Psychologists actually have a name for the shallow thinking that blinds people to the root cause of problems. It's called the fundamental attribution bias (also referred to as the "fundamental attribution error"). It's "fundamental" because it is so ubiquitous.

Researchers of the fundamental attribution bias have found that human beings tend to ascribe the cause of people's actions to the actors' personality traits rather than to external factors that may be influencing their actions. For example, when I see you slip on a floor, I conclude that you must be clumsy. Never mind that the floor was wet. You should have been more careful.

This bias is so strong that people will still attribute the cause of problems to an actor's character "even in the face of overwhelming evidence that the action was caused by the situational context."[1]

In one study, researchers randomly assigned participants to read essays for and against Fidel Castro.[2] Other study participants who observed the reading of the essays were then asked to estimate how the essay readers felt about Castro. When the observers thought that the pro-Castro readers were allowed to choose the essay they read, the observers believed the readers thought quite highly of Castro. What surprised the researchers is that when the observers learned that the readers were not allowed to choose but were randomly assigned their essays, the observers still believed the pro-Castro essay readers truly liked him!

Somewhat confounded, the researchers concluded that "it is difficult for the perceiver to assign appropriate weights to the situational context." In other words, human beings tend to believe that what people do is a direct reflection of who they are, not a reflection of the constraints they are under.

When someone cuts me off in traffic, my automatic assumption is that they did it because they're a jerk. The fact that I was driving in their blind spot for the last two minutes has nothing to do with it. They're a jerk, and that's that.

The reason my coworker didn't respond to my email is because she is lazy and unorganized. Never mind that her boss just gave her a week's worth of work today that needs to be done by tomorrow. She's lazy and unorganized. Don't confuse me with the facts!

This is the attribution bias in action. We naturally tend to believe that other people's behavior is a direct reflection of their personality and that external factors are irrelevant.

Our tendency to blame individuals instead of the systems they operate in is not limited to the attribution bias alone. Another psychological gremlin, called the self-serving bias, works in tandem with the attribution bias. The self-serving bias states that we tend to attribute other people's failures to internal factors (they're stupid or lazy) and our own failures to external factors (the dog ate my homework). We excuse ourselves for the same negative behavior that we blame others for doing.

For example, we've already established that when you slip on a floor, it's because you are clumsy. However, when I slip it's because some idiot spilled water on the floor and didn't clean it up. This is the self-serving bias in action.

We believe the opposite is true too. When we succeed, we believe that we succeed because we're awesome. When others succeed, we assume it's because they had everything going for them.

Working together, the attribution bias and the self-serving bias create a knee-jerk reaction to blame first and ask questions later—or not at all. In practical terms, we are wired to blame rather than explain.

When a University of Wisconsin professor taught his class about taking a systems-centered approach to managing safety, he used the following example.

> The US Food and Drug Administration (FDA) recalled a medication infusion device whose mechanical components were contributing to over-tenfold medication overdoses of hospital patients. The FDA recalled only those devices that were not yet installed in hospitals. For those devices that remained, the solution to the overdose problem was to train nurses to, essentially, "be safer," and to place warning labels on the devices. After what I thought was a convincing lesson on the absurdity of fixing a human device interface problem by focusing on anything but that interface, a student raised his hand, and dashed my hopes:
>
> "Yes, I see how the manufacturer could make their product fool-proof, but it's the user's responsibility to not be a fool, in the first place."[3]

Despite knowing that the nurses were given devices that essentially encouraged them to make mistakes, this student's initial reaction was to blame the nurses.

One researcher made the following observation: "In practice, getting away from the tendency to judge instead of explain turns out to be difficult."[4] That's an understatement.

One possible explanation for why we tend to focus on blaming people instead of looking critically at the situations they operate within is because, as one researcher put it, "it is easier to imagine rectifying human actions than environmental events."[5] This explains why, when things go wrong, management's first instinct to correct the problem is to provide more training. However, no matter how much training you give people, they can still make a mistake, and they are especially likely to do so when they operate within a system that is effectively laying a trap for them, as in the medication device example above.

Physiological Wiring

Today, about fifty years after the fundamental attribution bias was discovered by psychologists, we may have found the root cause of this psychological phenomenon. As it turns out, we aren't just psychologically wired to blame; we're also *physically* wired to blame.[6]

Recent brain imaging research out of Duke University has shown that when we witness an event, we use two different areas of the brain to decide whether it was intentional or not.[7] Bad events are processed by the emotional part of the brain. Good events are processed by the rational part of the brain.

Negative events immediately trigger the amygdala, which, as we learned earlier, controls the fight-or-flight response. When the amygdala gets to decide if the event was intentional or not, it has only one option to choose from, and it's a big red button labeled "The jerk did it on purpose!" (If you've seen the animated movie *Inside Out*, picture Anger when he's at the controls.)

Because the amygdala seems to have only one option to choose from when deciding if something was intentional, it's able to reach that conclusion lightning fast. So fast, in fact, that we are often unaware that a decision was made; we just *know* the jerk did it on purpose.

Positive events, on the other hand, are processed by an entirely different part of the brain—the prefrontal cortex. The prefrontal cortex acts like the brain's attorney. When we witness events that produce a positive outcome, our brain asks its attorney for its considered opinion on whether the act was intentional. The prefrontal cortex's answer is always "It depends."

Then the prefrontal cortex proceeds to do a thorough analysis of the facts, which, of course, takes a while. When it finally reaches a verdict, it prefers to assign good intentions sparingly. The prefrontal cortex tends to conclude that positive outcomes happened by chance, not because people are good, smart, or hardworking.

This is why we can assign fault and blame quickly and frequently, but we have to think long and hard before we decide to give praise.[8]

Researchers made this discovery by hooking up participants to a brain-imaging fMRI scanner and watched which parts of the brain lit up when they listened to scenarios like the following.

> The CEO knew the plan would harm the environment, but he did not care at all about the effect the plan would have on the environment. He started the plan solely to increase profits. Did the CEO intentionally harm the environment?

Most participants said "yes" at the same time the fMRI machine showed their amygdala light up.

When the brain perceives something bad, it routes the information to be processed by the amygdala, and the amygdala always concludes that whoever was behind it did it on purpose.

Then researchers changed a single word in the scenario and watched what happened.

> The CEO knew the plan would *help* the environment, but he did not care at all about the effect the plan would have on the environment. He started the plan solely to increase profits. Did the CEO intentionally help the environment?

In this case, most participants said "no" while the fMRI machine showed higher activity in the prefrontal cortex.

When the brain perceives something good, it routes the information to be processed by the prefrontal cortex. The prefrontal cortex tends to conclude that whoever was behind it did not do it on purpose. On the other hand, "blame the operator" seems to be the only response our amygdalae can come up with when our brains ask why a negative event happened. Our brains are wired to conclude that good things happen by fluke and bad things happen on purpose.

This means that when someone cuts us off in traffic, our brains route the decision of how to respond to the amygdala, which already has its finger on the big red "The jerk did it on purpose!" button. Not surprisingly, we tend to react accordingly by yelling, honking, or using sign language to communicate our outrage.

However, when you're trying to change lanes in tight traffic, and a spot opens up, your brain routes the information to the prefrontal cortex to determine if someone let you in on purpose or if they just weren't paying attention and didn't close the gap before you sneaked in. You may give a courtesy wave regardless, but your brain's attorney is still analyzing the facts to determine whether to press the "feel gratitude" button or the "feel smug" button while your conscious mind darts off in a different direction.

This is a profound discovery. It appears that the physical mechanics of how our brains process negative events is the reason for our natural bias to blame quickly and frequently. This is also why it's so hard for us to give others the benefit of the doubt. We're not only fighting our psychological instincts; we're fighting the actual physiology of our brains.

The next time you feel the instinct to blame, remember that what you're really feeling is your amygdala with its finger on the big red "The jerk did it on purpose!" button.

9. How to Stop Blaming

Before I describe some remedies for the blame virus, let's first consider the impact that blame has on our ability to lead.

Don't Give Away Your Power

Weak individuals allow fate to determine their outcomes. They blame their problems on circumstances and other people, effectively handing the power to overcome their problems to someone or something else. Their reasoning is essentially, "If this circumstance or person doesn't change on their own, I'm stuck in this situation forever. I'm a helpless victim."

For example, in 2017, after possibly the largest personal data breach in history, former Equifax CEO Richard Smith blamed a single IT employee who should have applied a patch to fix a vulnerability in their system but didn't.[1] Smith was basically saying, "What can I do if someone doesn't do their job?" Actually, he could have done a lot.

Equifax received more than fifty-seven thousand complaints from consumers between 2012 and 2017 about the accuracy of consumers' personal data that the company maintained, making Equifax the worst offender among its competitors.[2] This means that for years Smith knew Equifax had a data-management problem. Armed with this knowledge, here are a few questions Smith should have asked.

1. **Has the senior management team made data management and security a high enough priority?** The CEO and the senior management team are the catalysts and the custodians

of organizational culture. If the CEO and the senior management team don't take data management and security seriously, nobody else will.

2. **What processes do we have in place to make sure employees don't drop any balls?** For example, did everyone in the company use task-tracking software? Were managers held accountable for regularly reviewing employees' work progress? Were there consequences for repeated poor performance?

3. **What quality-control feedback processes are in place and are they working?** For example, were employees free to point out problems without fear of retribution or being labelled as troublemakers? Did senior managers know if their quality-control systems were working? (Equifax's quality-control system didn't work.) Do departments and business units regularly conduct lessons learned debriefs to improve organizational performance?

These are all factors that were within Smith's control. Equifax had an accountability problem, and it started at the top.

The moment Smith blamed an employee for the data breach, he disqualified himself as a leader. Why? Because leaders take outcomes out of the hands of fate by leveraging everything within their control to get the right results.

Leaders take outcomes out of the hands of fate by leveraging everything within their control to get the right results.

Blaming others for your problems is the equivalent of throwing your hands in the air and exclaiming, "I'm helpless. There's nothing I can do. Life is so mean to me." There is almost always something you can do to prevent or lessen the impact of your problems.

On the contrary, people who take accountability for problems are the most powerful people in the room. It takes guts to take the blame and it takes leadership to point people toward a solution. This is precisely what CEO Michael McCain did when his company found itself at the center of a national health crisis.

In 2008, when it was confirmed that twenty-three people had died after eating meat from Canada's largest meat company, Maple Leaf CEO Michael McCain took personal accountability for the tragedy, stating "the buck stops here." He went on to say, "Going through the crisis, there are two advisers I've paid no attention to. The first are the lawyers, and the second are the accountants. It's not about money or legal liability—this is about our being accountable for providing consumers with safe food." Maple Leaf acted quickly and decisively to reduce the impact of the contaminated food and took several measures to make sure it didn't happen again.

Psychology professor and author Susan Krauss Whitbourne put it this way: "Unlike other games, the more often you play the blame game, the more you lose. Learning to tell when you need to own up to your role in a bad situation will help you grow from your experiences, and ultimately help you achieve more fulfilling relationships."[3]

Now that you can see the impact that blame has on your ability to get the right results and to lead others, here are three key tactics you can use to resist the urge to blame.

1. Adopt the Mindset "We Are All Still Learning."

We all make mistakes from time to time. It's part of being human. Those who think they make fewer mistakes than others in one area often forget they weren't always as proficient in that area as they think they are now.

In the military, mistakes sometimes cost lives, so it's important to minimize them. However, even great military leaders recognize that making mistakes and learning from them is what got them to where they are.

Colin Powell explains the value that can be gained from mistakes: "Good judgment comes from experience, and experience comes from bad judgement."[4]

The reason why it may seem like we make fewer mistakes than others is because we've already made them. Now we're wiser. It's only fair to allow other, less experienced people the same opportunity we had to become wiser.

In the Harvard study described earlier about the detrimental effect that blame has on learning, researcher Amy Edmondson described how to combat the Cycle of Ignorance and instead create a Cycle of Learning: "The more readily errors are reported and discussed [by managers], the more willing unit members may be to report errors in the future, and the more they may believe that making a mistake will not be held against them. A feedback loop indicates how these perceptions contribute to a self-perpetuating cycle of learning."[5]

As a leader, it's essential to let others know that making mistakes is part of learning. What those in leadership positions communicate to others about making mistakes is quite possibly the most important thing they can do to encourage others to be more accountable—or less accountable. Leaders who help others become more accountable communicate two important messages about making mistakes: it's OK to make mistakes as long as a) we do everything in our power to mitigate the consequences, and b) we change the process to prevent making the same mistake again.

It's not OK to make a mistake and let other people bear the consequences of your mistake. That's the opposite of accountability. Upon discovering their mistakes, accountable people own up to them and then immediately go to work reducing the burden their mistakes have placed on others. Accountable people do everything in their power to mitigate the consequences of mistakes.

Learning from mistakes includes reflecting on lessons learned and putting systems or controls in place to prevent the same mistake from happening again. A lesson isn't truly learned until you've changed the process to prevent that mistake from happening again. As legendary industrialist Henry Ford once said, "Failure is simply the opportunity to begin again more intelligently."[6]

> A lesson isn't truly learned until you've changed the process to prevent that mistake from happening again.

2. Share Your Mistakes and What You Learned From Them

The most impactful way for leaders to stop blaming and instead demonstrate that mistakes are learning opportunities is to publicly admit their own mistakes and share what they learned from them.

A senior manager at one of my clients shared the following experience with me.

> I was coordinating a team that had just been given a new service offering they were supposed to provide to our clients. They were overwhelmed and concerned with the news, so I spent most of the meeting presenting all sorts of ways to solve their concerns. I could tell they left the meeting frustrated. Upon reflection, I realized that I prescribed the solutions before I gave them enough opportunity to discuss their feelings and concerns.
>
> I called another team meeting and started off by acknowledging that I screwed up and then I apologized to them. After they got over the initial shock of a manager admitting a mistake, I gave them time to express their concerns without me jumping in to solve them. Not only did they leave that meeting in a much better frame of mind than they had the previous meeting, but the trust that was built allowed each of them going forward to be vulnerable, admit their own mistakes, and learn from them.

Admitting your mistakes creates the psychological safety for others to follow suit. However, simply admitting your mistakes doesn't explain why they should want to do likewise. When leaders admit their mistakes *and share what they learned from them*, the reason for the confession becomes clear. We acknowledge our mistakes so we can learn from them. No acknowledgement, no learning. No learning, no improvement.

When leaders admit their mistakes and share what they learned from them, something magical happens. Others begin to feel that it is safe to admit their mistakes, and they begin to take ownership of problems. When people step up to take ownership of their part in problems, it eliminates the need or the desire for anyone else to blame them. This initiates a virtuous cycle that reinforces learning, improvement, and a positive workplace culture.

3. Remember the Systems Approach Mantra

What if, after you admit your mistakes, others don't act in kind and admit their mistakes? How can you help others see their mistakes without blaming?

Commit the following saying to memory:

> Weak leaders ask, "Who's at fault?"
> Strong leaders ask, "Where did the process break down?"

This simple question, "Where did the process break down?" is your secret weapon to fight the urge to blame. It reminds you that the problem is not usually with people; it's with the system.

When problems are identified, managers who ask this question enlist people as problem solvers rather than provoke them to become defensive or to deflect blame elsewhere. This question engages the prefrontal cortex instead of triggering the amygdala.

Remember, leaders care about people and results. Asking "Where did the process break down?" demonstrates they care about both. By focusing on the process instead of the person, leaders take care not to injure their team members' self-respect. By asking "Where did the process break down?" leaders also demonstrate they will not accept poor results. Leaders want to get the right results, and they expect their team members are smart enough to figure out how to change the process to ensure they get the right results next time.

In contrast, managers who insist on asking "Who's at fault?" with a serious intention to discover the truth will not like where that question takes them because it will likely lead back to them in some way, shape, or form.

In summary, 1) recognize and believe that we are all still learning, 2) admit your mistakes and share what you learned from them, and 3) remember the systems approach mantra. These three simple tactics will help you fight your natural reflex to blame and prevent the collateral damage it produces.

Resisting the urge to blame is the essential first step to becoming an accountable person and making it safe for others to take more accountability themselves. Eliminating blame allows everyone to access their prefrontal cortex to solve problems instead of becoming mired in the blame game.

Accountability, as we have discussed, is about achieving better results. In order to become better at solving our problems and achieving better results, we must first clearly see what's causing our problems. This brings us to habit two of personal accountability—look in the mirror.

HABIT 2 — LOOK IN THE MIRROR

Acknowledge your part in the problem

10. The Power to Overcome Our Problems

Throughout history, giving birth was a risky business. However, in the early nineteenth century, deaths of mothers during childbirth suddenly and inexplicably skyrocketed.[1]

An epidemic known as childbed fever swept through the western world in the 1800s, and it was only getting worse. By the mid-1800s, about one out of every ten women who gave birth in hospitals could expect to die an excruciating death from childbed fever within a week of delivering their child.[2]

At this time, the largest maternity hospital in the world was in Vienna, Austria. Within the maternity hospital were two clinics. One clinic was staffed by doctors and medical students, and the other clinic was staffed by midwives. Hospital staff began to notice a disturbing trend. Patients in the clinic staffed by doctors and medical students died 2.5 times more often than the patients in the clinic staffed by midwives.

This didn't make any sense. This was the golden age of medicine when doctors were beginning to abandon their superstitious traditions and embrace science.[3]

One doctor at the hospital, Ignaz Semmelweis, decided to find out why this was happening.[4] After isolating all the variables, he discovered that the only real difference between what the doctors were doing and what the midwives were doing was that the doctors would conduct autopsies in the morgue before doing their rounds of delivering babies *without washing their hands*! Semmelweis discovered that the doctors were transmitting the diseases from the mothers who had died from childbed fever to the healthy mothers in the maternity ward.

Once he made this discovery, Semmelweis insisted that all doctors at the hospital wash their hands and instruments in chlorine water before attending the maternity wards. Within months the mortality rate of the two clinics became comparable.

Armed with incontrovertible proof, or so it would seem, Semmelweis tried to convince the medical community that *they*, the doctors and medical students, were the problem. Far from being hailed as an important discovery, Semmelweis's message landed like a lead balloon. Nobody likes to hear they are causing their own problems. When Semmelweis told doctors they were *killing* their patients, the doctors were highly motivated to reject his message—so motivated, in fact, that the medical community made it their mission to shut him up. They called Semmelweis crazy and locked him up in an insane asylum, where he died in short order.

"Mission accomplished," the medical community must have thought. "Now let's get back to fighting this childbed fever epidemic *our way*."

Childbed fever continued to kill countless young mothers for more than fifty years before sterilizing instruments and washing hands became standard practice, at which point childbed fever essentially vanished.

The lesson in this avoidable tragedy is that the doctors were the carriers of the very disease they were battling every day. They were the problem! When this fact was pointed out to them, they refused to believe it. They refused to look in the mirror to find the solutions to their problems. The medical community's failure to take a hard look in the mirror resulted in the needless, excruciating deaths of thousands of young women.

Do you know someone who is obviously contributing to their own problems but refuses to see it? Of course you do. We can all see when others are contributing to their own problems, but can we see it in ourselves?

Is it possible that we are like those doctors who are creating our own problems, but we can't—or won't—see it?

To discover the solutions to your problems, you must train yourself to look in the mirror before looking elsewhere for answers. By looking for and acknowledging your role in problems, you obtain greater power to overcome your problems. Only when you see how you are contributing to your problems will you discover what you can do to improve your odds of getting better results in the future.

If you don't look in the mirror for answers, the solutions to many of your problems will continue to elude you. If you don't discover how you are contributing to your problems, you are doomed to remain mired in your problems, hoping that, by some miracle, something will change to improve your circumstances.

Here are two recent examples from my own life that demonstrate how I was contributing to my own problems but failed initially to see it.

Employee Performance Problem

I was on vacation in Hawaii when my consulting company was advertising for an upcoming webinar. Carrie, the staff member assigned to help me with the webinar, had helped me with a webinar once before. I was four time zones away from her, so by the time I got to my emails and responded, she had often finished for the day. Numerous technical issues needed to be ironed out before the ads went out, but I assumed Carrie knew what to do and would take the initiative to do it. However, we didn't specifically discuss the game plan.

To complicate matters further, Carrie and I discovered at the last minute that she missed an email from one of the advertisers who moved up the deadline for us to send them the ad materials. I was frustrated with Carrie for missing the email and deadline, but I knew she was quite sick that week. I also recognized that I hadn't given her specific instructions on what I wanted her to do until it became a crisis. I acknowledged these points in an email to Carrie, essentially saying, "We both screwed up."

Fortunately, the advertiser agreed to give us more time to send the ad materials, and Carrie was able to get all the technical issues and unforeseen problems sorted out in fairly short order. She also documented all the things that needed to get done for webinar ads for future reference. Knowing that we both dropped the ball to some degree, and knowing that Carrie now had a process for next time, I put the incident behind me, but something told me that she may not have put the incident behind her.

When I was back in the office, we had our weekly one-on-one meeting to go through our regular business. At the end of the meeting, I decided to ask her for some feedback on how I handled that situation. "Was there anything you wished I would have done differently last week that would have made this situation easier for you?" I asked. She thought for a moment. "Well, you usually send me *very specific* emails on what you want me to do for you, so when I didn't receive anything like that from you, I figured you had it handled," she replied, then quickly continued on to her next thought. "But now that we have a process nailed down, I will be able to run with this from now on."

I was inclined to say "Great" and end the meeting, but something told me I'd better investigate the words "very specific" a little more. "Do you sometimes feel that I'm too specific in my instructions to you?" I asked. Carrie paused and then opened up. "Well, actually, just yesterday when we were on the phone, you ended by giving me step-by-step instructions on a fairly routine task, and I was like, 'I know, Michael.' I'm fairly smart and can figure a lot of things out, but when you give me such detailed instructions all the time, it makes me feel like you don't trust me, or you think I'm stupid."

Without noticing, I had trained Carrie not to take the initiative because I was overly prescriptive when giving her assignments. Think about that for a moment. Carrie's performance was not meeting my expectations, but who's fault was that? To a large extent, it was mine.

It was difficult for me to ask Carrie what I may have done to make that situation worse; it would have been easier for me to blame her for this debacle. Had I not investigated how I contributed to the problem though, the same issue would have inevitably manifested itself in a different context. I would have trained Carrie not to take the initiative in another area of the business.

Looking in the mirror for the answer to this problem was painful (her feedback stung), but it gave me the power to create better outcomes in the future for us both.

Personal Health Challenge

The second example of how I was contributing to my own problems, but was slow to see it, relates to my health.

I developed chronic headaches the day my first child was born (Coincidence? I think not.) After suffering with no relief for some time, I accidentally discovered that anti-inflammatories helped relieve the pain. Anti-inflammatories, however, are not a long-term solution. I was prescribed some daily medication that helped reduce the frequency of my headaches to about two or three times a week. Then, when I'd get a headache, I would take a combination of painkillers and anti-inflammatories to alleviate the pain.

That was my treatment plan for thirteen years.

Here are some additional facts:

Fact 1: I ate a lot of sugar.

Fact 2: I knew sugar was inflammatory, but honestly, how much difference could reducing my sugar intake really make?

Fact 3: There was a strong correlation between my headaches and stress. I was pretty sure that stress was a contributing factor to my headaches, but I didn't think there was much I could do about that.

After some urging from my wife, I finally relented and for three days made a half-hearted effort to reduce my sugar intake. Result: no change. Ha! I was right! Reducing sugar didn't make a difference! So, I went back to my regular diet of treats after every meal and sometimes between meals.

Many years later, after overindulging during the Christmas holidays, I decided to lose a few pounds. Almost by accident, for two days in a row, I reduced my sugar intake to virtually zero. I noticed I didn't have a headache those days. Hmm . . . I did the same thing for a third day. Again, no headache. Three days without a headache for me was extremely rare, so I tried a fourth day with no sugar. Still no headache. Then the lightbulb went off. "I may be predisposed to headaches, but my sugar intake is making it worse!"

I didn't want to look in the mirror for the answer to this particular problem because blaming my headaches on genetics was easy, although it didn't improve my circumstances. Changing my eating habits (changing myself) was hard, but ultimately, looking in the mirror for my answer gave me the power to alleviate a lot of the pain I was experiencing.

What about the correlation between my headaches and stress? When I'm stressed, guess what I do more of? Eat sugary treats. For me, this was also a lesson on the difference between correlation and causation. My headaches were correlated with stress but only because they were also correlated with my sugar intake.

I still get headaches, but now they are far less frequent.

How many of us are suffering with chronic health problems that we are unknowingly making worse because we don't want to look in the mirror for answers? How many of our chronic health problems could be (or could have been) mitigated through better diet, regular exercise, and targeted stretching and muscle strengthening? Probably a lot, but those remedies require us to acknowledge our part in problems and the discipline to change our habits.

We contribute to many of our problems; we just don't want to look in the mirror for answers because it's usually somewhat painful.

Combatting the Victim Mentality

At one time or another, all of us have met or known people who believe deep down that life has been unfair to them. We all know *those* people.

People with a victim mentality. Their lives are in constant turmoil and filled with the drama of terrible ex-spouses, bosses who have the audacity to insist on medical evidence to justify their stress leave, and family members who allegedly take advantage of their good nature.

Know anybody like that? If you do, when was the last time they asked, "Do you see me doing anything that's contributing to these problems I keep having?"

They probably never have.

Most likely, any conversation you've had with them about their problems has gone something like the ninety-second video entitled, "It's Not About The Nail."[5] (Watch the video at youtube.com/watch?v=-4EDhdAHrOgat.)

Sound familiar? This video is so funny because we've all been there. While listening to someone complain about their problems, we get up the nerve to hint that perhaps they may be contributing to their problems. To them, the solution is a riddle wrapped inside an enigma, but to us the solution is painfully obvious. The cause of their problem is usually something they are doing or not doing. We can see it, but they can't.

How can people be so blind to how they are contributing to their own problems? Don't judge others too quickly.

People with a chronic victim mentality are easy to spot because their lives are usually a mess, but what about successful people like you? Could you, perhaps, be blaming other people or circumstances for your mistakes? Do you always notice the times when you slip into victim mode?

Here's a test to discover your propensity to do so.

When you encounter significant challenges in life, or when you discover problems at work, how often do you ask yourself "How may I have contributed to this problem?"

We learned earlier that the systems that cause undesirable results are usually invisible to most people, so people tend to blame others for problems instead of considering other factors that likely influenced the outcome. Guess what? Our own actions are included in the list of "other factors" that likely contribute to our problems. As someone once told me, people who are constantly fighting fires are often the arsonists.

As we move to habit two of developing personal accountability, we must remember this key systems thinking insight:

If you are part of the system in which a problem was discovered, you likely contributed to the problem.

If your child tends to bully his or her younger sibling(s), could the child be acting out how they feel you treat him or her?

If you and a colleague are embroiled in a never-ending blame war, could the fact that you keep talking to everyone else about your grievances be fueling the turmoil?

If one of your employees keeps making mistakes, could you be the one setting them up to fail because you delegate in a hurry and leave out important details?

If your team has a poor track record of following through on initiatives, could it be because you are constantly changing your priorities and firing off an email to them every time a new idea pops into your head?

I can hear Stephen Covey's wise, reassuring voice when I read this quote: "Remember, every time you think the problem is out there, that very thought is the problem."[6] Covey is teaching us not to be lulled into making the fundamental attribution error. He's teaching us to look in the mirror.

The more I have studied leadership and applied the principles I learn, the more I have noticed that many of my "employee performance problems" originated with me in some way. When the people who report to me fall short of my expectations, I often discover that I wasn't clear enough in my instructions, I forgot to provide a deadline, I didn't explain the context of what I was asking of them to do, I didn't follow up in a timely manner, or, occasionally, I actually made the mistake that I initially attributed to them. It is possible that I am just an exceptionally poor leader, but it's also possible that the more I improve my leadership skills, the more I notice how strong the link is between my leadership effectiveness and my people's performance.

Bob Chapman is the chairman and CEO of Barry-Wehmiller, a global supplier of manufacturing technologies and services. Chapman is a savvy business executive who managed to turn a struggling company into one that delivered over 16 percent compounded return to shareholders for over sixteen years—a record of value creation that compares favorably with the legendary Berkshire Hathaway during the same time period.[7] As he built his company, Chapman was like many other executives who are more concerned about making money than they are about the people who work for them, but then something happened. He had an epiphany that changed the way he saw his employees. As Chapman's desire to improve his leadership ability increased, he began to see his employees less as a human resource to grind value out of and more as someone's precious sons or daughters. Chapman's enlightened view of the people who worked for him compelled him to make many changes in the way his company operated to become a model of "truly human leadership." These changes are what helped Barry-Wehmiller outperform the S&P 500 by almost 400 percent for over sixteen years.

Taking stock of all he learned from his leadership journey, Chapman made the following observation: "One great truth that we've learned is this: The people are just fine; it's our leadership that's lacking. When people perform poorly, most leaders are quick to blame them, perhaps even fire them right away. It takes introspection and humility to admit, 'That might be a consequence of my poor leadership.'"[8]

The next time you have what seems to be an employee-performance issue, don't be too hasty in your analysis of the problem. First, ask yourself, "How may I have contributed to their unsatisfactory performance?"

We often create many of our own problems. Even if we didn't create a particular problem, we can usually influence the solution.

Leadership author Simon Sinek occasionally jokes that the common factor in all his failed relationships is him. As absurdly obvious as this statement is, many people never come to this realization. We often don't notice what we are doing to destroy our relationships with others, how we may be creating workplace enemies, or how we are contributing to our staff's poor attitude and performance.

Think of someone you know who has recently experienced a major relationship breakdown—be it a romantic relationship, a business relationship, or a friendship. When this person talks to you about their failed relationship, let me guess, you are left with the distinct impression that the other party in the conflict is primarily at fault for the relationship's demise, right? Coincidentally, every time a friend, family member, or acquaintance has described their relationship problems to me, I am tempted to think, *My poor friend is a saint, and their former partner is a horrible person.* Of course, I know the other party in that failed relationship is telling all their friends their own version of the facts and soliciting all kinds of sympathy for themselves and garnering disdain for my friend.

Wise confidants and relationship counselors know that relationship failures are almost never 100 percent the other person's fault. Even when an objective analysis of all the facts reveals that one party was more culpable than the other, it's usually more like 70/30. And yet, when we feel that we are the ones who have been wronged in a relationship, we can rarely see the 30 percent that we have contributed to the relationship's downfall.

The regional leadership of a service organization I belong to asked Grant, a member of our local chapter, to serve as the chapter president for a multi-year term. Grant was an obvious choice. He was eminently qualified and everybody who knows him respects him because of his genuine care and concern for people and because of his gentle, approachable nature. However, not even halfway through his term, Grant was asked to step down. It turned out that, despite his congenial nature and many other strengths, Grant only knew how to lead using a command-and-control style. The people assigned to support Grant complained that he paid lip service to their suggestions and that nothing could deter him from doing things his way. Grant's leadership style bred resentment among the members assigned to support him and created a fracture in our organization that deepened over time. Although Grant showed tremendous character by taking the demotion with grace and continuing to serve in our organization, he put the blame squarely on the regional leadership for his removal from office. To be fair, the regional leaders may have made some mistakes in the way they handled the situation. Nevertheless, Grant decided to focus on the mistakes he felt others made and the indignities he suffered as a result, instead of taking a hard look at how he behaved his way into that mess. Life handed Grant a gift-wrapped leadership lesson that his ego refused to receive. The lesson is this: leadership is elevating the voices of those you lead far above your own voice and being willing to course correct when they disagree with you. Forcing your will on others is coercion. Leadership is about consensus building.

Observing Grant's experience makes me wonder how many important life lessons I have missed because I failed to look in the mirror for answers to my problems. How many life lessons have you missed? If Grant, who is an intelligent, kind, and competent fellow, can miss an important leadership lesson because he failed to sufficiently look in the mirror, how can you and I expect to do any better?

The reason we often fail to notice that we are part of the problem is because we don't ask the following question often enough: "How may I have contributed to this problem?"

Why don't we ask this question? Because we want to preserve our self-esteem. Our brains will go to extraordinary lengths to ensure we maintain a high opinion of ourselves. The self-serving bias is one of the brain's primary tools to achieve this end. Remember how that works? When my coworker is late to work, it's because he is lazy and undisciplined. When I'm late to work, it's because I was having a bad morning and traffic was terrible.

Our brains do not process information impartially. They interpret information and tell us a story, typically one that places us in a generous light. Why do our brains do this? Because our brains know something that we often forget: confidence is essential to high performance.[9] Think about it; confident people outperform insecure people in virtually every context. Confidence is what separated our early ancestors who took on the woolly mammoth and won from those who faded out of the human gene pool. Confidence is what separates merely adequate performers from all-stars. Studies have consistently shown that knowing you are good at something increases your odds of future success in that activity and that, conversely, proven skills can be overruled by self-doubt. This phenomenon has been observed in virtually every context, including chess tournaments, on sports fields, on sales teams, and in management decision-making.[10, 11, 12, 13]

This need to believe we are good at things is why when we receive negative feedback, we instinctively get defensive. Our knee-jerk reaction is usually to look for reasons, *any* reasons, to discount or dismiss the negative feedback. This is our brain kicking in to protect our fragile egos.

Chris Argyris, the father of learning organizations, calls this phenomenon "skilled incompetence."[14, 15] He states that many people have become "highly skillful at protecting themselves from pain and threat posed by learning situations."[16]

In support of his conclusion, Argyris looked at the performance of Harvard Business School graduates ten years after they graduated. Virtually all of them thought they would be CEOs or senior executives by then, but most of them fell short of their expectations. In analyzing their lackluster performance, Argyris noticed a pattern: they failed to learn from their mistakes. Argyris explains their failure as follows:

> Those members of the organization that many assume to be the best at learning are, in fact, not very good at it. I am talking about the well-educated, high-powered, high-commitment professionals who occupy key leadership positions in the modern corporation . . . Put simply, because many professionals are almost always successful at what they do, they rarely experience failure. And because they have rarely failed, they have never learned how to learn from failure . . . [T]hey become defensive,

screen out criticism, and put the "blame" on anyone and everyone but themselves. In short, their ability to learn shuts down precisely at the moment they need it the most.[17]

Looking in the mirror for the solutions to your problems can be painful, but doing so gives you greater power to overcome your problems. Asking "How may I have contributed to his problem?" with a sincere desire to uncover the truth is essential to growth and your ability to be accountable.

11. We Aren't Very Self-Aware

If accountability is about striving to achieve the right results, and if we cause a lot of our own problems, then our ability to notice how we contribute to our problems is essential to getting the right results more often.

"True proactiveness," Peter Senge writes, "comes from seeing how we contribute to our own problems."[1] Unfortunately, as we will see, we aren't very good at noticing how we contribute to our own problems.

The following unbelievable but true story was reported in a 2010 *New York Times* article.[2]

A forty-five-year-old man from Pittsburgh named McArthur Wheeler became convinced that if he rubbed lemon juice on his face, it would make him invisible to cameras. Having come to this conclusion, Wheeler put lemon juice all over his face, went out, and robbed two banks without any attempt to disguise himself. Not much later he was arrested when his image was broadcast over the evening news. When police showed Wheeler the videos of him on the security cameras, he couldn't believe his eyes. "But I wore the juice!" he protested.

For decades, Cornell University scientist David Dunning has been studying how people like Wheeler can be so painfully unaware of how they appear to others. To determine whether this was a general problem, Dunning and his partner, Justin Kruger, invited college students to participate in a series of tests of various life skills and asked them to rate themselves on how well they thought they did. The researchers discovered that the students who performed poorly were the *least* accurate in evaluating their performance. Some students even estimated their scores to be five times higher than they actually were![3]

Simply put, those who are the worst at something tend to overestimate their ability the most.

Dunning and Kruger concluded that "when people are incompetent in the strategies they adopt to achieve success . . . they suffer a dual burden: Not only do they reach erroneous conclusions and make unfortunate choices, but their incompetence robs them of the ability to realize it."[4]

This phenomenon of not being able to see ourselves clearly is not limited to college students and half-wit bank robbers. The self-serving bias that I described earlier ensures that most of us, especially many successful people, routinely overestimate our own contributions and underestimate the contributions of others and disregard the constraints they are under. Our self-serving bias blinds us to how we contribute to our own problems.

I remember one particularly amusing incident while training a group of managers at an organization that provides various community social services. I happened to sit next to a manager at lunch who confided that he had the distinct impression that his manager (the director of the organization's largest business unit) held back and didn't really tell him how she felt about him. Not less than an hour later, during a group discussion about providing feedback, this same director declared to the whole group that everyone on her team knew where they stood with her. I did my best to keep a straight face and refrain from looking at the manager I had sat next to at lunch. This director was obviously delusional about how well she provided feedback to her staff.

Our inability to notice our shortcomings is particularly dangerous for people in leadership positions because leaders' actions ripple throughout the organizations they preside over and impact many other people. Alarmingly though, notwithstanding the greater damage that can be done by low self-aware people in leadership positions, unaware managers are the least likely to try to improve their leadership skills.

David Dunning conducted another study in which he tested the emotional intelligence of working professionals enrolled in an MBA program (many of whom were presumably managers). Not only did Dunning find that those with the lowest EI scores were the least aware of their weakness, they were also the least likely to seek to improve that weakness. When presented with concrete feedback about their performance, lower performers argued that the feedback they were given was either inaccurate or irrelevant. Consequently, when given the opportunity to purchase a book on improving emotional intelligence, they were the least likely to buy it.[5]

This is precisely the pattern I have seen in my consulting work. The worst managers (the ones that HR has warned me about before the engagement) are typically the least engaged in the workshops and the least inclined to improve their leadership ability. Those who need to strengthen their leadership skills the most are typically the least inclined to do so.

World-renowned leadership coach Marshall Goldsmith has worked with over fifty thousand successful people throughout his coaching career. His extensive coaching experience has led him to conclude that inaccurate self-perception is a general phenomenon and that it often becomes more pronounced in people with greater perceived social status. Put differently, people who think they're important tend to have less self-awareness than others. When Goldsmith asks the people in his training workshops to rate themselves against their peers, 80–85 percent of them rate themselves in the top 20 percent of their peer group, and 70 percent rate themselves in the top 10 percent.[6]

When we do look in the mirror, it's usually only when we are wearing rose-colored glasses. Until we take them off, the solutions to our problems will remain a mystery and frequently lead us to mistakenly believe that other people or circumstances are to blame for our problems.

There are many reasons why we aren't very self-aware, one of which is our innate need to protect our sometimes fragile egos. However, there are other, more tactical, explanations for why we aren't very self-aware—explanations that we can do something about.

1. We don't get enough feedback.

2. We think we are already self-aware.

3. Power dynamics make it even harder to see ourselves clearly.

While it may be more challenging to change our psychological wiring, we can change our beliefs and tactics in ways that will not only help us become more self-aware but also enable us to better navigate our way to personal greatness.

1. We Don't Get Enough Feedback

Without a regular flow of feedback, we don't have a mirror that reflects an accurate image. Without an accurate self-image, we aren't able to see what we must change to improve our outcomes. When we can't see how we are contributing to our problems, all we can do is hope that other people or circumstances change for our benefit. However, as someone once told Barack Obama, "Hope is not a strategy."

David Dunning noted that one of the key reasons why many people remain in the dark about their weaknesses is because they don't get enough specific feedback. In fact, receiving too little or unspecific feedback can lead us astray in our search for why we fail to achieve the results we want.

Take Wheeler, for example. You may be tempted to wonder how anyone could be so stupid as to believe that rubbing lemon juice on his face would make him invisible to cameras, but Wheeler wasn't quite as stupid as you might think. He actually tested his theory before putting his discovery to work.

Wheeler reported that he did several trials using a Polaroid camera. Although "the lemon juice was burning his face and eyes, and he was having trouble seeing," he snapped a picture of himself to prove his theory. As he presumed, his image was not captured by the camera. *Eureka!* he thought. *It works!*

Habit 2 – Look in the Mirror

Now, given the sheer idiocy of his hypothesis, there are a number of ways he could have conceivably botched the test, but emboldened by this initial piece of evidence, which seemed to confirm what he wanted to believe, he charged off, robbed two banks, and got himself arrested.

When it comes to requesting feedback, many people are like our dear friend, Wheeler. They come to conclusions about how others perceive them based on a small sample size of data from an unreliable source.

For example, when I run leadership workshops, and I cover the topic of feedback, it is not uncommon for me to hear comments like, "My staff all say nice things to me, they laugh at my jokes, and they tell me I'm a great boss. I guess I really must be a great boss."

One time I jokingly responded to a manager who made such a comment by asking, "And you really believe them?" Others in the room chuckled, but he didn't. He became indignant and said "Absolutely. My staff tell me everything." Sure they do.

While asking subordinates for feedback about yourself is a good practice, their feedback alone is not enough on which to base conclusions. People who report to you are highly motivated to embellish positive feedback and sugar-coat negative feedback. When people who report to you say nice things about you, take it with a grain of salt, but when they hint at an area you may need to work on, you are probably just seeing the tip of the iceberg. Your radar must be finely tuned to detect those hints, and you need the courage to pursue them.

It is shocking to me how many seasoned, intelligent people believe any feedback that seems to confirm their view of themselves no matter how superficial it may be. On the other hand, these same people often aggressively challenge and discount any feedback that contradicts their self-image. Most of us are in desperate need of additional sources of feedback.

In his landmark book, *Drive*, Dan Pink writes,

> An essential ingredient in achieving mastery [becoming excellent at something] is getting feedback on how you're

doing. And most of our lives are rich in this wonderful resource. When we play a video game, we get a score. When we press a button on an ATM, we see our bank balance. When we send a text message, a little sound confirms the message has been sent. Yet while we inhabit a landscape lush in feedback in most realms of our lives, when we step through the office door we enter a feedback desert.[7]

The reason why our workplaces tend to be a feedback desert is because at work, feedback has a bad reputation. Feedback has become associated with blame, with causing distressing conflict, and is regarded as the reason why we aren't getting a raise this year. People have learned to fear feedback, both receiving and giving it, because it often comes with negative consequences.

The purpose of feedback is to help others see themselves more clearly so they can achieve greater success. When people provide feedback for any reason other than that, it is bound to be received badly.

Here are a few common examples of how feedback has received a bad reputation in the workplace.

Example A
A manager believes that making sarcastic remarks to a certain staff member about his tardiness is the same thing as addressing poor performance. This employee is surprised to see an HR representative in his boss's office as he enters the room for a meeting initiated by his boss. The HR representative informs the employee that he is being put on a formal "performance improvement plan" because of his chronic tardiness. The employee leaves the meeting feeling blindsided and betrayed.

Example B
An employee relies on her coworker's documentation to complete her work. After several weeks of rewriting her coworker's sloppy and incomplete reports, she's reached her breaking point. When she finally confronts him about it, she's so angry she's shaking. In an obviously annoyed

tone of voice, she approaches her coworker and asks, "Can I give you some feedback?"

Example C
During the annual performance review, a manager presents her staff member's performance rating to him and explains that means he won't be getting a raise this year. When he asks her why his rating is low, she proceeds to point out problems with his work performance that he has never heard before. Knowing that this feedback is the justification for his salary increase, he rejects all the feedback and transforms into a defense attorney, systematically picking apart his manager's arguments to negotiate a better performance rating and, in doing so, a salary increase.

If senior managers truly understood how vital feedback is to performance, they would do everything in their power to change the bad reputation feedback has within their organization. They can do this by a) dissociating feedback with negative consequences (such as compensation), b) providing it solely for the benefit of the one receiving it (instead providing feedback to make themselves feel better by venting their frustrations), and c) publicly sharing feedback they have received and how it has benefitted them.

2. We Think We're Already Self-aware

Self-awareness is having an accurate sense of your abilities and how others view you. Most people think they're pretty self-aware, but few of us really are.[8, 9] "According to our research," says organizational psychologist and researcher Tasha Eurich, "with thousands of people from all around the world, 95 percent of people believe that they're self-aware, but only about 10 to 15 percent really are."[10]

When I share this fact with people in my workshops, most tend to believe they must be in the 10 to 15 percent. Before you jump to the same conclusion, remember that those who are the worst at something are more likely to overestimate their ability. Let that idea marinate for a moment.

Now, are you still inclined to believe you're part of the 10 to 15 percent who are truly self-aware?

One of the most documented findings in psychology, as stated earlier, is that we think we are better than we really are, which, ironically, includes overestimating our self-awareness.[11] For example, in a large-scale study, researchers analyzed the correlation between people's self-rated intelligence and their actual intelligence test scores. Their analyses included more than twenty thousand people. The results revealed that there is less than a 10 percent overlap between how smart people think they are and how smart they really are. In other words, we have no idea how smart we actually are.[12]

This general lack of self-awareness extends to virtually all other assessments of our abilities. For instance, another study showed that students who ranked in the bottom twenty-fifth percentile of the class on tests of grammar, logical reasoning, and humor rated themselves as above the sixtieth percentile.[13] Another example is driving ability. In 2018 the American Automobile Association surveyed a thousand adults and found that 79 percent of men and 68 percent of women believed they were better-than-average drivers.[14]

The bottom line is that we don't ask for feedback about ourselves because we think we already know the answer.

We don't ask for feedback about ourselves because we think we already know the answer.

This false belief—that we've got a pretty good sense of our abilities and how others see us—is an absolute performance killer.

A study involving fifty-eight teams and more than three hundred managers at a Fortune 10 company showed that teams with less self-aware individuals "made worse decisions, engaged in less coordination, and showed less conflict management."[15] The net result was that teams of self-aware people were *twice* as successful as their less self-aware colleagues. Self-awareness is critical to success. "Our self-awareness," Eurich affirms, "sets the upper limit for the skills that make us stronger team players, superior leaders, and better relationship builders."[16] When it comes to leadership ability, Eurich's extensive research on self-awareness led her to conclude that "self-awareness is the single greatest predictor of leadership success."[17]

When we don't have an accurate view of our strengths, weaknesses, and what others think of us, our behavior will constantly conflict with reality. The thorny thing about reality is that it delivers consequences. Consequences can serve as a great source of feedback to help correct inaccurate self-perceptions, except for the fact that our natural self-serving bias encourages us to mistakenly assign the meaning of negative consequences to external factors. The result is that we often come to the wrong conclusions about why bad things are happening to us. So, unless we are receiving feedback from numerous sources, the consequences of our actions may not even convince us to course correct when we should.

Low self-awareness can be as detrimental to individuals as haze can be to airplane pilots. Atmospheric conditions such as haze or a sloping cloudbank can disorient pilots and trick them into thinking they are level when, in fact, they are actually careening toward the ground. In aviation, this is known as "spatial disorientation."

A famous example of how deadly spatial disorientation can be to a pilot is the plane crash that killed John F. Kennedy Jr.[18] On July 16, 1999, Kennedy was flying his single-engine plane with his wife and sister-in-law on board to attend his cousin's wedding at Martha's Vineyard off the coast of Massachusetts. Kennedy did not hold an instrument rating and was, therefore, only certified to fly under visual flight rules. Although the weather was officially listed as clear skies, Kennedy encountered haze that one pilot that evening described as entirely obscuring the visual horizon. Kennedy's plane crashed nearly nose first into the Atlantic Ocean. The investigation by the National Transportation Safety Board concluded that Kennedy fell victim to spatial disorientation. He believed he was flying level when, in fact, he was not.

When it comes to assessing our own abilities and navigating other people's perceptions of us, we are all flying in a haze. The biases that kick in to preserve our self-esteem reduce our self-awareness and obscure reality. Commenting on this almost universal tendency to obfuscate our perception of ourselves, psychologist and prolific author Dr. Tomas Chamorro-Premuzic writes, "Our desire to understand reality is not as strong as our desire to think highly of ourselves."[19]

For example, Jim, the VP of sales in a company I worked with, was promoted to division president. He was a likable, gregarious guy who was quick to laugh and tell jokes, but I could tell Jim was insecure in his position as president, preferring instead to continue performing the functions of the VP of sales.

After I left the company, one of the senior managers who reported to Jim mentioned to me that "Jim always feels he has to have an answer to everything. Any time I bring an issue to him to discuss, he quickly dismisses it by telling me what he thinks the problem is and that it's not a big deal." The company effectively folded within a year of the senior manager making that comment to me.

Had Jim ever asked those who reported to him to give him some feedback on how he was perceived and how he could improve, he may have learned that he had a reputation of being a flippant know-it-all, always skimming the surface of issues and never taking a hard look at problems. Instead, Jim preferred to remain in ignorance as a way to maintain a high opinion of himself.

By soliciting multiple sources of feedback, we can learn to fly by our navigational instruments. As we identify common themes in this feedback, we can better ascertain reality, which will enable us to find the real cause of our problems, find solutions, and perform better. Those who insist on relying on their gut to evaluate themselves will eventually crash in one aspect of their life or another. However, the real tragedy is that when they do crash, they won't know why!

3. Power Is Blinding

Isn't it interesting that our spouses are so willing to tell us what we're doing wrong and how we are contributing to our own problems, but the people who report to us hardly ever point out the stupid things we say and do?

Come to think of it, our staff are so much nicer to us than our spouses. They stroke our egos all day, telling us how great we are. Why can't our spouses be more like our staff?

Possibly because healthy marriages involve an equal balance of power. Marriage is a partnership. Each person has an equal opportunity to help or hurt the other, but that is not the case in the workplace.

The perceived imbalance of power in the workplace all but stops feedback from traveling up the hierarchy. Robert Steven Kaplan, Harvard Business School professor and former vice chairman of Goldman Sachs, describes the problem this way:

> Lots of people are willing to complain to their colleagues about the CEO, and talk about what the CEO is doing wrong and should be doing differently. Ironically, many of those same people turn to mush when given the opportunity to speak up directly to the CEO. Why? They want the CEO to have a positive impression of them, and not making waves seems like the safe 'default' approach. As a consequence, the leader is often the last to hear constructive criticisms that may be circulating widely through the organization.[20]

This imbalance of power creates a dynamic that insulates those higher up the food chain from receiving as much feedback as those lower down the food chain.

> The higher you climb, the less feedback you receive.

This general principle of organizational behavior manifests itself perfectly in the emotional intelligence scores of managers.

Emotional intelligence researcher and author Dr. Travis Bradberry analyzed the emotional intelligence profiles of over a million people according to job title and discovered a disturbing trend.[21] Emotional intelligence scores climb with titles from the bottom of the corporate ladder until middle management, but from that point on, emotional intelligence falls steadily the higher up the corporate ladder one goes. "CEOs," Bradberry writes, "on average, have the lowest EQ scores in the workplace."

EMOTIONAL INTELLIGENCE AND JOB TITLE

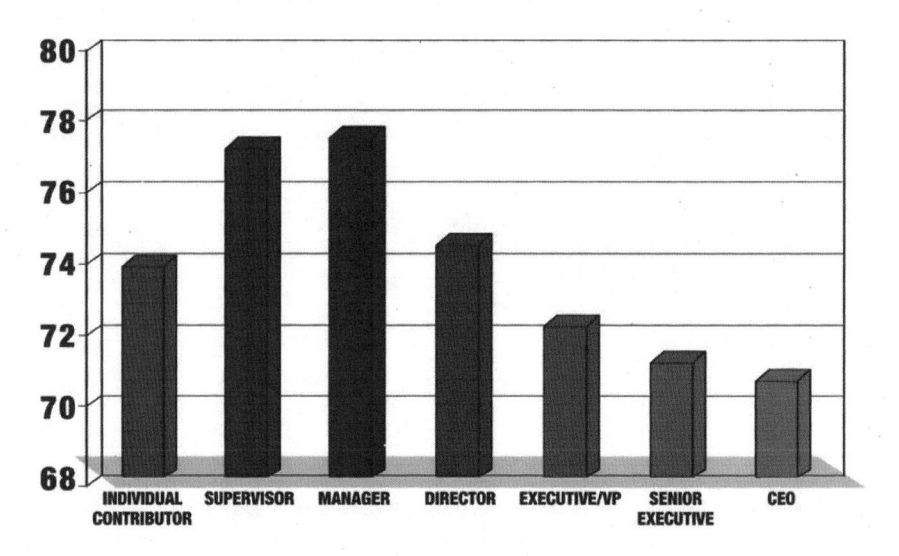

Job Title	EQ Score
Individual Contributor	~74
Supervisor	~77
Manager	~77.5
Director	~74.5
Executive/VP	~72.5
Senior Executive	~71
CEO	~70.5

(Graph provided courtesy of Dr. Travis Bradberry)

Self-awareness is a key component of emotional intelligence and has been shown to be the most over-estimated one by executives.[22]

A study entitled "It's Lonely At The Top: Executive's Emotional Intelligence Self [Mis] Perceptions" found that "higher-level participants consistently rate themselves higher than others." The researchers compared the 360-degree feedback of over 1,200 participants with the participants' self-assessment on a variety measures of emotional intelligence. The greatest discrepancy between "self" and "other" ratings was among senior executives. Now take a guess which competency senior managers are most delusional about. That's right, the biggest gap between self and other ratings among senior managers was in the self-awareness category. Not only are senior managers more delusional about how others view them, they have no idea how delusional they really are!

The study's authors concluded that the reason for this gap between self and other perceptions of emotional intelligence is primarily because of a lack of feedback. There are two reasons for this. Not only are people less inclined to give senior managers feedback, the more senior someone is, the fewer people there are in a position to directly observe the person's work and provide feedback. That's what the expression "It's lonely at the top" means.

This was Robert Kaplan's experience during his time at the top of Goldman Sachs, one of the largest companies in the world. Throughout his career, Kaplan mentored and coached many people in prestigious leadership positions. Concerning the impediment that formal authority imposes on self-awareness, Kaplan writes, "As executives become more senior it becomes far more difficult to get timely and constructive feedback, maintain an accurate self-perception, and develop early warning systems for emerging problems."[23]

Think of power or formal authority as a spatial disorientation amplifier—a fog machine that increasingly obscures our visibility the higher we rise. However out of touch with reality we were before we had any formal authority, we are bound to be flying off kilter once we fly into the thick fog produced by the endowment of formal authority. The higher you climb in the organization, the thicker the fog gets, and the more critical it becomes to rely on multiple instruments and tactics to ensure an accurate perception of reality.

The Beginning of Wisdom

I once heard a wise man say, "Seeing ourselves clearly is the beginning of wisdom."[24] When I heard that phrase, I was struck with its profoundness.

Ancient Greek philosophers recognized that to "know thyself" is a key step on the path to greatness. Perhaps this is because we can't influence others effectively until we know what we must change about ourselves to have greater impact. Or perhaps Greek philosophers knew thousands of years ago what systems thinkers today are trying to share with the world: we cause a lot of our own problems; we just don't realize it.

The habit of looking in the mirror for answers before looking elsewhere is how you can gain the wisdom to overcome your greatest challenges and become your best self. It is how you can shake off the victim mentality to obtain the power to design a better future for yourself and others.

12. How to Look in the Mirror

There are a number of ways that you can become more aware of how you contribute to your own problems and gain the insight you need to improve future results. Here are four important steps you can take to look in the mirror.

1. Build Your Confidence

Insecure people don't want to look in the mirror for answers to their problems. As Jack Nicolson said in the movie *A Few Good Men*, they "can't handle the truth."

Insecure people view negative feedback as a judgement of their worth, and it shatters them to pieces. In contrast, confident people can not only handle feedback, they actively solicit it. Confident people believe that feedback can help them improve, so they seek it out. This is what leadership research firm Zenger Folkman discovered. Drawing from their firm's database of over a million 360-degree reviews, Jack Zenger and Joe Folkman identified a strong correlation between a person's confidence level and his or her preference for giving and receiving improvement feedback.[1] This means that confident people are generally more comfortable giving and receiving feedback than less confident people.

Self-awareness expert and best-selling author Tasha Eurich refers to the correlation between people's level of self-confidence and their ability to receive feedback in her book, *Insight*. Speaking about the importance of focusing on our strengths and values to build the confidence necessary to receive potentially hard-to-hear feedback, Eurich writes, "when we remember the greater picture of who we are, we can put seemingly threatening information in its proper perspective."[2] Indeed, when we look in the mirror to see how we may have contributed to our problems, we are purposely seeking out potentially threatening information. In doing so, we are making a conscious choice to lower our psychological defenses and seek out information that might make us look bad. Before any self-respecting person would dare do that, they must believe that the core of who they are is good and strong enough not only to withstand this threatening information but also resourceful and smart enough to leverage this threatening information to produce better outcomes for themselves in the future. The question, then, is how can we help ourselves feel confident enough to shine a light on our faults, so we can learn from them and overcome them?

Psychologists have learned that the ultimate source of self-confidence is past success because success supplies our brains with hard proof that we are good at something.[3] When people believe they are competent in a certain area, they become motivated to set higher goals and continue to work on improving that ability, even in the face of adversity and setbacks.[4] Simply put, we are naturally motivated to continue challenging ourselves in areas we think we're already good at. When people are motivated to try harder and persist longer at an activity, they tend to get better at it. This additional success reinforces their belief that they are competent in that ability, which motivates them to continue working on it. Success, therefore, can create a virtuous cycle of confidence and higher performance.[5]

PERCEIVED COMPETENCE → MOTIVATION → SUCCESS → (SELF-CONFIDENCE) → PERCEIVED COMPETENCE

The self-confidence cycle, however, can backfire if we let our successes lull us into believing we don't have more room to improve. As noted earlier, highly successful people tend to be bad learners for this very reason. They shut their brains off to potential learning situations because being right has become a core part of their identity, and they refuse to accept any evidence to the contrary. Remember what Chris Argyris taught us: because many successful people eschew the idea of being wrong, they tend to "become defensive, screen out criticism, and put the 'blame' on anyone and everyone but themselves."

A GROWTH MINDSET – KEY TO BUILDING TRUE CONFIDENCE

How can you build your confidence without allowing your successes to blind you to additional avenues that will lead to even greater success? Researcher Carol Dweck suggests that to push through insecurity and defensiveness, we need to develop and strengthen what she calls a "growth mindset."[6] People with a growth mindset believe they can develop their abilities through effort. When they fail, people with a growth mindset believe their failure is a result of lack of preparation or effort, not ability. People with a growth mindset are more concerned with learning than with looking smart. Perhaps counterintuitively, when a person focuses more on learning than on performing, they tend to perform better, both in the classroom and in the workplace.[7]

At the other end of the spectrum, people with a "fixed mindset" believe their abilities are innate, and when they fail it's because they lack natural ability in that area. They gain their confidence from being right and looking smart. For example, Jim, the president of the company I once worked for whom I introduced earlier, felt compelled to appear like he had the answer to every question. He was more concerned with looking smart than with learning. Had he ever uttered the words "I don't know. We should look into that" when asked a puzzling question, the company might have avoided some of the problems that led to its demise.

Because people with a growth mindset value learning more than they value looking good, they are more willing to look at how they may have contributed to less-than-stellar results. In other words, a growth mindset makes one more willing to look in the mirror. On the other hand, people who value performing more than they value learning will be more inclined to distance themselves from poor results by blaming other people or circumstances.

In addition to helping us be more *willing* to look in the mirror, developing a growth mindset helps us be *able* to look in the mirror in two ways.

1. By prioritizing learning over performing, we protect ourselves against overconfidence, which blinds us to opportunities to improve.

2. Developing an ability to learn can become a source of confidence in itself.[8]

Let's say you are attempting something new and don't yet have confidence in your ability to accomplish it. A growth mindset can become a substitute for past success in that area, thereby activating the self-confidence cycle into motion. Here's why. Those who demonstrate a growth mindset are more motivated to set higher goals, try harder, and persist longer in the face of adversity.[9] As luck would have it, these are precisely the same motivations that are generated by past success.[10] By focusing on learning instead of looking good, you create the motivation to try hard things and learn from them. This improves your odds of success, which builds your self-confidence, as the following graphic illustrates.

Diagram

PERCEIVED COMPETENCE → MOTIVATION ← GROWTH MINDSET

SELF-CONFIDENCE

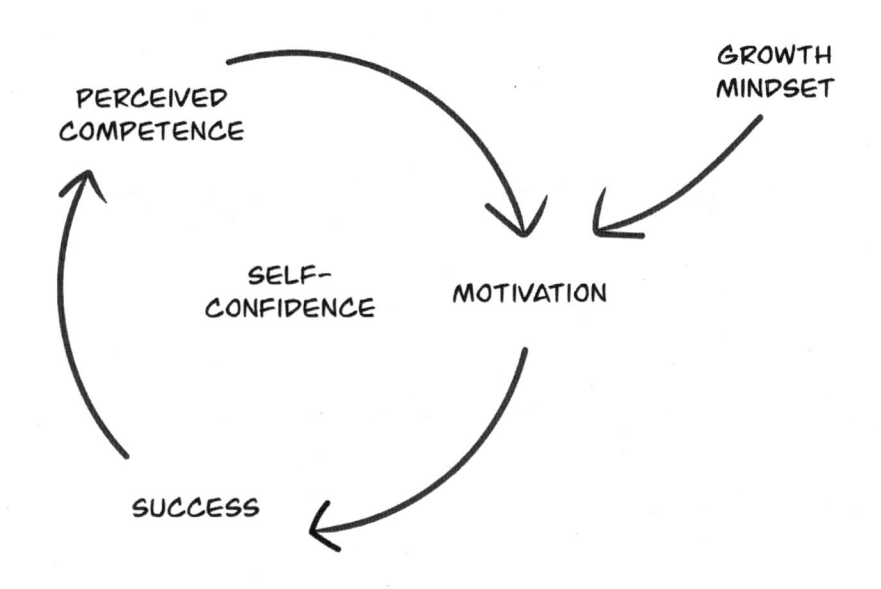

SUCCESS → (cycle back to PERCEIVED COMPETENCE)

Developing a growth mindset not only guards against overconfidence, which can sabotage you, it can also kick-start the self-confidence cycle into motion. The more you develop a growth mindset, and the more success you achieve, the more your confidence will grow. As your self-confidence increases, so does your capacity to accept critical feedback, acknowledge your role in problems, and apply what you have learned to improve future results.

No longer is your confidence dependent on how smart you think you look—a perception that can be shattered the moment you are proven wrong. True confidence is built upon the belief that you can learn from your mistakes and failures to become better. Critical feedback might sting, but it only makes you stronger, so bring it on!

Your confidence now becomes built on your potential for greatness, not your current proximity to it. It doesn't matter how good or how smart other people are and how you think you compare. What matters is that with this newfound belief in your ability to learn and grow, and with your new appetite for feedback, you are accelerating toward greatness, and nobody can stop you!

The belief in your ability to learn and grow is the only reliable and sustainable source of confidence. True confidence is the quiet assurance that comes from knowing your strengths and being determined to learn from your mistakes to become even stronger and bring you closer to personal greatness.

> True confidence is the quiet assurance that comes from knowing your strengths and being determined to learn from your mistakes to become even stronger.

If you want to increase the confidence of those you lead, help them find success by focusing on their strengths, and strengthen their belief in their ability to learn. Encourage those you lead to pursue work and interests that are aligned with their strengths instead of harping on them about their weaknesses. Teach them that developing new strengths takes time and hard work. Share how you have benefited from learning from your mistakes. Point out how much progress they have made and the effort they invested to make that progress.

As people build their confidence—true confidence—they will see their capacity to accept critical feedback increase along with their willingness to acknowledge their role in problems.

2. Solicit Feedback from Multiple Sources

Remember our simple-minded friend, McArthur Wheeler, who put lemon juice on his face and, believing he was invisible to cameras, robbed two banks? It's hard to forget that ridiculous story. Wheeler made a poor attempt to prove his theory by looking at only one data source (the botched Polaroid camera experiment), which led him to embrace a false belief. Then he acted on this inaccurate belief, only to discover that it was in conflict with reality.

Although we may laugh at this story (with good reason), most of us begin living Wheeler's story any time we hear feedback we don't like. We all hold beliefs about ourselves that are inaccurate. Most of us, particularly those of us in leadership positions, believe we are better than we really are. We tend to believe we are more skilled than we are and that we have a pretty good idea of how others view us.

When our beliefs about ourselves meet any resistance from disconfirming feedback, most people tend to recoil, seeking refuge in the opinion of their cronies. Researcher Paul Green calls this "shopping for confirmation." Green conducted several feedback studies in which he observed an interesting pattern.[11] When people receive negative feedback, they tend to distance themselves from the person who gave them the feedback, both in physical proximity and by forming different social networks. They do this in order to find people who will give them feedback more consistent with their self-image. In other words, they moved away from people who gave them negative feedback to find people who would give them more positive feedback. Green discovered that, as people do this, they essentially create an echo chamber that feeds them only positive information about themselves, thus reinforcing potentially inaccurate self-perceptions.

"But any form of echo chamber ultimately weakens us," Green says. "If you surround yourself with those who constantly prop you up, you're willfully being blind to any aspect of yourself . . . that might need improvement."

As discussed earlier, you need to rely more on your navigational instruments to make sure you are flying level rather than relying on your gut. Requesting multiple perspectives about your strengths and your performance are those navigational instruments. The people around us see us more clearly than we see ourselves. For instance, one study collected leadership self-assessments from 155 US Navy officers. Then the researchers collected performance and promotion data from these officers' superiors and also asked the officers' senior subordinates to provide an assessment of their bosses' leadership. The ratings of the officers' subordinates closely matched the performance data provided by the officers' superiors. However, the officers' self-assessments were generally inflated. Not surprisingly, the officers who performed the best were those whose self-assessments were more congruent with those of their superiors and subordinates.[12] Individuals are more successful when they have an accurate self-perception, and the best way to accomplish this is to ask for feedback from multiple sources.

Commenting on this tactic, Tasha Eurich writes, "Feedback from one person is a perspective; feedback from two people is a pattern; but feedback from three or more people is likely to be as close to a fact as you can get."[13]

Here are a few ways you can get feedback from multiple sources so you don't make the "lemon juice mistake."

I. REQUEST INDIVIDUAL FEEDBACK

One of the best sources of specific feedback is the people who we interact with on a regular basis. However, before you go about randomly asking for feedback, consider who you should ask. Not all perspectives are equally valid or important. You probably don't care what some people you work with think about you. Ask for feedback from the people whose perspectives you *should* care about. These are your key relationships, such as your boss, the people who report to you, the colleagues who rely on your work, your clients, your spouse, and close friends. They hold the opinions that matter most to you.

Once you know who to ask for feedback, it's critical to know how to ask. Casually asking work colleagues "How did I do?" after a presentation probably isn't going to yield rich data. Nor will asking your best friend "Am I a good friend?"

There are many ineffective ways to ask for feedback, but without a doubt the worst way is to ask, "Do you have any feedback for me?" This closed-ended question begs the response "No" or "I can't think of any right now." Asking for feedback in this way is worse than not asking for feedback at all because you will be tricked into thinking that since nobody ever has any improvement feedback for you, you must be as awesome as you always thought you were!

There are basically two types of feedback: reaffirming feedback and improvement feedback. Reaffirming feedback, such as praise, teaches us what our strengths are, lets us know that we are on target, and encourages us to continue to do what's working. Improvement feedback gives us ideas on how we can do better.

Celebrated leadership coach Marshall Goldsmith advises that the best way to request feedback is to ask, "How can I do better at . . . ?"[14] Phrasing it this way encourages people to provide you with specific advice instead of destructive criticism.

Building on Goldsmith's suggestion, here are several tips for requesting feedback like a pro.

- **Explain why you are asking**. Before people will give you improvement feedback, they need to be convinced that you want it for the right reason, and the only right reason is so you can improve. Make sure to be clear about this up front, so they don't come to any other conclusions.

- **Ask for Advice, Not Criticism**. Criticism is focused on the past. Advice is focused on the future. You will usually get more helpful and less hurtful feedback if you ask for advice instead of asking what you are doing wrong.

- **Focus your request**. People are far more likely to give you useful feedback if you give them a specific area about which you'd like feedback. For instance, you might ask, "How can I do better at running meetings?" "How can I improve the way I communicate?" or "How can I do better at providing you with feedback?" By narrowing the focus of your request, you make it easier for people to provide you with more specific and actionable feedback.

- **Ask for positives**. Ask people to start by telling you what you're doing well. This makes them feel more comfortable providing improvement feedback. If you suspect someone may be uncomfortable giving you improvement feedback, double down on this behavioral hack by asking for two things you're doing well and one thing you could do differently to get better results.

- **Give them time to think about it**. It's usually best not to ask people to give you a response right away. Instead, ask if you can follow up with them in a few days. This gives them time to think about it. You may even consider adding "sharing feedback" to your regular one-on-one meeting agenda with your staff.

- **Receive it in person**. Don't ask for feedback to be delivered through email. Requesting feedback initiates an important conversation where tone of voice and body language adds clarity and reveals sincere intentions. As Eurich says, "the richness and detail you get in a conversation is unmatched by written feedback."[15] Although feedback can be delivered over the phone, it works best in person or over video conference.

- **Receive feedback with gratitude**. The old saying is true that "People who shoot the messenger stop getting messages." The only correct way to respond to feedback is "Thank you." You may also want to add something like "I hadn't considered that" or "You've given me something to think about." Any defensiveness in your response will be interpreted as a sign that you don't really want improvement feedback.

- **Make it private**. It's best to ask for feedback in a private one-on-one conversation, not in a group setting.

To put these tips into practice, try the following exercise that I give to my workshop participants.

    a) Over the next month, ask your boss and three or more peers (if you are a manager, ask three people who report to you) to provide you with feedback.

b) Let them know you are trying to improve your performance and would like their help. You might say something like "I'm learning about how feedback can help me improve, and I was wondering if you would be willing to give me some honest feedback on a specific area of my performance if I gave you time to think about it."

c) If they agree, ask them to provide you with feedback in a specific area, such as how well you interact with others, how you come across at meetings, how you communicate, how you can improve your relationship with different departments, how well you are living the company values or leadership competencies, etc.

d) Ask them to think of two things you do particularly well in the area you specified and one way you can do better in that area.

e) Let them know you will follow up with them in a few days to hear what they've got for you.

f) When they provide their feedback, sincerely thank them for it, even if it stings.

g) Record your notes from those conversations onto one document. Writing notes during a feedback meeting can give you a few extra moments to process the feedback before responding, and it demonstrates that you are taking the feedback seriously.

h) Look for common themes in their responses.

i) Select one or two common themes to work on improving.

j) Follow up with the people who provided you with feedback to let them know what you have decided to work on. Ask them if they would provide you with feedback in a month or two on how well you are doing in the area you are working on.

Participants in my workshops who perform this exercise for the first time report that they occasionally get some truly helpful feedback. For example, Leslie learned from a coworker that she is sometimes too loud on the phone, which can distract others. Leslie doesn't want to be known as the loud, annoying office mate. Now that she knows this, Leslie is monitoring her volume more closely. Because Leslie tried the feedback exercise, she and her office mate feel that their respect and concern for each other has increased.

The first time you ask for feedback will likely be the most difficult for you and may feel a bit awkward. This is because it's a new experience for you and for the person you are asking. They may have some reservations about your motives and sincerity. Before others will give you improvement feedback, they must feel that it's safe to do so—that you won't react poorly when they hint at an area in which you could improve.

It's clear from those who attend my workshops that those who have actively solicited feedback in the past end up receiving far more helpful feedback from this assignment than those who are trying it for the first time. Like most skills, the more you practice, the better you'll get, and the better the feedback will get. Asking for feedback should not be a one-time exercise; it should be a lifelong habit.

Those in senior leadership positions have a few more options to facilitate feedback throughout the organization. Here are two important tools they can employ.

II. CONDUCT EMPLOYEE ENGAGEMENT SURVEYS

Employee engagement surveys are the most basic way that organizations can receive feedback from multiple sources about how well their leaders are doing. The key to making employee engagement surveys a useful feedback tool is by requiring responders to identify their manager. The greatest influence on employee engagement is not the perks and benefits an organization offers its employees or its organizational policies but how individual managers treat their staff.[16] Not parsing employee data by manager is like having someone tell you how many calories you ate that week but not telling you which foods they came from. All you'll know is whether or not you are meeting your weekly calorie goal, but you won't know specifically what foods are contributing the most to your weight loss or gain.

In like manner, the best way to influence overall employee engagement scores is to provide each manager with their team's engagement score and to let them know where their team's score ranks against other teams. This gives managers a sense of how their leadership effectiveness stacks up against their colleagues. For example, Google discovered that when managers know they are in the bottom half of their peers, this knowledge alone is enough to motivate managers to improve their leadership effectiveness.[17] Improving leadership effectiveness is the most powerful way to improve employee engagement. Organizations should also provide managers with their team's average rating of specific engagement items to let managers know which areas they need to work on.

Most executives claim they care about employee engagement, but many organizations only conduct employee engagement surveys every two or three years. For organizations that only conduct employee engagement surveys sporadically, I have two thoughts for you:

- **You get what you measure**. You won't be able to move the needle on employee engagement if you aren't regularly measuring it. If you want to lose weight, weighing yourself once a month isn't very effective. Likewise, organizations should measure employee engagement several times a year.

- **What you measure reveals your priorities**. If you only measure employee engagement every couple of years, then you don't really care about it. And if you don't really care about employee engagement, then you don't really care about improving your leadership. It's that simple.

Some CEOs I speak to explain that they don't conduct regular employee engagement surveys because they believe that if they don't act on the feedback, it's worse than if they didn't ask at all. Here are two thoughts for senior managers who believe this.

- **That's not true.** Think of it this way: would you rather have a boss who asks you how she can improve and doesn't act on your feedback or a boss who never asks you how she can improve? People who ask you how they can improve are at least signaling that they care about their leadership ability and how it affects you, even if they don't act on your feedback. People who never ask you how they can improve are telling you that they don't care how their leadership affects you.

- **Why accept defeat?** Senior managers who believe they won't act effectively on employee feedback are perpetuating a self-fulfilling prophecy. Decide to make one simple change based on employee feedback. Don't overcomplicate your response or make it bigger and harder than it needs to be. Commit to making one simple change based on employee engagement survey data and explain to employees why you made it.

III. INITIATE 360-DEGREE FEEDBACK

"Multi-rater" or 360-degree feedback is the ultimate feedback mechanism. Typically, a contracted consultant interviews about a dozen or more people who work with the person being evaluated. The feedback group includes people within the organization and can also include customers and suppliers. The consultant asks standard questions, records the responses, consolidates the common themes, and shares the feedback with the person being evaluated—keeping the participants anonymous.

Three-hundred-and-sixty-degree evaluations can also be conducted through anonymous surveys. If this feedback focuses on specific behavioral competencies, it will likely provide more specific and useful feedback.

Some have questioned whether 360-degree feedback is fair and accurate. Such concerns largely disappear when organizations commit to using 360-degree feedback only for development purposes and not for employment-related decisions, such as for promotion or compensation.[18] Substantial research shows that 360-degree feedback provides a far more accurate picture of one's strengths and weaknesses than other tools and that this feedback facilitates performance improvement.[19, 20, 21] There is virtually no evidence to the contrary.

When we acknowledge how we have contributed to our problems, we become like detectives looking for clues to determine all the factors that led to our present situation. Regularly requesting feedback is like interviewing witnesses. A solid case is rarely based on only one or two testimonies. No single perspective is 100 percent reliable, but the common themes in the testimonies of many witnesses provide compelling evidence of the truth.

Regularly requesting feedback and accepting it with gratitude is critical to developing personal accountability. Knowledge is power, especially knowledge about yourself.

3. When things go wrong, ask, "How may I have contributed to this problem?"

As noted earlier, insecure people tend not to ask this question very often, if at all. It's too dangerous. The answer could destroy their fragile egos. Only confident people are willing to look at how they have contributed to their problems. They want to know, so they can produce better outcomes for themselves in the future.

Colin Powell's infamous speech to convince the UN that Iraq was producing weapons of mass destruction provides a great example of how confident people deal with their mistakes.

In the summer of 2002, Powell caught wind that President Bush was planning to invade Iraq because of intelligence claims that Saddam Hussein was manufacturing weapons of mass destruction (WMDs).[22] However,

Powell hadn't heard very much discussion about what the president planned to do after the invasion. Powell famously told the president "If you take over a government, guess who becomes the government and is responsible for the country? You are. So if you break it, you own it."

Instead, Powell convinced Bush to try to resolve the WMD issue diplomatically through the United Nations.[23] From that point on, Bush gave Powell that responsibility. The primary source of Iraq's WMD program was a partially completed national intelligence report. This report was circulated around Washington and was accepted by America's military commanders and most of Congress, but the evidence contained in the report was mostly circumstantial and inferential.

On January 30, 2003, President Bush told Powell that he wanted Powell to present their case against Iraq to the UN on February 5, just a few days away. However, Powell's staff didn't have a copy of the report. When they received it later that day, they discovered it was a disaster and completely unusable. They had four days to prepare their case to the UN, essentially having to start from scratch!

Powell moved his staff to the CIA to work with the CIA director and his team to piece together the report from the raw materials on which the original report was based. They worked day and night trying to come up with solid evidence and discard any items that seemed like a stretch. They finished their case the night before Powell was to present it to the UN, and the CIA director stood behind every word of it.

Powell presented a powerful case to the UN, and the war began six weeks later. The rest is history. No WMDs were ever found. Powell's case to the UN is regarded as one of the worst intelligence failures in US history.

Powell calls this part in his personal history "One of my most monumental failures, the one with the widest-ranging impact."

How did Powell respond? He could have blamed the shaky sources the CIA passed off as reliable intelligence. He could have blamed Vice President Cheney for pressuring him to use less than credible sources. He could have blamed the unusable intelligence report he was given or the lack of time he had to prepare his case. Instead, Powell blamed himself. "I am mad mostly at myself for not having smelled the problem," he said. "My instincts failed me." Powell didn't stop there. Acknowledging your role in problems is next to useless unless you also extract lessons learned. "I learned from this experience," he writes. "I learned to be more demanding of intelligence analysts. I learned to sharpen my natural skepticism toward apparently all-knowing experts."

Powell provides the following recipe for dealing with failure: "Learn from it. Study how you contributed to it. If you are responsible for it, own up to it. Though others may have greater responsibility for it than you do, don't look for that as an escape hatch. Once you have analyzed what went wrong and what you did wrong, internalize the lessons learned and then move on."

Powell's example teaches the rest of us a great lesson. Those who acknowledge how they contribute to problems become more powerful than their problems because they are able to learn from their mistakes. On the other hand, people who don't want to see how they are contributing to their problems are held captive by their ignorance. You can't overcome your problems if you don't know what's truly causing them.

4. Take the Blame

Leadership is about going ahead of others to show them the way. Leadership is inherently risky. That's the social contract we make with leaders. They take the risks to make it safe for others. They take ultimate accountability for the success and welfare of the group, so the rest of us can focus on doing our jobs.

To compensate leaders for this act of heroism, we accept that they will receive more pay and more perks than us, and we allow them to make decisions that impact us, believing their decisions will have our best interests at heart.

Of course, as Simon Sinek masterfully explains in his TED talk, "Why Good Leaders Make You Feel Safe," this social contract is often broken.[24]

Many people in leadership positions sacrifice the people who work for them to save their own skin. They are cowards who are not living up to their end of the bargain. The sad truth is that employees follow those in leadership positions not necessarily because they *want* to follow them but because their livelihood depends upon it.

Fortunately, leadership is not a position. Anybody can be a leader if they are willing to change. Anyone can be a hero, even in the workplace, but heroism takes courage. One of the simplest (and hardest) ways to be a leader is to take the blame so that the team can move on to focus on the solution.

"Contrary to what you may feel in the moment," says leadership coach Peter Bregman, "taking the blame is the power move, strengthening your position, not weakening it."

Bregman goes on to provide an example.[25]

> I was running a strategy offsite at a high technology company with a CEO and his direct reports. We were looking at some problematic numbers from the previous quarter. One by one each leader was trying to argue that he or she was not, ultimately, responsible for the issues, pointing to the other areas that contributed.
>
> Then Dave, the head of sales spoke up. He proceeded to list the mistakes he felt he personally made and what he wanted to do differently in the future.
>
> His colleagues didn't pile on. In fact, they did the opposite. They began to say things to dilute his blame. One by one, they started taking responsibility for their role in the challenges the company was facing.
>
> By taking the blame, Dave changed the course of that meeting and, as it turns out, the course of the company. He also got promoted.

Only strong people can admit when they make mistakes. We know this when we see others acknowledge their role in problems, and our respect for them instantly increases. Our challenge is to remember this fact when the pressure is on us to take the easy road and blame someone or something else for our problems. Will we succumb to the pressure to blame someone or something else and give away our power to overcome our problems, or will we look in the mirror, acknowledge our role in problems, and move forward?

Former US president Barack Obama consistently demonstrated that he was willing to do the latter. Speaking of her former boss, former senior adviser to President Obama Valerie Jarrett said of him, "I have always observed he is the first to say, 'What could I have done better?' His willingness to be introspective, to be tough on himself, yet show grace to others, is, I think, one of the leadership qualities that others should look up to."[26]

Rarely are we 100 percent the cause of problems. This means that whenever our actions contributed to undesirable results, we can usually point to other people or circumstances "as an escape hatch," to use Powell's words. Accountability is owning up to our role in problems and finding a solution. Being a leader means resisting the urge to shift the burden of accountability to other people or other factors even when some of it may be deserved.

Now that you have some new tactics to help you look in the mirror, I'd like to share another tip for you to keep in mind as you build your accountability muscles. To enhance your ability to look in the mirror, you need to understand the difference between using facts as an explanation versus using them as an excuse.

13. Heroes Look for Explanations, Not Excuses

Everybody loves a great story. Our favorite stories often involve a protagonist who is dealt a bad hand but who manages to rise above their circumstances because of his or her remarkable character and unconquerable spirit. These are stories of a hero's journey, stories that many famous leaders have lived.

In our everyday life, however, we don't often see these heroic stories unfold. This is partly because it's hard to notice the heroic journeys transpiring around us that take decades to play out. Another reason why we don't see very many heroes is because when these pivotal moments come into our lives, providing us with an opportunity to become a hero, most of us have not developed the habits necessary to respond to such challenges in heroic ways.

We build our capacity to act like a hero by the way we respond to the daily challenges that aren't necessarily our fault. When those times come, we basically have two options. We can either try to excuse ourselves from the problem, or we can look for explanations to help solve the problem. Learning to be a hero begins by focusing on what you can do to overcome your challenges instead of focusing on what you can't do.

> We build our capacity to act like a hero by the way we respond to the daily challenges that aren't necessarily our fault.

The Difference Between Explanations and Excuses

Some people in leadership positions believe they are teaching others to be accountable for problems by slamming a fist on their desk and barking, "Don't bring me excuses; bring me solutions!" This is not leadership, and it definitely won't create a culture of accountability. What it communicates is "I don't care about you. I only care about results." True leaders care as much about the people they lead as they do about achieving the desired results.

According to global CEO coach Sabina Nawaz, the "only bring me solutions" approach often prevents problems from surfacing until they're full-blown crises.

Nawaz describes a CEO who used to lose his temper and raise his voice any time his team members brought problems to light. Not surprisingly, the CEO's employees stopped bringing him problems, leaving him blind to potential issues.[1] Instead, leaders who model accountability teach people that problems can be valuable because they provide an opportunity to learn and improve.

They key to surfacing problems in a way that doesn't sound like an excuse is to bring them forward with the intention of being part of the solution.

An excuse is a justification for poor behavior and unacceptable results. An excuse is something someone offers in exchange for bad results in an attempt to extricate themselves from the debacle. "I can't deliver what you want," the thinking goes, "so let me offer you some excuses instead. That should satisfy you."

A person who provides an excuse has no intention of mitigating the unacceptable results. They are essentially washing their hands of the situation and saying, "I'm out." An explanation, on the other hand, is an analysis of the problem with the intent to salvage the situation as best as possible and attempt to turn things around. Leaders encourage people to

Habit 2 – Look in the Mirror

bring forward explanations for problems, so the team can use them to find solutions or prevent the same problem from recurring.

Giving excuses for bad results is like losing someone else's dog and bringing them back the broken leash, expecting that to appease the dog's owner. "The leash broke," you say, "and your dog ran away. I hope you find your dog. See you later." In this case, the broken leash is being used as an excuse.

On the other hand, after an accountable person tells the dog's owner that the leash broke and their dog ran away, she continues, saying, "I have called three of my friends to come help look for your dog. I need you to come help us, and could you possibly ask your husband to start making flyers for us to post if we don't find your dog before nightfall?" In this instance, the broken leash is used as an explanation because it leads to a solution.

The difference between an excuse and an explanation is how you intend to use it. If you think that providing a reason for poor results absolves you of accountability, then it's an excuse. If you use the reason for poor results as the starting point to find a solution you intend to implement, then it's an explanation.

The difference between an excuse and an explanation is how you intend to use it.

Excuse making has almost become a sport in some organizations. No matter what problem is thrown at some people, they can find a reason why it's not their fault. Who hasn't heard excuses like, "Traffic was brutal today," "I didn't have time to get that done," or "I told him to do it, so I assumed it got done properly"? There may be an element of truth in each of these statements, but they are excuses because they don't acknowledge what could have been done to mitigate the undesirable outcomes, nor do these statements imply that the person providing them intends to be part of the solution.

Most people in leadership positions know how maddening it is to be offered excuses instead of results, but is it possible that those who report to you are learning this behavior from you?

Exercising Accountability Builds Hero Habits

I once read a story about two fast-food restaurant CEOs who were interviewed by the same news reporter. The reporter summed up his two interviews with the following commentary.

> I had a conversation recently with the CEO of [ABC] Corporation, and the entire conversation revolved around how the company is being pounded by the economy. Their CEO spent our entire conversation complaining and crying about their challenging environment. My conversations with their biggest competitor were dramatically different. As I spoke with their CEO, he did not see any problem with the environment in which they are operating. Their entire organizational focus centers around what else they can do to create growth opportunities. That's why their business is thriving.

The reporter concluded with this observation: "The shareholders of these companies don't care how the food tastes. They care about how the leaders are leading their companies to achieve results in spite of the current economy."[2]

To the first CEO's credit, when he was confronted with the reporter's reproval, he publicly acknowledged his mistake and vowed to stop offering excuses. Instead, he encouraged his team to focus on what the company *can* do to improve results instead of on what they *can't* do. This courageous act of looking in the mirror marked a major turning point for the company.

Building personal accountability increases your capacity to be a leader and respond to your challenges in heroic ways. Think of the following three practices as exercises to prepare you to become a hero when those pivotal moments come in your life.

1. **Look for explanations, not excuses**. Make a list of all the factors that contributed to your problem, and don't stop until you've listed all the things you did or didn't do that may have contributed to your problem.

2. **Reward people who surface problems**. Never punish people for bringing forward problems by labeling them as "troublemakers." If people don't feel it's safe to bring problems to your attention, you'll stop hearing about them. Then you will be blindsided when the problems are much harder to deal with and when it's become more difficult to diagnose the root cause. Instead, teach others that problems are opportunities to improve. Publicly praise people who bring forward problems, and, when necessary, coach them on how to turn their excuses into explanations.

3. **Model being part of the solution**. If you want others to come to you with more solutions, model what being part of the solution looks like. This includes being willing to invest the time necessary to teach people how to find their own solutions when they come to you with problems instead of solving it for them or unsympathetically saying, "Don't bring me excuses; bring me solutions."

Heroes rise above their challenges to accomplish great things. So do great leaders. Exercising personal accountability in how you respond to the daily challenges that aren't necessarily your fault is how you build your capacity to act more like a hero that others can look up to and strive to emulate.

14. Accurately Diagnose Before You Prescribe

Before you can find lasting solutions to your problems, you must accurately diagnose them.

As you move from habit two to habit three, you must recognize that any diagnosis of problems that doesn't include looking in the mirror will miss a large chunk of the possible causes, and your solution will likely miss the mark.

Once again, Colin Powell shows us how looking in the mirror is an essential prerequisite to finding sustainable solutions to our problems.

When Colin Powell was secretary of state, a congressman attacked the State Department's annual report to Congress about trends in terrorist incidents. The congressman claimed that Powell and his team intentionally understated the terrorist problem.[1]

Initially, Powell's staff circled the wagons to defend their position, but Powell wanted to first make sure that there weren't any problems with the process they used to create the report. "I thought we should listen to his criticism, concede that he might be right, and fix the problems he'd spotlighted so they would not end up in lurid display before his congressional committee."

After using a process called an after-action review (AAR), which I will discuss later, Powell and his team discovered significant errors in the way the CIA recorded and counted terrorist incidents. The State Department further compounded the mistakes by not doing an adequate job of analyzing the CIA's draft report.

The result? After Powell called the congressman to inform him of the problems Powell's team discovered, the congressman publicly congratulated the State Department and dropped the issue. "More importantly," Powell states, "we fixed the report-making system to avoid future problems."

The best way to get an accurate diagnosis of your problems is to follow Powell's example and begin by looking in the mirror. This is the first fork in the road of diagnosing problems. If you don't explore that path first, you'll never be certain your solution will work or if it will last.

Remember, accountable people care deeply about the desired results. This is why they are willing to own the results and do what it takes to achieve the right results. People who sincerely look in the mirror for answers demonstrate that they care about the results more than they care about their egos. The act of looking in the mirror is an act of humility—a trait we would all like to see more of in our leaders.

Looking in the mirror is the discipline of asking, "How may I have contributed to my present situation?" Once you have asked that question to help diagnose your problem, you will be able to confidently move on to engineer the solution, which is to ask, "How can I improve my situation?"

HABIT 3 – ENGINEER THE SOLUTION

Fix processes, not people

15. Engineer Solutions to System Problems

Mike loves being a fireman. Every day he gets to do things that will help people in emergency situations and save lives. Mike has an easygoing disposition and is quick to make a joke, but he takes his job very seriously. He approaches his work with the discipline of a soldier and has the leadership style of a hockey coach—tough but approachable, caring for his team members without being permissive of poor performance.

Earlier in Mike's career, he worked with Chuck, who ran the fire hall's preventative maintenance program for all their equipment and vehicles. When he started, Chuck was an outgoing, gregarious guy who was described as "the life of the party." Chuck would plan after-work events and enjoyed the tight-knit community of the firehall staff and their families.

Within a short while, Chuck's performance began to decline. He just couldn't seem to get his work done on time. Chuck became so slow at his job, in fact, that unbeknownst to him, his coworkers began calling him "sloth" behind his back.

Unfortunately, nothing was done about Chuck's lackluster performance. The fire chief and the deputy fire chief assumed that's just how he was. They didn't feel that addressing Chuck's performance was worth going to battle with the union.

Over the years, Chuck's reputation as a sloth developed from a flippant nickname to characterize his entire work identity. After years of failing in his job and sensing he had lost the respect of his colleagues, Chuck began to change. His upbeat nature turned to pessimism, and his confidence turned to self-doubt. Not only did Chuck begin to disengage at work, he also began to withdraw from social activities outside of work.

Chuck's decline at work followed a common pattern: poor performance led to low self-confidence, which led to even poorer performance. Chuck spiraled downward in this vicious cycle of low confidence and low performance for almost twenty years.

When Mike was promoted to deputy fire chief, Chuck became his problem. Like his predecessors, Mike thought that there must be something wrong with Chuck, so he tried every person-approach solution he could think of, which included conducting a job analysis and providing Chuck with time-management training. Then the fire department brought in a records-management system that enabled management to glean insights from the data it produced. When reviewing the data from Chuck's area, Mike noticed a pattern. Chuck fell behind his work schedule every Wednesday. He fell so far behind schedule that Chuck couldn't catch up on Thursday or Friday. His backlog then spilled into the following week, putting Chuck behind the eight ball right away, only to fall further behind the next Wednesday.

Once he discovered this pattern, Mike suspected that the way they organized the maintenance schedule was creating a backlog on Wednesdays from which Chuck could never recover.

When Mike approached Chuck with his theory, Chuck was skeptical that a simple change to the schedule would make a difference. Chuck had been defeated time and again. These successive defeats led Chuck to believe something was inherently wrong with him, eroding his self-esteem and his dignity. Like his managers before Mike, Chuck was convinced that *he* was the problem, so he didn't want any more evidence to confirm this widespread belief.

After some encouragement from Mike, Chuck agreed to try the new schedule. "Within no time," Mike said, "Chuck was coming to me three quarters of the way through the day, saying, 'I'm all done. What else can we do?'"

Not only did Chuck's work performance improve immediately, but his jovial self also began to remerge. "People weren't looking at him the way they did before," Mike said. "He was no longer feeling like an outsider. He was back to having a sense of pride in his work."

Chuck's poor performance was not the result of a personal defect after all. Chuck had been set up to fail from the outset by a poorly thought-out schedule. The problem wasn't the person; it was the system!

This story is both heartwarming and gut-wrenching. Imagine if that story was about your wife or husband, your mother or father, your sister or brother, or your daughter or son. Consider the emotional damage this work situation was causing and how it must have affected Chuck's whole life. Misdiagnosing this system's problem as a person problem eroded Chuck's sense of self-worth and dignity for twenty years![1] (Watch a short video of this story at AvailLeadership.com/inspire-accountability-resources)

This tragic story didn't have to happen. It's possible to avoid unintentionally causing so much emotional devastation and emotional suffering. You can prevent yourself from making the same mistake that Chuck's former managers made.

The next time you discover a problem, and you think you know who caused it, pause for a moment, and walk yourself through the three habits of personal accountability.

Remember, when you witness a negative event, your brain automatically routes the information to your amygdala to process, and your amygdala only comes to one conclusion: "The jerk did it on purpose!" Our psychological and biological wiring steer us toward incomplete or incorrect conclusions. Don't let your amygdala suck you into looking at your problems from a person-centered perspective. Train yourself to look at your problems from a systems perspective.

When you feel the urge to blame someone for a problem you've discovered, remember what we learned in habit one: "Weak leaders ask, 'Who is to blame?' Strong leaders ask, 'Where did the system break down?'" Strong leaders resist the urge to blame the person closest to the mess and instead consider how the process, environmental factors, or their own actions may have contributed to the problem.

Changing other people is hard. Changing the process, the environment, or your own behavior is far easier because you have much more control over them. This is what it means to engineer the solution. Engineers solve problems by fixing things; they do not try to fix people. Engineers assume that people make mistakes and will always make mistakes, so they design processes and products to account for human fallibility. They don't assume people will follow the instructions 100 percent of the time, so smart engineers build fail-safes into their products to make it difficult for people to get the wrong results and make it easier for people to get the right results.

Here is another way to look at what it means to engineer the solution. When you look at successful people or organizations, you'll most often find that they are highly disciplined. For example, to generate optimum creativity, Stephen King follows the same morning routine of drinking water, taking his vitamins, listening to music, and keeping his workspace organized in the same way.[2] To keep himself focused, Steve Jobs looked in the mirror every morning and asked, "If today were the last day of my life, would I want to do what I am about to do today?" As a company, Google is religious about goal setting.

Discipline is the practice of consistently doing things that bring about long-term benefits. Admirers of disciplined people and organizations often mistakenly attribute their success to super-human willpower. Willpower is not the same thing as discipline. Discipline is about consistent behavior, whereas willpower is about impulse control. Exercising willpower is physically exhausting. Discipline, on the other hand, is liberating. Successful people and organizations aren't successful because they necessarily have more willpower than the rest of us. They are successful because they establish and follow processes to ensure they do the things they know will make them successful and to keep them accountable for doing those things. In fact, successful people and organizations create processes so they don't have to rely on willpower to do the right thing. They put their trust in processes, not willpower, to get the right results. This is the essence of engineering the solution.

Engineered Solutions Exist for Most Problems

Engineered solutions strike at the root of problems. They are more reliable and more sustainable than trying to train people to "be more careful." Instead of trying to fix people, engineered solutions aim to change the environment people work in to help them produce the right results more often. Engineered solutions, therefore, are environmental interventions.

Person-centered solutions are like trying to teach a toddler not to stick things in an electrical socket. You may have some success for a while, but sooner or later, she'll forget, or she'll forget that you meant don't stick *anything* in *any* electrical sockets. That's a dangerous and foolish way to solve the problem. A systems solution is to insert childproof outlet covers on all electrical sockets.

Not all problems are systems problems, however. Some problems simply require people to own the results and come up with a creative solution. As a case in point, one of my clients, AdvantAGE Assist, manages care homes for seniors. One day a lady named Pearl approached the front desk at one of their care homes and asked if she could rent a room for a month while her house was being renovated. She didn't need the care services, just a room. Unfortunately, that's not the way these care homes work. Resident contracts are long-term agreements and include various services depending on the level of care requested. However, sensing an opportunity, or perhaps simply out of the kindness of her heart, the care home manager agreed to a one-month term and created a new contract just for Pearl.

During her stay, Pearl was cared for so well by AdvantAGE Assist employees that at the end of the month, she decided to sell her house and move into the care home permanently. Had the care home manager demonstrated low accountability, she would have said something like, "Sorry, it's not our policy," and turned Pearl away. However, because she decided to own the results, the care home manager helped a person in need, added some quick and easy money to her company's bottom line, and invented an entirely new revenue stream. This is how you own the results!

Some problems are unique and only require a desire to own the results and the creativity and know-how to find a solution. However, an engineered solution exists for many, if not most, of our people-related problems. We just need to look for it instead of focusing on fixing people.

More often than not, the one-off problems that you need to troubleshoot will reoccur in some form in the future. After you troubleshoot your one-off problems, ask yourself what you learned, what you can do to prevent the problem from happening again, and how you can implement the solution in a simpler, more efficient manner next time. This is how you can pivot from owning the results of a problem to engineering a solution.

In the case of AdvantAGE Assist, the practice of renting a room for a month has now become a standard procedure. Pearl's contract became the template for such arrangements. The "engineering" in this case was simply: a) informing staff that they are able to accommodate such requests from now on, b) changing the sales process, c) creating a temporary resident rental agreement template, and d) saving it in an easily retrievable location.

Engineering solutions is not just for the workplace. Problems are all around us and provide us with ample opportunity to engineer the solution in any area of life. When constructing our home, we had cabinets built to hold the stereo equipment for the large-screen TV in our front room. One of the cabinets holds the amplifier, which, we discovered, gets extremely hot when the cabinet door is closed. This presents a problem. If someone forgets to turn off the amplifier after watching TV, it could overheat, which could break it, and there is a chance it could even set the cabinet on fire.

Habit 3 – Engineer the Solution

Of course, my initial remedy was a person-centered solution. For several months I regularly reminded everyone to keep the cabinet door open while watching TV and make sure to turn off the amplifier after watching TV. When my wife or kids inevitably forgot to leave the door open, I would remind them to "be more careful." In essence, I expected everyone to remember to behave differently with this stereo equipment because my design oversight created a hazard. Several months later after numerous supposed "human error" incidents, I finally decided to engineer the solution and cut air vents in the side of the cabinet!

Remember, any time you hear or think the words "be more careful," that's your cue to engineer the solution. Whether you are protecting yourself and others from physical danger or simply trying to prevent avoidable mistakes, engineering the solution can help you get the right results more reliably than trying to change human behavior.

Any time you hear or think the words "Be more careful," that's your cue to engineer the solution.

Strategies to Engineer Solutions

Engineered solutions address the root cause of problems. Person-centered solutions simply hack at the branches.

An assistant who keeps making mistakes is a problem. A manager who gets angry at her assistant and berates him every time the assistant makes a mistake is hacking at the branches. A systems approach to solving this problem requires the manager to ask, "Why does my assistant keep making mistakes?" and ignore the knee-jerk response provided by her amygdala: "Because he's an idiot." The real answer may be "Because he gets distracted" or "Because he often forgets at least one step in any given process." Now that the manager has confirmed that her assistant is a human being who makes mistakes and not a robot, then what? What can this manager do to help her assistant remember every step in every process regardless of whether he gets distracted? In this case, one strategy will address both matters. An engineered solution is to create a checklist for every process the assistant will likely repeat, then use it every time. A checklist is a simple form of a standard operating procedure (SOP). Any time you find an organization that consistently executes well, you will find an organization with well-used SOPs. In contrast to what some people may think, SOPs don't restrict creativity or ingenuity; they free the mind from having to focus on the mundane so it has the capacity to direct its attention to look for ways to improve.

Creating a checklist or SOP is just one strategy to engineer the solution. There are many ways to change the environment to produce better results. Instead of blaming others, leaders consider how they are contributing to problems and leverage the following four key strategies to engineer solutions.

1. **Make reality transparent**. Implement feedback mechanisms to help people adjust their behavior to get better results.

2. **Clarify the critical steps**. Create simple, clear, standard operating procedures for anything you want done flawlessly.

3. **Automate the right behaviors**. Establish triggers that remind people of the right thing to do.

4. **Design the environment**. Design workflows that make it easy to do the right thing and hard to do the wrong thing.

The remainder of this section explains how you can engineer the solution using those four strategies to help you achieve the right results more often.

16. Strategy 1 – Make Reality Transparent

Implement feedback mechanisms to help people adjust their behavior to get better results.

To consistently get the right results, whether in your workplace or elsewhere, you must first determine how close you are to achieving them. You need to see reality clearly if you are to accurately diagnose the problem.

In the story earlier about Mike and Chuck, did you notice that Mike was only able to diagnose the problem accurately once his fire hall implemented a records-management system? This intervention provided them with the data they needed to see reality clearly enough to identify patterns in Chuck's work performance.

As we learned in habit two, Look in the Mirror, we tend to keep ourselves in the dark about what other people think of us simply because we don't ask. We also inadvertently keep ourselves in the dark about other important information that could help us get better results. Creating transparency is a deliberate choice to make important information available and visible.

Let me share an example of what I'm talking about. For years, my least-favorite parenting responsibility was getting my kids ready and out the door in the morning for school or church.

One Sunday I was doing my regular follow-up and nagging the children while my wife was getting ready. Our church started at 10:30 a.m., and I knew we needed to be out the door by about 10:10 to take our seats five minutes before the service started. Having prodded my girls about four times in the last hour, I was nearing the end of my patience.

We live on a slope with a walk-out basement, and the girls' bedrooms are all on the bottom floor. At about 10:00, I went downstairs to tell the girls to come upstairs because we were almost ready to leave. I found my oldest daughter, age thirteen at the time, outside on the patio enjoying her hanging chair on a nice fall morning. I told her to come upstairs and put on her shoes. When I came back upstairs, I heard my middle daughter playing the piano. I gave her the same message and asked her to come and put on her shoes. "It's time to go," I said.

When I came back to our living room, there was no trace of my oldest daughter. I discovered she went back outside and was sitting in her hanging chair again. At that point I was about to lose my mind. "What are you doing?" I asked angrily. "I told you to come upstairs. We're leaving!"

"Oh," she said, "I didn't hear you."

"Get upstairs *now* and put on your shoes!" I shouted.

When I came back upstairs, I discovered that my middle daughter had, in fact, left the piano room, but she only left to ask my parents and my aunt, who were visiting, to come listen to her play a song. When I found my middle daughter back in the piano room playing for my parents and aunt, I was livid. I turned the power off the electric piano and, not wanting to make a scene in front of my parents and aunt, used my most deathly serious, barely calm dad voice and said "Get . . . your . . . shoes . . . on . . . now!"

Needless to say, it was not an enjoyable Sunday morning. We made it to church on time, but I'm pretty sure I gained a lot of gray hairs from the stress and frustration I experienced. If you have children, perhaps you can relate to this scenario.

In the moment, I felt like my children were either brain dead or purposely ignoring me to make my life miserable. When I'm thinking calmly, I know my children want to please me. They want to be treated like adults. They want to be accountable. So, why weren't they acting accountable? When I stopped to think about what went wrong that morning, I realized my children had a few disadvantages.

1. There was no clock in the main room downstairs. If they wanted to know what time it was, they had to look at their alarm clocks in their rooms, which may or may not have been facing the right way. I knew I needed to make it easier for them to know what time it was.

2. I knew the schedule of when they needed to be done breakfast, when they needed to be dressed, when their hair needed to be done, and when we needed to leave, but they didn't.

3. Although I thought I was clear that I wanted them sitting at the back door at a certain time with their shoes on, they didn't know that, which meant I hadn't communicated it well enough.

4. There were no consequences for being on time or being late. They had no reason to care about being on time.

I realized that all these factors were within my control.

After church that Sunday, I hung a giant clock on the wall of the main room downstairs. On Monday morning, I ordered a large whiteboard to hang beside the clock on which to write the morning schedule in large print. Every weekday morning for a couple of months, I set the oven timer for 7:20 to cue the girls to stop eating and begin cleaning up. (I don't have to do this any longer because it's become a habit for them.) We also held a family council about accountability and consequences. We decided that every day they were on time for school and church, they got to add fifteen minutes to their bedtime on Friday night. Every time they were late, they were deducted fifteen minutes.

Getting out the door on time in the mornings is still not a flawless process, but it happens far more often now that I've provided the conditions my daughters need to be accountable.

While this story highlights several conditions of organizational accountability (the subject of a future book), perhaps the one change that made the biggest difference was the giant clock we hung in the main room downstairs. My children weren't aware of what time it was, so they couldn't adjust their behavior accordingly. That simple environmental intervention was designed to provide my daughters with critical information so they could get the right results more often (being ready to go on time), and it worked!

There are numerous examples of how to make reality transparent in the workplace to get the right results more often.

Real-Time Work Status

One of my clients, New World Medical (NWM), is a biomedical manufacturer in California. They shared the following story with me about how they injected more transparency into their manufacturing process and how it helped them get better results more often.

Each week the NWM production team met to discuss what they produced versus what they should have produced and how much of what product they needed to produce next week. It was supposed to be a one-hour meeting, but it ended up turning into a two-hour meeting each week because they had to spend an hour and a half cleaning up the data. Production data changed every hour, but the production report was produced only once a week. By the time it was in people's hands, the data was outdated.

Outdated data was not their only problem. They also didn't have a method to track the completion of each individual's tasks. Each production employee was responsible for his or her own portion of different batches of different products. It wasn't clear when one person had completed his or her portion and when the batch was ready for the next person to work on it. Production employees derisively referred to their production data as the "production management black box."

Employees could have blamed management for not providing them with a solution. Instead, a production employee named Billy came up with a low-tech solution that worked beautifully. He brought in a large whiteboard with magnets. Each production batch was represented by a card stuck on the whiteboard under the appropriate production stage. Every time production employees completed their portion of each batch, they would move their production batch card across the white board to the next stage so everyone knew the status of the entire production process in real time. Now that they had accurate data and could track their assignments in real time, their two-hour meeting turned into a fifteen-minute meeting. But that's not all. "Now everyone can see what is happening upstream and downstream to their task," Billy said. "If a task is delayed, it's obvious to the entire team where the issue is so they can work together to mitigate the delay. This now happens spontaneously without the intervention of a supervisor."

By simply injecting more transparency into the production process, Billy and his teammates enabled themselves to take greater ownership of results. New World Medical's experience highlights an important principle of accountability: transparency makes it easier for people to take initiative with confidence.

Billy's white board intervention is essentially a physical version of the solution that project management software offers on a digital platform. A multitude of project-management software platforms are available to organize projects and assignments and to make it clear who is doing what and to what stage assignments have progressed. At Avail Leadership, we use Trello to stay informed of the status of all the assignments we are each responsible to complete. As soon as my assistant completes a portion of a project she's working on, she moves the project card to the next stage in the process. At a glance, I can see the real-time status of every project she's working on and whether she's waiting for something from me to move the project to completion.

If you aren't using some sort of project-management software to manage your assignments and the assignments of your team members, you are missing out. If cost is holding you back, many of these software platforms have a free version or a relatively inexpensive paid version.

KPI Dashboard

Key Performance Indicators (KPIs) are critical pieces of information that provide evidence of performance. Leading indicators predict future performance. Lagging indicators are historical data that show outcomes.

If you're trying to lose weight, for example, there are two key leading performance indicators: calories consumed and calories burned. Managing these well will lead to your ultimate goal of losing those unwanted extra pounds around your middle. Your weight on the scale is the lagging indicator. Until the advent of smartphones and apps like MyFitnessPal, it was extremely difficult to manage the "calories consumed" KPI. Having successfully lost weight several times, I can confirm that accurately tracking my calorie intake is strongly correlated to my weight loss success.

Before I began using MyFitnessPal, my estimate of how many calories were in one of my homemade peanut butter chocolate chip cookies, for instance, was way off. It was disheartening to learn that each of my cookies was about 350 calories. This meant that eating three cookies (which, hey, if you're going to eat one, you've got to eat three) blew through more than half of my daily calorie target! Simply becoming aware of how many calories I was eating throughout the day helped me make real-time choices about what to eat. Having this information readily available on my phone substantially improved my odds of making better eating choices.

The same principle applies at work. When people have easy access to the KPIs that matter to achieving their goals, they will make better real-time choices to help them achieve those goals. Too often, however, only senior management is aware of the organization's KPIs. In most organizations, managers only review the status of KPIs every week or month. This is a mistake.

In the case of my daughters getting out the door in the mornings on schedule, time was a KPI. I knew the time, but my daughters didn't. Without this critical piece of information, I was the only person who felt a sense of urgency in the morning. My daughters couldn't possibly meet my performance expectations without this critical piece of information.

One of my clients, Alberta Pension Services (APS), provides a great example of how to make KPIs transparent so everybody has the critical information they need to make better decisions and get better results.

APS administers the pensions for all Alberta government employees. On a number of measures, including accuracy and timeliness, their service was not up to the standards they wanted. So, they came up with an ingenious way of helping everyone focus on the most important measures of success.

The executive team asked APS's business intelligence and analytics team to come up with a way to collect all the performance data related to their KPIs and post it on monitors throughout the organization so everybody would know what was truly important and be able to decide what the priority was based on the status of each metric.

The APS dash looks like this:

KPI NAME	CURRENT	TARGET	KPI STATUS
KPI 1	95.9%	95%	+0.9%
KPI 2	93.8%	95%	-1.2%
KPI 3	98.3%	97%	+1.3%

Within a year of implementing the APS dash, they slashed file-handling time by three quarters, increased their accuracy, and reduced one quarter of their staff in their processing department (they were reassigned, not terminated).

The APS dash keeps everyone informed about key performance data, thus enabling employees to stay accountable for achieving the right results.

You don't need a business intelligence and analytics team to make reality more transparent for your department or even for you personally. Just define what success looks like and then begin measuring it and making that measurement visible to everyone who needs to know. For instance, if customer service is a key performance measure, make sure you measure it and share that metric with the whole organization.[1] An annual survey won't cut it. By the time you discover customers are unhappy with your company, it'll be too late. At the very least, you should be tracking customer service on a quarterly basis, surveying different samples of customers each quarter to avoid survey fatigue.

Feedback Mechanisms

One time when I was in Mexico on vacation, I stayed at a high-end, all-inclusive hotel. I was so impressed with the customer service I received that I asked to interview the hotel manager. She kindly obliged. The manager was a lovely lady, and she let me in on a few of their customer service secrets. One key to their exceptional service is that customer service is the most important measure they track. The owner of the resort calls twice a week to review key performance measures. The first thing he asks for, before financial data, are the customer comments from TripAdvisor and their customer survey. These comments are also shared with employees. Nothing communicates that customer service is a top priority more than sharing a regular flow of nearly real-time customer feedback. Now that's making reality transparent!

If you are in supply-chain management, are you tracking your suppliers to determine which suppliers are delivering on time and which ones are providing the best service and products? If not, why are you treating your poorest suppliers as well as your best suppliers? If you are tracking their performance, are you communicating their scorecard metrics to them so they can see where they rank among your other suppliers? By making reality transparent for suppliers, you create competitive tension. Nobody wants to be at the bottom of anyone else's list. Don't believe me? Try it and see how it affects their performance.

Habit 3 – Engineer the Solution

Google learned how to improve teamwork and cooperation by making reality transparent. One team developed a reputation for discord and antagonism. Some members refused to work with other members and would undermine their teammates by withholding resources and information. When senior management addressed it with them, they refused to hear it, each convinced it was the other person's fault.

So, Google's people operations department decided to introduce the following two-question survey to help individuals in this unruly department see reality.

1. "In the last quarter, this person helped me when I reached out to him/her."

2. "In the last quarter, this person involved me when I could have been helpful to, or was impacted by, his/her team's work."

Each member of the department was given a report that showed their ranking among their teammates. All other rankings on the report remained anonymous. Without any further intervention, the lowest-ranking team members worked to improve their teamwork skills. Within two years the entire team went from 70 percent favorable on these questions to 90 percent.[2]

If Google tried to tackle this problem using a person-centered approach, they'd probably start by sending an email to tell everybody to work together better. When that didn't work, they'd try putting teamwork posters on the wall and providing teamwork training. This is the equivalent of hacking at the branches of the problem. Engineered solutions get to the root.

As Google's experience illustrates, sharing survey data is an extremely effective way to make reality transparent.

There's a way you can leverage Google's success to improve your department's performance and reputation: create a department scorecard for your department. Here's how.

1. Ask the other departments what they need most from your department. Consolidate and simplify the list, and voila! You'll have your department's scorecard.

2. Once a quarter, send a survey to key internal customers throughout the company asking them to rate your department on each of the scorecard items.

3. Identify the consistent themes in survey responses.

4. Ask some of your key internal customers if they would form a focus group to help you figure out how to improve your performance in a few of the key areas identified in the survey.

Not only will you likely get some great ideas, the very act of asking others for feedback will elevate you and your department in their eyes. Furthermore, using survey data to highlight some friction points that others may have with your department opens up dialogue in a non-confrontational manner.

When it comes to customer service feedback, perception is reality. It doesn't matter if you think you are providing timely delivery of what your internal customers need from your department. If your customers don't feel they are receiving the expected service or deliverables from your department in a timely manner, that is the reality you need to deal with. The response to your internal customers should not simply be "Get used to disappointment." Accountability is about focusing on what you *can* do, not what you can't do. When you see themes of critical feedback from internal customers, the only question you need to ask your internal customer focus group is "How can we change this negative perception?"

When you and representatives from your department are looking at the same data that your internal customers are looking at, you're on the same team trying to find a solution. Your key internal customers will be more motivated to provide helpful feedback, and this continuous improvement meeting may provide you with an opportunity to explain some of the constraints you are under that they may be unaware of. The focus group will then serve to leverage additional brainpower from different perspectives to increase understanding and reduce perceived friction points.

Once your department has taken the brave first step to ask for feedback from other departments, senior managers may like the idea so much that they might encourage other departments to do the same. When every department is sharing performance feedback with every other department, there is no room for hidden agendas, undiscussable issues, or elephants in the room. Teamwork and cooperation are the natural results when reality becomes transparent. Dialogue replaces silent resentment and passive-aggressive provocations as everybody gets the message that they are on the same team.

Getting better performance through feedback mechanisms is not rocket science. It's an environmental intervention that works. Make reality transparent by implementing mechanisms that make feedback and improvement automatic.

Lessons Learned Debriefs

Offering a slight twist on feedback mechanisms, lessons learned debriefs take advantage of 20/20 hindsight and provide another way to make reality more transparent.

War is a high-consequence business. The US military has learned how to execute its missions with an incredibly high degree of consistency and effectiveness, but they didn't always execute consistently. After the disaster of the Vietnam War, the US Army faced a crisis. It had failed to achieve its ultimate reason for existence, success in war. As a result, Army officials set out to completely overhaul an institution that was failing to achieve the desired results.

Colin Powell credits the success of the rebuilding of the US Army after their defeat in Vietnam to a technique called the after-action review (AAR). "The goal of an AAR is to get everyone around a table to review the battle, learn what went wrong, learn what went right, and work out how to train to do better. Learning and improvement are the sole focus, not the units' success or failure in the mission. It's not a blame game."[3]

Similarly, after every mission, US Air Force pilots walk directly from their jets to the debriefing room to examine their execution and incorporate lessons learned.[4]

Teams and organizations can easily instill the rigor and discipline of military-level execution when their leaders create a tradition of implementing lessons learned debriefs. An effective lessons learned debrief asks four questions.

1. What went particularly well?

2. What can we do to make sure these things continue to happen?

3. What didn't go well?

4. What can we do to make sure these things don't happen again?

The final, and most frequently neglected, step of conducting a lessons learned debrief is to incorporate lessons that have been learned into existing procedures (or use them to create new procedures). Remember, a lesson isn't truly learned until you've changed the process to make sure good things continue to happen and to prevent mistakes from recurring. This is precisely why airline manufacturers put a publication date on all their checklists. Standard operating procedures are expected to change with time after new lessons are incorporated.[5]

Lessons learned debriefs are a proven method to increase organizational intelligence, execution, and innovation. In his book *Good to Great*, Jim Collins refers to this practice as conducting "autopsies without blame." "When you conduct autopsies without blame," Collins writes, "you go a long way toward creating a climate where the truth is heard." Doing so can have a tremendous impact on the bottom line. In fact, research has shown that companies that conduct lessons learned debriefs after new product launches average 100 percent more revenue from new products

Habit 3 – Engineer the Solution

than companies that don't regularly debrief.[6] Think about this statistic for a moment. Can you think of any other simple organizational habit that will double your revenue? Your organization simply won't learn and grow if you don't make time to extract lessons learned on a regular basis and record them in SOPs that are used regularly.

Those in leadership positions who bemoan their people's apparent inability to learn from their mistakes have no room to complain if they haven't implemented regularly scheduled lessons learned debriefs at the conclusion of every project or quarter.

When people see their current reality, they are in a much better position to improve their future. Wise leaders fix their people problems not by fixing people but by changing the environment to get the right results more often. Making reality transparent is one of the best ways to do this.

Go to AvailLeadership.com/inspire-accountability-resources to download a free Lessons Learned Debrief template.

17. Strategy 2 – Clarify the Critical Steps

Create simple, clear, standard operating procedures for anything you want done flawlessly.

What do you suppose is one of the primary reasons people fail to do what you want them to do or what they know they should do? The answer is surprisingly basic. It's not because people are inherently belligerent, don't like change, are lazy, or any of the other common person-centred amygdala-produced responses. The most common reasons why people don't do what you want them to do is because they don't know exactly what to do, or they forget to do it. It's that simple.

We Don't Know Exactly What to Do

Brothers Chip and Dan Heath are students of human behavior. They are both researchers, graduate-level professors at prestigious universities, and have coauthored a handful of best-selling books. In their smash hit *Switch: How to Change Things When Change is Hard*, the Heath brothers boil down their vast body of research into one compelling conclusion: when it comes to getting the right behaviors from people, attitude or competence is generally not the issue. The conditions they are asked to work under are the problem. In short, behavioral change is mostly about changing systems, not people.

One of the essential conditions people need to produce the right results is clarity. "If you want people to change," the Heath brothers say, "you must provide crystal-clear direction." Their advice sounds almost too simple. Besides, you may think, "I always give crystal-clear direction." And that's the *real* problem: we assume we always communicate clearly.

When we screw up, it's easy for us to point out the ambiguous direction we received from our superiors. However, when someone fails us, it's hard to notice how our poorly worded email doomed them from the beginning. That's our self-serving bias hard at work.

Every Monday morning I meet with my assistant to discuss what needs to get done that week and to make assignments. By the end of our meeting, we have both added tasks to our to-do list on Trello where we can both see and edit them. Before we end the meeting, I arrange my assistant's assignments based on priority, with the highest-priority items at the top of the list.

On one occasion I wanted my assistant to make some changes to a document and send it to a client immediately, so I put that assignment at the top of my assistant's list. I got busy and didn't check my email until close to noon. When I did, I noticed the email to the client hadn't gone out. I called my assistant to find out what the hold-up was, but I couldn't get a hold of her. Frustrated, I made the changes to the document and sent it to our client.

My assistant called me back shortly after I sent the document. "Why didn't you send that document this morning?" I asked in an annoyed tone.

"I was finishing up a top-priority assignment left over from last week," she replied. "I planned to send the document this afternoon."

The previous week's assignment was important, but I specifically told her I wanted her to send the document to my client that morning—Oh, wait a minute... whoops! That's when I remembered I didn't actually ask her to send it that morning, nor did I explain why that document needed to be sent that morning. When I put it at the top of her list, I assumed she knew that meant "immediately." I also assumed she didn't have anything else pressing that she needed to do.

Habit 3 – Engineer the Solution

My assistant failed me that morning, but who's fault was it? Mine! My lack of clear direction set her up to fail to meet my expectations.

Notwithstanding this example of poorly communicated direction to my assistant, writing instructions is a big part of my job. I teach senior management teams how to change organizational culture to get specific results. As part of these change efforts, I frequently give the entire senior management team homework assignments. It's no small feat to get twenty very busy people to take time out of their schedule to do an assignment when I'm not the one signing their paychecks. After doing this for many years, I've learned that the quality and simplicity of my instructions is directly correlated with the degree to which the senior management team completes the assignments.

Before I begin a change initiative with an organization, I often receive well-meaning warnings from their HR team cautioning me that it's next to impossible to get the senior management team to complete assignments. When I sample some emails from these HR folks, I soon learn why. Their emails to senior managers are often long, convoluted, and poorly formatted (yes, formatting matters!). Don't expect people to do what you ask them to do unless you give them simple, clear instructions.

(Check out AvailLeadership.com/inspire-accountability-resources for a guide on how to compose a crystal-clear email.)

Standard Operating Procedures Are a Mental Hack

I once read a story about a car that lost a wheel during a test drive on a major auto manufacturer's company track.[1] As you'd expect, the quality-control department conducted an investigation into the accident. It didn't take them long to determine that the reason the wheel fell off is because the lug nuts were not tight enough.

For most people, that would be the end of it. Their amygdala would kick in and say, "We need to find the idiot mechanic who put that wheel on and fire them!" Fortunately, that's not what happened. The quality-control investigator asked a few more questions.

Q: Why were the lug nuts not tight enough?
A: Because the tool was used at the wrong setting.

Q: Why was that?
A: Because the person who usually did that kind of work was sick, and someone covered for him.

Q: Why did the replacement worker not use the tool at the correct setting?
A: Because the person who was sick had not communicated that he would be sick, and the last-minute replacement worker was not properly trained for that particular procedure.

Q: How could that situation be anticipated and avoided?
A: Create a standard operating procedure for that step on the production line.

Standard operating procedures (SOPs) are one of the easiest ways to engineer a solution. An SOP is a document that describes how to complete the steps of a certain task.[2] Similarly, a checklist is used to ensure the key steps of that process are completed. A checklist can also be used as a simple SOP on its own if the "how to" is already known or obvious. With this distinction in mind, I will use the term SOP when discussing the general principle of documenting processes, and I will use the term checklist when discussing the tool that helps you adhere to your SOPs.

Checklists are among the most reliable ways to help people get the right results more often. Why? Because the primary reason people don't do what they know they should do is because our memories are far from perfect and we have too much information to keep track of at once. In other words, our mental capacity is limited and fallible. Checklists reduce the mental burden of having to remember everything and free up mental space so we can stay focused on the big picture.

"The volume and complexity of what we know," writes checklist crusader Atul Gawande, "has exceeded our individual ability to deliver its benefits correctly, safely, or reliably."[3] Our work and the world we live in overloads us with more information and options than we can handle. Our mental processing capacity is simply not powerful enough to manage all the information we need to do our jobs flawlessly.

In addition to our amygdala problem, another reason we tend to find the people closest to the mess and blame them for it is because quite often we think the people involved "should have known better." We know they knew what to do; they just didn't do it for some reason.

The answer to why people make avoidable mistakes is clear: the brain's processing capacity is limited, and concentration is an exhaustible resource.[4,5] People can only wrap their heads around so much information at once, and that limit is surprisingly low.[6] Working memory is the name given to the component of our short-term memory used to hold the information we can pay attention to at the same time. Scientists used to think our working memory limit was around seven items. More recent research shows that the most items we can consistently remember in any given list is about three or four.[7,8] That's why our phone numbers and credit card numbers are conveniently broken into three or four groups of three or four digits; it makes it easier for us to remember them.

Checklists reduce our reliance on the limited capacity of our working memory so we can save our mental capacity for more strategic thinking, such as paying attention to where we are going instead of having to focus on how to get there. Even the most respected, highly trained professionals sometimes make mistakes and poor decisions because of biological constraints. We forget things, we get tired, and we get distracted. This is part of being human.

For instance, one study found that parole judges tended to grant almost twice as many parole requests immediately after a meal break. After each meal, judges approved about 65 percent of parole requests. The approval rate dropped steadily to about zero right before the next meal break. The study's authors concluded that when judges get tired and hungry, it's easier to fall back on the default position of denying requests for parole.[9]

If the results from the parole judge study concern you, then you really don't want to know this. A 2016 study showed that doctors and nurses wash their hands less than half as often as they know they should.[10] (Let's hope that statistic has changed since COVID-19!) Handwashing has long been known to be one of the best ways to prevent infection, but doctors and nurses are human, and sometimes they either forget to wash their hands, or they are too tired to do so.

"How could they be so careless?" you may wonder. Don't judge too quickly unless you too have had someone counting the number of mistakes you make in a day when "you should have known better."

British Petroleum (BP) executive Ian Vann commented on the "you should have known better" phenomenon when he said, "I can give you a hundred examples where people made a mistake because they didn't use knowledge they already had, for every one example where we learn something that is valuable for next time."[11]

BP revolutionized oil drilling in the 1990s when they established a goal to avoid making preventable mistakes drilling "dry holes" (locations where there was no oil). By 2000, BP had an industry-leading hit rate of two out of three. They accomplished this, in part, by establishing an SOP for deciding where to drill. (It's too bad they didn't apply the same rigor to safety protocols, which might have prevented the *Deepwater Horizon* accident.)

Similar to how BP uses an SOP to assess drilling locations, Cisco Systems uses a checklist to analyze potential acquisitions.[12] Some items on their acquisition checklist include: a) Are the company's key engineers willing to relocate? b) Will we be able to sell additional services to its customer base? c) What's the plan for continuing to support the company's existing customers?

Smart, highly trained people can make bad decisions when they forget to consider all the variables. You can bet that many items on Cisco's acquisition checklist were added after examining why certain acquisitions didn't go well. Checklists ensure that you consider all the relevant information when making decisions so you can avoid blind spots in a fast-paced, complex environment.

If judges, surgeons, and business executives get sloppy and make mistakes when they should know better, you can bet we all do.

The solution to "you should have known better" problems is clear: create an SOP for anything you want done flawlessly and use the corresponding checklist every time you complete that process. Use the checklist even when you feel like you don't need to anymore, so you can save your mental processing energy for higher-level thinking.

A Checklist Ensures the Important Things Get Done

Atul Gawande is on a mission to make the world a better place by getting people to use checklists. His argument is essentially that human beings have become experts at many things, but being an expert or specialist doesn't make people perfect. Even the best of the best still make mistakes from time to time. So, why not accept that all of us occasionally make mistakes, and introduce a simple checklist to help us get the right results more consistently?

For example, the average patient requires 178 individual actions by doctors and nurses each day. Close examination has revealed that doctors and nurses are remarkably accurate, only making a mistake with one of these actions only one percent of the time. Unfortunately, even such a high degree of precision still amounts to an average of two errors per day with every patient. In medicine, as in other high-stakes industries, mistakes can be costly.

Central (intravenous) line infections are one of the most common complications in medical treatment and among the most preventable.[13, 14] At the beginning of the twenty-first century, ICUs in the United States inserted five million intravenous lines into patients. Statistics showed that after ten days, 4 percent of those lines became infected, causing complications in eighty thousand people per year. Those complications became fatal 5-28 percent of time, depending on how sick people were to begin with. That translated into four thousand to twenty-two thousand avoidable deaths each year due to central line infections.

A critical care specialist at Johns Hopkins Hospital named Peter Pronovost decided to see if a simple checklist could reduce some of these avoidable medical mistakes. So, he created a five-point checklist to prevent central line infections—basic things that everybody already knew and knew well. After a month of observing how well doctors followed each of the steps on the checklist, Pronovost discovered that doctors skipped a step more than a third of the time. So, he persuaded Johns Hopkins Hospital administration to give nurses the authority to stop doctors if they saw them skipping a step.

After a year of observing the effect of providing a checklist and giving nurses the authority to enforce it, the ten-day line-infection rate in that hospital went from 11 percent to zero! They determined that in one year this one simple checklist prevented forty-three infections, eight deaths, and saved two million dollars in costs in one hospital.[15]

Pronovost tried to persuade others to adopt his checklist, but some doctors were offended at the notion that they needed a checklist to improve their performance. Others were skeptical because it had only worked in one hospital. Recognizing he needed a larger sample size to prove that his simple checklist worked, Pronovost got a taker in 2003. The Michigan Health and Hospital Association invited him to test his central-line checklist across the state's hospitals. Within three months of launching the program, central line infections in Michigan's ICUs decreased by 66 percent. After eighteen months, Michigan's hospitals saved an estimated 175 million dollars in costs and more than 1,500 lives as a result. Not a bad return on a five-point checklist!

The more complicated the process, the more beneficial checklists become.

In 1934, the US government requested proposals from major aircraft manufacturers to build a new type of bomber that was faster, could fly longer, and could hold more bombs than previous aircraft.[16] In response, Boeing developed the mighty B-17 bomber, which was clearly superior to the designs submitted by other aircraft manufacturers.[17] It was also substantially more complicated than previous aircraft.

The competition for the Air Force contract was to be decided by a "fly off" between Boeing and the other hopeful suppliers. Boeing enlisted two of

Habit 3 – Engineer the Solution

the most accomplished test pilots available to pilot the prototype B-17 "flying fortress": Major Ployer Peter Hill and Boeing employee Les Tower. Tragically, the B-17 crashed shortly after takeoff, killing Hill and Tower and dashing Boeing's hopes of being awarded the contract.

The B-17's controls turned out to be so complicated that even the highly experienced Major Ployer Hill forgot to release the gust locks, thus causing the fatal crash. There were simply too many controls and dials in the new aircraft than the pilots could manage successfully. As one newspaper put it, the B-17 was "too much airplane for one man to fly."[18]

Would more training have prevented the crash? No! They had some of the best trained and most experienced pilots in the cockpit. No amount of training can eliminate the possibility of human error. In response to this failure, Boeing created the first documented pre-flight checklist. Once the pre-flight checklist was in place, pilots went on to fly the B-17 a total of 1.8 million miles without one accident. The US Air Force subsequently ordered close to thirteen thousand B-17s, which ultimately helped the Allies gain a decisive advantage in WWII.[19]

When things go terribly wrong, many people in leadership positions instinctively look for someone to fire and/or order more training, assuming these are the only ways to solve their people-related problems. While an appropriate amount of training is essential to perform effectively, you can't train human fallibility out of humans.

Any time you want to increase your chances of getting the right result and reduce your chances of making mistakes, a checklist can help. Checklists guard against distraction and prevent lapses in memory. As Gawande puts it, "checklists simply make big screwups less likely."[20]

Even with SOPs and checklists in place, mistakes will happen as unanticipated circumstances and problems arise. However, errors only need to occur once. Once the SOP is updated to consider that particular problem, you never have to make the same mistake again. Using a checklist to follow your SOPs is the essence of discipline and the means of consistently executing to a high standard.

SOPs Manage Complicated and Complex Processes

Most people can accept that SOPs and checklists help people manage complicated processes where there are too many actions to remember to do them all correctly 100 percent of the time, such as flying a plane. However, we live in a complex world with dynamic variables that sometimes combine to create unanticipated problems, such as building a skyscraper while accounting for geological issues, weather, changing city regulations, environmental considerations, and material deficiencies. Surely checklists can't help us with those sorts of problems, right?

Checklist expert Atul Gawande believes they can. His research reveals that checklists don't just help people manage *complicated* processes with a lot of variables to consider. Checklists can also help people manage *complex* situations where there is no "correct" way of doing things, only the "best" way to do things depending on the circumstances.

A lot of our problems come out of left field, can't be anticipated, and possibly wouldn't otherwise be a problem under different circumstances.

According to the academics, the solution to complex problems is to learn, try, and adapt.[21] However, individuals almost never have a clear line of sight to all the variables in the complex problems that besiege them. Teams, on the other hand, can manage complexity better than individuals. They do this by harnessing their collective brainpower. They share their individual perspectives, insights, and specialized knowledge with the group within the context of all the known variables and constraints before deciding how to proceed.

Gawande argues that the solution to complex problems is to schedule times for team members to come together to discuss and troubleshoot issues. In other words, you can add a few line items at key points in any SOP and checklist to bring the appropriate people together to proactively address potentially complex issues before they become unmanageable.

A good SOP, therefore, accounts for complexity by building points of contact and coordination at natural transition points within the process.

For example, when constructing a skyscraper, the schedule specifies certain times when the heads of major trades must meet to inspect certain aspects of the project, identify potential problems, and come up with solutions to mitigate those problems. Here is how one of those line items might read: "May 31 – Electrical contractors, elevator installers, and elevator engineers to test elevator cars traveling from floors 1-10, identify unacceptable variances, and develop mitigation plans as needed. Submit any required change orders by June 3."

One box on the checklist gets checked for having the meeting on May 31. Another box gets checked once all the required change orders are submitted. This is how the construction industry manages complicated processes and the complexity that emerges when weather, geological conditions, material deficiencies, and human behavior combine to produce unpredictable problems.

The medical field is also catching on to how checklists can help manage the complexity of the operating room. The World Health Organization's (WHO) "Surgical Safety Checklist" has three sections signifying the different stages of surgery: "Before induction of anesthesia," "Before skin incision," and "Before patient leaves operating room." The whole surgical team must verbally review each item together to confirm that all nineteen items on the list have been addressed by the entire team, not simply by one individual on the team. The checklist even specifies the questions each member of the team must answer, such as:

Surgeon: "What is the anticipated blood loss?"
Anesthetist: "Are there any patient-specific concerns?"
Nurse: "Are there equipment issues or any concerns?"

These questions on the Surgical Safety Checklist are included to identify and prevent potential problems before they happen. The WHO trialed their new Surgical Safety Checklist in eight hospitals located throughout the world among rich and poor countries. Within one year of implementing the checklist in these hospitals, the rate of major complications fell by 36 percent, and the mortality rate of operations fell by 47 percent.[22] This translated into preventing 158 patients from developing serious complications and saving the lives of twenty-seven people.

I have experienced the peace of mind that comes from knowing that the people I was relying on to get things right used a checklist. I recently had surgery to fix a broken clavicle after a biking accident. At various times during the forty-five minutes preceding my surgery, the nurse, surgeon, and anesthesiologist each came to see me to run through the same questions from the same checklist. They each confirmed that I was the right patient and confirmed the type of surgery I was about to receive and the location on my body that was to be operated on (my right shoulder, not my left!). Any one of those three people could have had an off day and either forget to run through the checklist or write down the wrong information. That would have been a high-impact mistake if it happened. So, they triple-check each other to eliminate any chance of error. As far as I could tell, the nurse was not offended that the surgeon double-checked her work, and the surgeon was not offended that the anesthesiologist double-checked his work.

Anywhere you find a high degree of discipline and execution, you will find current SOPs and well-used checklists. Gawande notes that even posh restaurants build team troubleshooting into their processes to ensure the highest quality of service and food. For example, a restaurant manager at a high-end Italian restaurant holds an all-hands meeting every evening before opening to expose and mitigate any potential hiccups that might occur that night.[23] Agenda items include: a) Reservation count? b) Any unusually large parties? c) Special requests or dietary concerns? d) Menu changes? e) Staffing issues? These variables are built into the process in the form of a meeting agenda. When you think about it, an agenda is simply a checklist to keep everyone on point.

Anywhere you find a high degree of discipline and execution, you will find well-used SOPs.

Habit 3 – Engineer the Solution

Things can still go awry in the kitchen, so the restaurant manager has another quality checkpoint inserted into the process. Right before the dish goes to the dining room, the head chef checks it based on pre-established criteria: a) made to order, b) presentation, c) temperature, d) smell, and e) taste. With this final check, the restaurant manager builds a second quality-assurance process into the overall process.

In the military, they call these touchpoints "briefings." One happens immediately before the mission is carried out. Another briefing occurs immediately after the mission is completed.

The pre-mission briefing reviews: a) the mission objective, b) the scenario/important context, c) weather and environment, d) threats and intelligence, e) standards of success, f) tactics and timeline, g) contingency plans, and h) final questions.[24]

The pre-mission briefing is the process the military uses to manage the extreme complexity of war.

Do you notice the common activity running through the methods by which various execution-focused organizations manage complexity? It's called a *meeting*. That's right, execution-focused organizations use meetings as a tool to manage complexity. In most organizations, meetings have a bad reputation. That's because many meetings are unfocused and poorly managed. They frequently include pointless exercises such as "ring around the table" where each person speaks in sequence to provide an update on their area of responsibility. The result is wasted time multiplied by the number of people in attendance.

On the contrary, execution-focused meetings have carefully designed agendas that are effectively checklists. Like every good checklist, meeting agendas identify the key aspects that need to be considered before it's safe to proceed. Recurring meetings provide an opportunity to refine the meeting agenda repeatedly until it becomes so sharp that it cuts all the fat off that particular meeting.

Effective meetings can serve as quality touchpoints and should be built into just about every process to ensure potential problems are anticipated and mitigated. SOPs and highly focused meetings are the key to getting consistently high-quality execution no matter how complex the environment.

Before people will become converted to the power of SOPs, they must first embrace the idea that no matter how well trained they are, and no matter how much experience they have, they are human and will, therefore, make mistakes from time to time. SOPs make mistakes less likely and help people proactively deal with complex problems.

Create Your Own SOPs

Do you want to make fewer mistakes? Do you want your team to be more execution focused? Then do the following four things.

1. **Select a standard format to access your SOPs.** At Avail Leadership, we have a shared folder labeled "SOPs" and save our SOPs as Word documents that are easy to access and edit. If you store your SOPs in various locations, people will be confused about where to look for them and won't use them.

2. **Create an SOP for anything you want to do flawlessly.** Identify repetitive activities that have high consequences. These might include activities such as hiring decisions, promotion decisions, payroll, quality assurance, shipping and delivery processes, or business acquisitions. At Avail Leadership, we have various SOPs that describe critical steps for activities such as client engagements and putting on a webinar. Our SOPs include things such as instructions, email templates, and meeting agendas. We use a corresponding checklist for each process to ensure those SOPs are followed.

3. **Regularly update SOPs by incorporating lessons learned.** An SOP will quickly become obsolete unless it is updated every time a mistake is made. Once SOPs and checklists are in place, mistakes generally happen when the SOP hasn't accounted for a

particular event or situation. Simply update the SOP every time a mistake is made (and the checklist too if needed), and you should see the degree of flawless execution increase over time.

4. **Hold people accountable for results.** This means letting them feel the impact of the results they produce by consistently addressing poor performance and praising and rewarding progress and good performance. People who resist following SOPs will soon change their tune when they see the connection between SOPs, performance, and results.

Start with Yourself

Before trying to convert others to SOPs, you must become a true disciple yourself.

I learned the value of SOPs in my personal life before I became an SOP advocate in my business. I love the outdoors and enjoy going on multiday hikes to remote wilderness locations. Packing everything you need for a four- to seven-day backpacking trip can be stressful. If I discover on the trail that I forgot to pack a waterproof/windproof jacket, the consequences can be life-threatening. By creating a checklist, I eliminate a lot of the guesswork and stress.

I have refined my backpacking pack list over the years as I have discovered which items are essential and which are not worth the weight. One time, I did, in fact, forget my waterproof jacket. It was on the pack list and I brought it out to the garage where I was packing. However, I planned to bring it in the vehicle with me, so I didn't put it in my pack. Four hours down the road when we stopped for gas, it was a little chilly, so I looked for it to put on. Only then did I realize I had forgotten to put it in the vehicle. Fortunately, I was able to find an adequate substitute at a second-hand store in the town where we stopped for gas.

When I got home from the hike, I added one last item to my backpacking checklist: "Do a final checklist review once pack is loaded in the vehicle."

Since packing for a business trip rarely has life-threatening consequences, I didn't think to create a checklist for business travel. That is, until I consistently forgot to pack my pajamas. Although not a big deal, it was annoying enough that I decided to engineer the solution and create a business travel pack list. After using it for several years, something interesting happened. I felt that I knew everything on the list and that I didn't need to use it anymore. Guess what happened? That's right, the next time I packed without using my checklist, I forgot to pack my pajamas! That was a perfect example of a time that I "should have known better" but still failed to take the right action.

We all make dumb mistakes occasionally because we are human. SOPs and checklists are the best way I know of to engineer a solution to guard against human fallibility and our mental capacity and processing limits. Remember, anywhere you find a high degree of discipline and execution, you will find well-used SOPs.

18. Strategy 3 – Automate the Right Behaviors

***Establish triggers that remind people of
the right thing to do.***

Most of us don't like to entertain the idea that external forces are controlling our behavior. That idea usually conjures up images of Ivan Pavlov conditioning dogs to salivate or B. F. Skinner training rats to pull a lever. However, much of our behavior is, in fact, in response to some sort of external stimuli. When we get in our vehicles, we only get a few seconds before a beeping sound tells us to put on our seatbelts. When we hear a text message alert, we feel an urge to glance at our phones. And we'd probably miss a lot of meetings if we didn't receive an auto reminder fifteen minutes in advance.

Most of us have a lot going on in our lives, and if we didn't have some sort of automatic reminder to trigger the right behaviors, we'd probably become pretty flaky pretty fast. Accountability is taking ownership of results and working to improve future results. The more you can automate the right behaviors, the more likely you will follow through with your commitments and intentions, thereby enhancing your reputation as a reliable person.

There are several ways you can automate the right behaviors in your life and in the lives of those you lead. Some of the best ways to do this are to create traditions, establish recurring meetings, and to set reminders.

Create Traditions

Earlier in my career I worked for a modular construction company that we'll call Canco Modular Buildings. When I first joined, it was still being run by the original owners some thirty years after the company had been established.

I was hired as their first head of HR. One of my initial tasks was to convince the owners that with three hundred employees working at three different manufacturing facilities, they needed a safety manager. The executive team told me not to bother trying because it took them two years to convince the owners to hire my position. Despite their warning, I persisted, unsuccessfully, for some time.

Canco was growing substantially and had tentatively won a major long-term contract with a large general contractor. The contract was a massive boon for the company and would provide steady work for several years. For a company that was used to having only a three-month backlog of work, the contract was a major victory.

Just before the general contractor signed the deal, they reviewed our safety record as part of their due diligence. What they found stopped the deal dead in its tracks. Canco's safety record was deplorable. To be clear, it was shockingly bad. Canco had accrued many safety problems over the years, including inconsistent reporting, inadequate personal protective equipment (PPE), no enforcement of using PPE, and poor handling of safety incidents, to name a few.

Fortunately for us, the general contractor agreed to move ahead with the contract under the provision that Canco meet certain safety targets within six months. The general contractor graciously mentored Canco to improve our safety practices and safety record. Our new customer also invited Canco executives and key employees on tours to see how they managed to maintain one of the best safety records in the industry.

Among the many things we learned from our largest client about how to achieve an impeccable safety record, one idea surprised us. Our safety tutor explained that a key to successfully implementing their safety culture was the "safety moment" tradition. At the beginning of all meetings, someone was selected to share an example of how they witnessed employees taking ownership of safety. The safety moment only took about two minutes at the beginning of each meeting, but it focused people on a crucial aspect of their work: keeping themselves and others safe. Nothing else matters if someone is seriously injured on the job.

What was the most surprising to us about this tradition is that safety moments weren't only held on site for construction workers. Our client explained that *every* meeting in their company began with a safety moment, including executive meetings, management meetings, staff meetings, and company events. The purpose of the safety moment was to a) make an unmistakable statement to staff and other stakeholders that management took safety seriously and b) to focus everyone in the company on the right behaviors.

I have never witnessed a more dramatic culture change in my life than when Canco incorporated the safety moment tradition into all of its meetings. No message from senior management was ever communicated as forcefully or received as clearly: *safety is our top priority.*

As a result, we not only met our safety targets, we exceeded them. In fact, in fairly short order, Canco went from having one of the worst safety records in the industry to one of the best. Everybody knew that safety was a top priority with senior management, but that's not all. Employees were provided a constant flow of positive examples, so they knew exactly what they had to do to fit in and be successful. Employees were given both the "why" and the "how" of safety in these safety moments.

To automate the right behaviors, a trigger is required. A trigger is any event that *must* occur in a given process to initiate a mechanism to remind people to do the right thing. Starting the ignition on your vehicle triggers the beeping to remind you to put on your seatbelt. The trigger is starting the ignition. The mechanism that reminds people to do the right thing is the automatic beeping.

The trigger for the safety moment tradition was meetings—any and every meeting. Meetings, therefore, triggered the safety moment, which was the mechanism to remind people to do the right thing.

As mentioned earlier, I work with many of my clients to identify predictive leadership competencies that articulate the leadership behaviors that produce the greatest positive impact on people and performance. Then we make these leadership competencies the primary criteria used to evaluate candidates for promotion to key leadership positions.

My clients establish a policy that nobody gets promoted to key leadership positions unless the executive team unanimously agrees that the candidate consistently demonstrates the organization's leadership competencies. This provides some incentive for employees to demonstrate the leadership competencies. Motivation without clarity usually leads to the wrong outcomes, so how do these organizations help their employees remember what to do? Many clients choose to incorporate a "leadership moment" tradition into their management meetings. At the beginning of every management or executive meeting, someone takes a moment to share how they have seen someone in the organization demonstrate one of their leadership competencies.

Like starting a car to go to work, the management meetings are the trigger. Like the beeping in our cars that reminds us to put on our seatbelts, the leadership moment is the mechanism to remind people of the highest impact leadership behaviors in that particular organization.

Another corporate tradition I have witnessed that produces tangible results occurred on a flight from Winnipeg, Canada, to Calgary. I was sitting in row two reading a book on my phone while the passengers boarded. I noticed several business executives file through the cabin door, one after another. The man sitting next to me noticed the people filing in and then waved excitedly to the next gentlemen who walked on the plane and said, "Hi, Ed, nice to see you again." Ed greeted him warmly, then walked past me and took a seat somewhere around row six. The fellow next to me leaned over and explained that the man who just walked by

Habit 3 – Engineer the Solution

was Ed Sims, CEO of WestJet, the airline we were flying. WestJet is a Canadian airline modeled after Southwest airlines.

The gentleman seated beside me said that he and several other frequent flyers were invited to meet with WestJet's executive team to give them feedback on WestJet's frequent-flyer program. Sims and some of the executives happened to be catching the same flight back. I thought that was pretty neat and then promptly went back to reading my book. Within a few minutes, my reading was interrupted by the unusual excitement I felt from fellow passengers as the flight attendant read the announcements. When I looked up, I noticed it wasn't the flight attendant reading the announcements; it was Ed Sims on the mic. When the plane was in the air, Sims was back up at the front of the cabin donning an apron over his business attire. Before I knew it, he was serving me my drink!

Later, I learned that this is a tradition among WestJet executives. When they fly, they usually fly coach, and quite often they help frontline staff with their tasks.

Having never seen firsthand this demonstration of humility and pragmatism from the CEO of a major company, I asked some WestJet employees why they think WestJet executives do this. This is what a former WestJet employee told me.

WestJet executives established this tradition for a few reasons:

a) So that they know what it's like to be a frontline employee.

b) To show their support and appreciation to the frontline employees—to show that they matter.

c) To live a moment in a guest's shoes—most of their loyal guests don't get to fly business class, so they want to experience what a typical guest experiences.

d) They don't think of themselves as "executives"; they are just another WestJetter (WestJet employee), so why should they get special privileges?

e) To speak to the guests and hear their stories, concerns, questions, etc.

> They've been doing these types of things for years—no matter who the CEO is. They do this for the same reason that all WestJetters on every flight are expected to assist in cleaning the aircraft. This includes pilots and all other WestJetters, whether they are on duty or off duty. When everybody pitches in to clean the aircraft, it demonstrates their value to 'Act like an owner' by saving money, helping reduce turnaround time, and helping other crew members. It's just the right thing to do.

Clearly, this executive tradition and WestJet's culture made a strong impression on the former "WestJetter" to whom I spoke.

In this instance, the trigger for the tradition is when a WestJet executive boards a WestJet flight. The mechanism to set the right example is threefold:

1. Sit in coach.

2. Make the announcements.

3. Serve drinks and snacks to guests.

When executives do these things, it models the type of behavior they want to see in others: doing work they don't have to do to help out their teammates.

Here is a similar example. I recently spoke to the executive director of a non-profit organization who asked me to advise them on an accountability initiative they wanted to undertake. This organization had already

Habit 3 – Engineer the Solution

established a culture of "shared accountability" and was looking for my help to promote and amplify this cultural value.

"Shared accountability," the CEO said, "is where everybody believes that every role is important, and where people pitch in to help their colleagues regardless of their place in the hierarchy." Not surprisingly, one of the ways they established a culture of shared accountability was by implementing a simple tradition. Each month, every member of the senior management team takes a one-hour shift at reception. This straightforward act of service sends a far clearer message about how senior managers feel about shared accountability than any speech or motivational poster could. It also provides employees with a model to emulate.

The trigger for this tradition is the email sent to the senior managers by the CEO's executive assistant reminding them to schedule their shift. The mechanism to encourage the right behaviors is the humble calendar. Even if senior managers forget to look at their calendars, they will receive an automated reminder fifteen minutes before their shift.

Just like in the WestJet example, this tradition is impactful because it involves a small but visible sacrifice of time and convenience. While many executives believe their position exempts them from performing mundane tasks and making sacrifices, true leaders demonstrate that shared accountability starts with them, and it often involves making small sacrifices for the benefit of others.

Many business leaders would love to see their employees act more like owners, but most executives and managers don't notice how, by eschewing work outside their normal scope, they reinforce the opposite behavior in those they lead.

A clerical employee at a medical office once told me that her boss frequently complained that his staff members don't take enough ownership of workplace problems. "He got mad at us one day for not taking the initiative to put a box away that had been sitting by the back door all morning," she said. "But this same manager walked past that box *five times* without picking it up. Why should we take ownership of the little things when he doesn't?"

This employee's boss made it clear to his staff that he felt certain work was beneath him. When employees take note that their manager believes performing lower-status work makes one lower status, people will begin avoiding any work outside their normal job duties. WestJet executives established a tradition of service and pragmatism precisely to combat the natural tendency to allow rank to induce feelings of superiority, which leads others to demonstrate the same pretentious behavior.

Traditions help remind people of the right thing to do. When those in leadership positions observe the traditions and model the behaviors these traditions were intended to inspire, cultural norms emerge. If you want to see others take more ownership of results, establish a tradition to remind yourself to do the same, and set the right example.

A final illustration of how thoughtfully designed traditions can trigger the right behaviors is a parenting example. My good friend Steve has four daughters and no sons. Since I have three daughters and no sons, Steve and I like to joke that we specialize in girls. In addition to having four young daughters to keep him busy, Steve runs an extremely active investment business and holds an important and time-consuming responsibility in his church. His work responsibilities alone would consume his every waking moment if he allowed it.

To ensure he spends enough quality one-on-one time with his daughters, Steve has established several traditions. Besides being the primary tucker-inner at bedtime, he began having daddy-daughter dates with each of his daughters when they were all very young. About once a month, Steve asks each daughter what they would like to do just with him for about thirty to sixty minutes. When they were younger, they asked him to play Barbie dress-up or go to the playground. As they got older, they asked to go to a coffee shop for hot chocolate or to work on a project together.

By establishing the tradition of daddy-daughter dates, Steve created a mechanism to establish and maintain a safe and direct communication line with each of his children. Steve recognized that this communication line is essential if he was to have some influence on his daughters' decisions during their teenage years. Daddy-daughter dates also demonstrate to each of his girls that they are a top priority in Steve's life. How we spend our time reveals our priorities.

As Steve's other responsibilities have grown, sometimes he forgets to book his daddy-daughter dates each month. Fortunately, his girls don't let him off the hook for long. Since Steve established the tradition with them when they were younger, his daughters have come to expect regular daddy-daughter dates and will remind him if he drops the ball.

Once thoughtfully designed traditions are established, they create their own inertia. Traditions move individuals and teams to behave in the ways they want to behave in order to get the desired results more consistently.

Establish Recurring Meetings

One of the best, most underutilized tools to automate the right behaviors is a calendar. That's right; getting the right behaviors can be as simple as putting the right action on the calendar. In his landmark book, *The 7 Habits of Highly Effective People*, Stephen Covey popularized the notion that we need to focus less on urgent activities that aren't very important and focus more on important activities that are not so urgent.

In a dramatically simple yet poignant analogy of how to use calendars as an accountability tool, Covey produced a video called "Big Rocks." In this video, a woman from a live audience was invited to fit all the important things in her life, represented as big rocks, into one bucket. However, before he let her do that, Covey poured a lot of small pebbles in the bucket, representing all the small things that we must deal with on a daily basis that consume the majority of our time. The pebbles filled more than two thirds of the bucket. This poor woman was then left to try to squeeze all of the big rocks into that bucket. It was an impossible task. After allowing her to struggle in vain for a while, he suggested she consider changing her approach. When she was given the option to start again using a different bucket, she wisely chose to put the big rocks in the bucket first before pouring in the smaller rocks.

What's striking about this demonstration is that after she finished putting her big rocks into the new bucket, it looked as though the bucket was full. It seemed as if there would be no way she could pour in another two thirds worth of pebbles into the bucket. However, appearing to defy the rules of physics, she was able to fill the bucket with all of the big rocks and all the small pebbles without overflowing the bucket.

Those of us who travel a lot for work understand this seemingly magical principle well. When packing your bag, if you put the big stuff in first, you can fit more in. Managing time is the same. If you don't put the big rocks on your calendar first and religiously complete your most important tasks when scheduled to do so, you will quickly get lost in the "thick of thin things," as Covey taught.

Remember, accountability is taking ownership of results and working to improve future results. Time management is a huge part of doing both. With this in mind, consider how well you apply the principle of time management in your personal and professional life.

In my work with executive teams, I often see a lot of room for improvement. Many executives and executive teams cannot hold themselves accountable for completing critically important tasks for no other reason than they fail to put those tasks on the calendar and discipline themselves not to reschedule them. That's it!

The following three simple steps ensure the most important stuff gets done.

1. Differentiate between your most important activities and less important activities. (You can download a free activity analysis at AvailLeadership.com/inspire-accountability-resources)

2. Put important activities in your calendar (assigning enough time to complete them).

3. Do not cancel or reschedule them!

Step 3 is the most difficult step. When you identify an activity as a higher priority, and you put that activity on the calendar, it takes precedence over everything else, except in the case of illness or true emergencies.

These three steps of time management are helpful not only for you but also for anyone else who may have influence over your calendar. Discuss with your boss (and your assistant, if you have one) what the big rocks are among your responsibilities. Let them know what meetings you are willing to reschedule and what meetings you would like them not to ask you to reschedule except in cases of illness or true emergencies.

Here are a few examples of "big rock" activities that many managers, executives, and executive teams need to automate to get the right results more often.

ONE-ON-ONE MEETINGS WITH STAFF

I have yet to meet a manager who doesn't wish their staff would be more engaged and take more ownership of their work. However, I find that most managers do not schedule weekly meetings with each of their staff members to talk about the things that are important to them and help them stay accountable. Do you notice a correlation? The Gallup organization certainly does. The Gallup organization has found that employees who have regularly scheduled one-on-one meetings with their manager are three times (that's 300 percent!) more likely to be engaged than those who don't, and they also perform at a higher level.[1] The same study shows that employees who have managers who help them set and monitor performance goals are *seventeen times* (that's 1,700 percent!) more likely to be engaged.

Gallup's conclusion, and that of myself and others who study accountability and employee engagement, is that holding regularly scheduled one-on-one meetings with staff is critical to employee engagement and the ability to hold employees accountable for performance in a positive and productive way. You will not be able to hold others accountable unless you have established a regular one-on-one meeting schedule for them to report on their accountability.

STRATEGY TUNE-UPS

Executive teams almost universally agree that devising corporate strategy is very important. Consequently, most executive teams coordinate an off-site retreat for a couple of days and return to the office with a new business plan in hand. However, research has shown that by the end of the year, many, if not most, of the plans they have made are not achieved.[2] Why is that? Answer: because there is no follow-through mechanism.

Strategy expert Rich Horwath provides a simple mechanism for executive teams to hold themselves accountable to the corporate strategy they devise. Horwath suggests that executive teams schedule monthly or quarterly strategy "tune-up meetings" to review their progress and make adjustments.[3] This includes identifying any gaps between what they have accomplished to date compared to what should have been accomplished, discussing any changes in the external landscape and how those changes may affect their strategy, and making the necessary adjustments.

PEOPLE STRATEGY MEETINGS

Having written a book on succession planning, I frequently receive calls from HR executives who ask me to diagnose why succession planning isn't working in their organization. "We have certain people identified to take over certain critical positions," they say, "but when it actually comes time to fill those positions, the people we identified for those roles are rarely, if ever, selected to fill them." I hear this story all the time.

One of the questions I ask them in response is "How often does your executive team meet to discuss your organization's top internal candidates for key roles and what the executive team can do to fast-track their development?" The answer I usually hear is "Never."

In many organizations, executives get together once a year to decide which employees they think are good candidates for management positions, and that's where their succession planning ends. Executives at organizations with a world-class leadership and career-development program meet quarterly to review internal candidates for key positions. At such meetings, executives also brainstorm creative development activities for these candidates to increase the candidates' chances of being prepared to step up when the time comes.

As simple and impactful as people strategy meetings are, they only happen if the CEO has the discipline to put them on the executive team's calendar.

LESSONS LEARNED DEBRIEFS

I have already discussed the importance of lessons learned debriefs and how to conduct them (refer to "Lessons Learned Debriefs" under "Make Reality Transparent"). These won't happen unless you make them a tradition and put them on the calendar. Here is how to weave lessons learned debriefs into the fabric of your culture.

Establish a trigger. I suggest scheduling a lessons learned debrief following every project, after every quarter, or both. The meeting becomes the mechanism to remind people to do the right thing. Lessons learned debriefs won't get off the ground if people don't know what to do when they get to the meeting, so make sure to create a lessons learned debrief agenda to clarify the critical steps. The agenda should include a reminder to incorporate lessons learned into the appropriate SOP.

Remember, a lesson isn't truly learned until you've incorporated that lesson into an SOP to make sure good things continue to happen and to prevent mistakes from recurring.

The humble calendar is among the most effective accountability tools ever invented. When used effectively, it allows people to accomplish the most important things in life and achieve the right results more often.

Provide Follow-up Reminders

When discussing organizational accountability with executives, I commonly hear them complain that follow-through on assignments is inconsistent. For instance, when a VP of sales asked her branch managers to solicit some specific feedback from key clients, few got back to her with the requested data. Of the handful of branch managers who did send her some data, most provided incomplete or vague responses from key clients.

I hear stories like this all the time from frustrated executives.

Now think for a moment, is there anything this VP of sales could have done to improve her odds of getting the right results? Accountable leaders follow the three habits of personal accountability and look in the mirror to see what they can do differently to produce better results.

Here is a simple rule that helps me obtain the right results more often when I give assignments to busy people:

**If you want someone to do something for you,
make it as easy as possible for them to fulfill your request.**

Scheduling yourself (or asking your assistant) to send a reminder to people on an important assignment is a simple way to improve your odds of getting the right results. If you think you shouldn't have to send people reminders, let me ask you this: how's that assumption working out for you? Scheduling reminders is one of many ways you can automate the right behaviors to help you and others get the right results more often.

Most of us use meeting reminders to make sure we don't miss meetings we have committed to attend. Some of us use the reminders function on our phones to prompt us to pick up the groceries on our way home from work. I even use reminders to make sure I don't set the house on fire. When I finish using the barbeque, I turn the heat up full blast for five minutes to incinerate food particles on the grill and sanitize it for the next use. On more than one occasion, I've forgotten to turn it off after five minutes. Consequently, I now set the timer on my phone for five minutes immediately before I crank up the barbeque dial.

Habit 3 – Engineer the Solution

Similarly, anyone in sales should be using the follow-up feature in their customer relationship management (CRM) application. For example, I use an app called Pipedrive. Every time I make a change to a client's record, I receive a prompt to schedule another action. The program is essentially saying, "When are you going to follow up with them next?" This automated feature makes it far less likely that I will drop the ball and let prospective clients slip through the cracks.

You most likely already use reminders to help you automate the right behaviors in many areas of your life, but you can extend this accountability tool even further.

Google's People Operations Department learned that adding an automated email reminder to an existing process can make a big difference. New hires at Google are encouraged to onboard themselves by taking the initiative to learn their team's names, schedule one-on-one meetings with their managers, and actively solicit feedback. As an experiment, a sample group of new hires was provided with an extra fifteen-minute segment of their new-hire orientation to explain five specific actions they could take to onboard themselves. Two weeks later they received a follow-up email reminding them of those five actions.

The result? New hires who received the extra training and follow-up email were more likely to take the actions and became about 5–10 percent more productive in their first three months on the job than those who didn't. Google calculated the savings of the productivity gain and discovered that the additional fifteen minutes of orientation and the email reminder increased productivity for the whole workforce by 2 percent.[4]

By clarifying the critical steps and automating the right behaviors though a reminder email, Google made it easier for new hires to do the right thing, and both the new hires and the company benefitted.

Now, there's a critical difference between an automated reminder and being nagged to death by a micromanager. The difference is this:

> A reminder is scheduled and expected.
> Nagging is unscheduled and unexpected.

Most of us need reminders to keep the important things on our radar screens. When I give an assignment to an executive team to complete before I meet with them again, I do two things to improve the odds of them completing it. First, after showing them the assignment on a PowerPoint slide and verbally explaining it to them, I tell them that I will email them the assignment and that I will send a follow-up reminder about completing the assignment. Then I make sure to send them the initial email that evening or the next morning and a follow-up reminder a few days before we meet again. If it is a few weeks between the time I give them the assignment and when I meet with them again, they will likely receive two follow-up reminders from me. When I delegate an assignment that is particularly important to me, I make it as easy as possible for people to fulfil my request.

Reminders are a simple and effective way to automate follow-up and improve follow-through.

Engineering the solution means creating environmental interventions to help you get the right results more often. Leaders who understand accountability get the right results more often because they automate the right behaviors by creating traditions, establishing highly focused recurring meetings, and taking advantage of follow-up reminders.

19. Strategy 4 – Design the Environment

Design workflows that make it easy to do the right thing and hard to do the wrong thing.

It has long been known that larger plates and packaging lead to overeating.[1] Studies have consistently shown that whether people are offered a medium or large bucket of popcorn, bag of M&Ms, or box of pasta to cook, people unwittingly eat 20 to 50 percent more when offered food in the larger packages.[2, 3, 4] Intuitively, we know this is true. Give me a bag of chips when I'm watching a movie at home, and surprise, surprise, the bag is empty when the lights are turned back on. However, when I pour an appropriate portion of chips into a bowl, I eat far fewer chips. This is because when the chips are in the bowl, I have a greater ability to control the portion size. It also means I'd have to stop the movie to go to the kitchen to refill the bowl.

Anybody who's tried to lose weight knows that a poorly designed environment can lead to bad choices and lousy results, whereas a cleverly designed environment can lead to better choices and results.

I'm an amateur when it comes to nutritional science and consumer behavior. Since I have no training in this area, my eating behavior is much more likely to be influenced by my surroundings than, say, PhDs who study, lecture, and write research papers on nutrition, right? That question was the subject of a *20/20* television episode in 2001.

20/20, the longstanding investigative journalism program, paid a visit to a food research lab at Cornell University to film a segment on how container sizes affect food choices. After filming wrapped, all of the distinguished professors and PhD students from the Nutritional Science Division at Cornell were invited to an ice cream social "wrap party." Except, the filming wasn't over. Unbeknownst to the party guests, the cameras continued to roll while the real experiment began.

The guests were given either a medium-size seventeen-ounce bowl or a large thirty-four-ounce bowl and invited to make their way through the buffet line of ice cream to dish themselves as much of the various kinds of ice cream as they wanted. Different size serving spoons were placed in each ice cream container too. Some were two-ounce scoops, and others were three-ounce scoops. After serving themselves, the guests completed a brief survey as their ice cream was weighed.

The result? You guessed it! Those who were given a large bowl dished themselves 31 percent more ice cream, which amounts to about 127 more calories. Those who were given a large bowl *and* a large scoop dished themselves 57 percent more ice cream than those with the smaller bowl and ice cream scoop![5] Simply changing the size of the bowl and serving scoop made a tremendous, unconscious difference in how much people scooped themselves. What's striking about this example is that the people in this study should have known better.

Our environment influences our behavior
more than we think it does.

The author of the study concluded, "We simply need to shift our surroundings to work with our lifestyle instead of against it."[6]

Three Techniques to Design Your Environment

I discussed earlier that when problems happen, our default response is to blame the people closest to the mess and tell them to be more careful

Habit 3 – Engineer the Solution

next time. However, as explained in habit two, Look in the Mirror, people are rarely the primary cause of people-related problems. Human error is most often a symptom of bad systems. In other words, *systems produce behavior.*

The Heath brothers highlighted this truth in their book, *Switch,* which is about how to change human behavior. "What looks like a people problem," they write, "is often a situation problem."[7] Armed with this knowledge, you can engineer the solutions to your problems by designing the environment to help you and your team make better choices and get the results you want more often. Here are three techniques you can use to do that:

1. **Add barriers**. Determine what you don't want to happen and then set up barriers that make it harder to make the wrong choice.

2. **Clear the path**. Determine exactly what you do want to happen and then remove potential barriers to make it easier to make the right choice.

3. **Make the wrong behavior irrelevant**. Assume that mistakes will happen and then determine how to eliminate the problem if they do.

In the following pages, I share a number of examples of how people have designed their environment to help them get the right results. I also provide a few illustrations of how people failed to do so. Let's see which of the three techniques was used, or could have been used, in each situation.

A CFO named Wendy was surprised when she received the quality and productivity numbers from a recently reengineered assembly line.[8] The company had just made a huge investment in new equipment and reorganized the assembly line to make it more efficient. Instead of seeing quality and productivity gains from these changes, the numbers fell far short of expectations. When Wendy inquired what the problem was, she learned that frontline workers believed it was management's fault. Wendy decided to go to the manufacturing floor to see the problem for herself.

Wendy went directly to an outspoken senior assembler who she knew would give it to her straight. When she asked the assembler why she thought quality and productivity had declined, the assembler pointed down the line and asked, "What do you see, Wendy?" Wendy responded that she saw the assemblers working to put things together. The assembler shook her head. "Look again." Then Wendy noticed that all the assemblers were women. "Look how high the bins of parts are compared to the height of the women," the assembler said. That's when Wendy realized the problem. The part bins were placed so high that the assemblers had to use a stepladder to reach the parts they needed. Wendy surmised that the maintenance workers, who were mostly men, must have placed the bins at their height, not the height of the women who would be using the bins.

When Wendy shared this discovery with the operations manager, he had the maintenance crew lower the bins to the assemblers' height, eliminating the need for a stepladder. As a result of Wendy's investigation, the operations manager cleared the path for the assembly workers. As expected, productivity improved immediately.

These kinds of environmental design oversights happen all the time when building or renovating hospitals and medical clinics. For instance, an MRI technologist told me that in one hospital she worked at, the MRI area was not sealed off from the rest of the medical imaging department. MRI machines use powerful magnets that can turn metallic objects into deadly projectiles. Because of the way the department was designed, other medical imaging professionals could walk right through the MRI magnetic field. If they happened to be carrying scissors, for instance, or had a medical implant, they could cause serious injury to themselves or others.

A person-approach solution would be to send an email to non-MRI medical imaging staff informing them that they must stop walking through the MRI department, effective immediately. When that didn't work, the next step would be to provide training for all non-MRI medical

Habit 3 – Engineer the Solution

imaging staff to instruct them not to walk through the MRI department or to remove all metallic objects before they did. In other words, train them to "be more careful." Of course, this training fails to consider one important fact: people are human and will make mistakes regardless of how much training they receive. The obvious way to engineer the solution was to design the environment by adding barriers, such as enclosing the MRI area and putting a door on it with a security code that only the MRI technologists knew.

A former X-ray technologist shared a similar experience while working in a newly renovated X-ray department. Before X-rays were done digitally, X-ray technologists would take X-rays on film cassettes and hand them off to another technologist to process. There were several advantages of having one technologist process the films while the other completed the prescribed series of X-rays for each patient. Not only was it more efficient, the technologist who was processing the film could flag any unclear scans and inform the technologist taking the X-rays to rescan the patient before the patient left.

At the newly renovated clinic, however, there was no doorway from the scanning room to the processing room, nor was there a pass-through window connecting the two rooms. Technologists, therefore, had to walk a fair distance to get from one room to the other, reducing their ability to communicate with each other and slowing the process considerably. Multiply that inefficiency by several hundred X-rays each day, and this clinic was not only wasting a lot of money, it was inhibiting the number of patients it could scan.

A simple and easy way to engineer the solution would be to clear the path by adding a pass-through window between the X-ray room and the film-processing room.

Grocers have long understood the principle of designing the environment to get the right results. They know that the more time people spend in their store, the more products they will see, and the more products they will buy. So, they cleverly design their stores by positioning the milk coolers at the back of the store, which contain the most perishable and frequently purchased items, such as milk and eggs. This means customers must walk past 237 other items that they wouldn't have seen had the coolers been positioned in the front of the store. By positioning essential items at the back of the store, grocers clear a path to their less-essential items. Case in point: high-margin, impulse-purchase items such as candy bars and magazines are placed by the checkout. You are more likely to purchase a brightly packaged candy bar or the magazine you're flipping through while you wait than if you walked past them on your way to the milk. Have you ever noticed that the candy rack happens to be situated at eye level for a young child? Coincidence? In both cases, grocers have cleared the path to non-essential, high-margin items.

We've seen several examples of how designing the environment can improve efficiencies in the physical movement of work, but is it possible to design an environment to solve "soft" problems, such as strained work relationships?

Take Amanda Tucker, for instance, the country manager for Nike in Vietnam.[9] Amanda traveled frequently, visiting factories throughout the region. When she was back in the office, she had to catch up on work that was piling up as well as make time to meet with her direct reports. When she was in the office, Amanda established an open-door policy, thinking this would make her staff feel she was more accessible to them. After nine months on the job, Amanda solicited feedback from her team members about her performance as a manager. She was shocked to discover that despite her effort to make herself accessible to her staff, they complained that she didn't seem to have time to talk to them. Several of her direct reports commented that Amanda had a habit of continuing to work on her computer while people were talking to her. Naturally, these people felt slighted by this behavior.

Amanda knew she needed to change this habit, but she also knew herself well enough to know that if her computer monitor was in sight when people spoke to her, she would be tempted to glance at it. Once she recognized that the layout of her office was enabling this bad habit, Amanda redesigned the environment to make it impossible for her to see her computer when people came in to talk. She moved her desk, so it no longer separated her from her guests, and added a meeting area with two small couches and a table. Now when she spoke to people who dropped by, her computer was directly behind her. She could also move to the meeting area for longer discussions. In either case, Amanda was able to give her full attention to the people who reported to her when they came to her office. Amanda cleared the path for herself to do the right thing.

This example shows that it is possible to design your environment to improve the impact you have on people *and* the impact you have on efficiencies.

If you look closely, many areas of our environment have been carefully designed to encourage us to do things that other people want us to do. Here are a few more examples of problems and how clever people engineered the solution by designing the environment to get the right results. Each example includes a common person-approach solution and a more effective environmental-design solution.

Computer Power Waste

- *Problem*: People frequently leave their computers on for long periods of time. In the past, the computing functions and monitor consumed power unnecessarily.
- *Person-approach Solution*: Put up a sign above every computer monitor in the office reminding people to turn off their computers when they are done.
- *Environmental-design Solution*: Computer companies built in a "sleep mode" that shuts off most power-consuming functions. This substantially reduces the power consumed when computers aren't being used. In essence, they made the wrong behavior irrelevant.

Increase Casino Revenue

- *Problem*: Like grocers, casino owners know that the more time people spend in a casino, the more money they will spend. How do casino owners encourage people to spend more time in the casino?

- *Person-approach Solution*: Provide promotions, incentives, and free giveaways during slow times.
- *Environmental-design Solution*: Add barriers by eliminating windows to make it easier for people to lose track of time and by designing the floor layout like a maze to obscure the exits. Clear the path by providing plenty of food and beverage options at reasonable prices, so people don't have to stop gambling when they're hungry.

Table Saw Accidents

- *Problem*: Table saws are especially dangerous because operators hold the wood being cut instead of holding the saw. This makes it easier to accidentally move hands into the spinning blade.
- *Person-approach Solution*: For over a hundred years, the primary method to keep operators safe was to provide safety training.
- *Environmental-design Solution*: Several safety features were designed for the table saw over the years, including blade guards and anti-kickback pawls, but these had drawbacks. Finally, in 1999, an amateur woodworker with a doctorate in physics designed a saw that stops in less than five milliseconds when it comes in contact with skin.[10] Simply put, he made the wrong behavior irrelevant.

Lost ATM Cards

- *Problem*: People kept forgetting to take their ATM cards out of the machine. When these people requested new ATM cards, banks had to spend time and money to reissue them.
- *Person-approach Solution*: Charge customers high fees to replace their ATM cards.
- *Environmental-design Solution*: Banks began designing ATMs so customers can't take their cash until they remove their card. In other words, they added a barrier to make the wrong behavior more difficult, if not impossible. Result: no more lost ATM cards.

Distracted Nurses While Administering Medication

- *Problem*: When nurses administer medications, they are frequently interrupted by passing doctors, nurses, or patients. These distractions can cause nurses to make unnecessary mistakes resulting in preventable medical complications and deaths.
- *Person-approach Solution*: Train the nurses to be more focused and not be so careless.
- *Environmental-design Solution*: Hospital management at Kaiser South San Francisco Hospital asked nurses to don a high-visibility vest right before they administered medication to signal to others not to distract them. Result: hospital management cleared the path to reduce medicine administration errors by 47 percent.[11]

Increase Amazon Revenue

- *Problem*: Amazon wanted people to buy more products on their website.
- *Person-approach Solution*: More advertising.
- *Environmental-design Solution*: Amazon cleared the path by making the checkout process easier with one-click purchasing.

Opportunities to engineer the solution through environmental design are all around us; we just don't usually notice them. Here's a key to identifying them. Any time you think or hear the words "be more careful" or "be more disciplined," look for an engineered solution.

Your environment is not usually designed to help you get the results you want. Sometimes your environment is designed by others to help them get you to do what they want. However, for the most part, opportunities abound for you to make your surroundings safer, more efficient, and less distracting, enabling you to make fewer mistakes and encourage others to do things that will be in their best interest and yours.

Become more aware of how your environment is influencing you so you can take control and change it to get the results you want. The next time you discover that you are not getting the results you want, look at how your environment is working against you. Then consider how you can use each environmental design tactic—clear the path, add barriers, make the wrong behavior irrelevant—to engineer the solution.

20. Engineer the Solution to Set Others up for Success

One of the primary responsibilities of leaders is to set others up for success. Far too often though, those in leadership positions do not see how they are setting others up to fail.

Here are a few common examples of how those in leadership positions set up those they lead to fail.

- Managers expect their subordinates to accept critical feedback when the managers never ask for any themselves.
- The CEO of a pizza chain berates his VP of sales for falling market share when the company forces customers to order their pizza online using a cumbersome checkout process.
- A business owner gripes about his employees who won't do simple things to help their teammates, yet he has made it crystal clear that certain work is beneath him.
- An HR executive writes an email asking managers to use the new human resources information system, expecting these managers to piece together what they are supposed to do from a four-page, poorly formatted email.
- To save money, business owners fail to supply technology that would automate certain activities and instead tell their workers to "just be careful" not to make mistakes.
- Top executives demand employees be more innovative but make no time for lessons learned debriefs.

- Parents expect their children to manage their time wisely when they don't put the clock and schedule in a place where their kids can easily see them.

Those in leadership positions who are not getting the results they want from the people they lead must first look in the mirror to see how they are contributing to the problem. Once they do, these leaders can set their people up for success by strapping on their systems-thinking hat and looking for ways to engineer the solution.

In conclusion, leaders have four key strategies at their disposal to engineer the solution.

STRATEGIES	HOW	EXAMPLES
Make Reality Transparent	Implement Feedback Mechanisms	• KPI Scoreboard • Survey Feedback • Lessons Learned Debriefs
Clarify the Critical Steps	Document the Steps of Important Tasks	• SOPs • Checklists • Meeting Agendas
Automate the Right Behaviors	Establish Triggers and Follow-up Mechanisms	• Create Traditions • Reminder Alerts • Recurring Meetings
Design the Environment	Make the Right Behaviors Easy and the Wrong Behaviors Hard.	• Simplify Workflow • Automatic Shutdowns • Add Barriers to Wrong Behaviors.

As you encounter people-related problems in your life, your approach to solving these problems can be either ennobling or degrading, uplifting or defeating. Great leaders resist the urge to blame people for mistakes and instead ask, "Where did the process break down?"

The more those in leadership positions shift from a person-centered view of problems to a systems-view of problems, the less defensive people will become, and the more willing they will be to take ownership of results and work to improve future results.

21. Putting the Three Habits Into Action

As Jocko Willink walked onto the stage to deliver his TED talk, entitled "Extreme Ownership," his imposing physical presence hinted at the strong tone of the message he was about to deliver.[1] Jocko is a former US Navy SEAL who now uses lessons he learned on the battlefield to teach corporate executives how to be better leaders. The following story that he shared in his TED talk perfectly illustrates the three habits of personal accountability when the stakes are high.

In the spring of 2006, Jocko was the commanding officer of a Navy SEAL team in charge of an operation in Ramadi, Iraq. Jocko's team was directing multiple units, including allied Iraqi soldiers, US Army operatives, and US Marines, when a horrendous firefight broke out. When the shooting began, Jocko described the chaos that ensued as "the fog of war" rolling in.

When the battle was over, and the fog of war lifted, they realized they weren't fighting the enemy; they were fighting each other, which is considered the mortal sin of combat. As a result of this friendly fire incident, one Iraqi soldier died, two more were wounded, and one SEAL was wounded. It was a miracle that more people weren't killed.

When the incident was reported up the chain of command, Jocko was ordered to shut down all operations, return to base, and prepare a debrief for the commanding officer, the master chief, and the investigating officer, who were on their way. He knew this meant someone was going to get fired.

In preparing his debrief, Jocko detailed every mistake that was made and who made it. So many things went wrong, and so many people made small errors that there was plenty of blame to go around. However, he was having a tough time deciding who was the most at fault and who deserved the most blame for this incident. After he prepared his brief, he thought, *Something doesn't seem right*. He struggled for an answer. Then about ten minutes before he was to give his debrief, the answer hit him. There was only one person to blame, and he finally knew who it was.

Armed with this knowledge, Jocko walked into the debriefing room to face his commanding officer, the master chief, the investigating officer, and his entire SEAL team, including the wounded SEAL who was wearing a bandage around his head and face.

Jocko asked the team one question: "Who's fault was this?"

One Navy SEAL raised his hand. "It was my fault," he said. "I didn't keep control of the Iraqi soldiers that I was responsible for, and they left their designated sector. That was the root of all these problems."

"No, it wasn't your fault," Jocko replied.

Another SEAL raised his hand. "It was my fault. I didn't pass our location over the radio fast enough, so no one knew what building we were in, and that's what caused all this confusion. It was my fault."

"No, it wasn't your fault either," Jocko replied.

Another SEAL raised his hand. "Boss, this was my fault. I didn't properly identify my target, and I shot and killed that friendly Iraqi soldier."

"No, it wasn't your fault either," Jocko replied. "And it wasn't yours or yours or yours," he continued, pointing to each of his teammates in the room. "There was only one person at fault and only one person to blame. And that person is me. I am the commander. I am responsible for the entire operation. As the senior man, I am responsible for every action that takes place on the battlefield. There is no one to blame but me."[2]

By resisting the urge to blame and looking in the mirror, Jocko set the stage for the real magic to occur. After promising he would make sure nothing like this ever happened again, Jocko went on to engineer the solution. He explained some new tactics, techniques, and procedures that they were going to implement to ensure their mistakes would never be repeated.

Can you see how Jocko instinctively followed the three habits of personal accountability (don't blame, look in the mirror, engineer the solution)?

The outcome? He didn't get fired. His commanding officer, who had expected excuses and finger-pointing, came to trust him even more, and his teammates didn't lose respect for him. In fact, they knew for certain that he would never throw them under the proverbial bus, even when his own career was on the line.

Have you ever experienced leadership like this? If not, try to imagine the respect you would have for someone in a leadership position who took the blame for a colossal team failure and then spelled out the lessons learned to set the team up for future success. This sequence of behaviors—don't blame, look in the mirror, and engineer the solution—is precisely what we need to see in our leaders so we will trust their leadership and feel safe to follow them.

I share Jocko's story because it is dramatic and supremely impressive. I also share his story because it brought the discrete behaviors of personal accountability sharply into focus for me as I was developing the personal accountability framework. Although the context of Jocko's application of the three habits of personal accountability may seem "extreme," to use his word, we can all become Jocko-like leaders in our own spheres of influence if we develop the same three habits.

Now that you know what the three habits of personal accountability are, you will begin to notice precisely why some people tend to garner more respect than others. A case in point is the immediate respect Dr. Anthony Fauci gained for President Joe Biden during their first meeting under Biden's leadership. Dr. Anthony Fauci is the top infectious disease expert in the US. He has advised seven US presidents and gained international attention by guiding the United States through the COVID-19 pandemic using his characteristically calm, practical, and fact-based approach. Fauci, who is a widely respected person himself, paid homage to the leadership style of the newly elected president, Joe Biden. When Biden came into office, he explained to Fauci how he planned to continue fighting COVID-19. "We're going to make some mistakes along the way." Biden said. "We're going to stumble a bit and when that happens, we're not going to blame anybody. We're just going to fix it." After recounting that conversation, a grateful Fauci said, "Boy, was that refreshing." [3]

People notice when you demonstrate personal accountability. They might not recognize exactly what you are doing that makes them admire you, but they will feel their respect for you increase as you demonstrate the three habits. More importantly, they will want to emulate you. They will feel it's safe for them to admit their own mistakes and focus on solutions instead of protecting their ego. Make it easy for others to emulate you by teaching them your formula for facing life's challenges with integrity.

Applying the Three Habits in Your Life

I had the good fortune of teaching the three habits of personal accountability to the management team of Canada's premier chocolate maker, Purdys Chocolatier. The company is based in Vancouver, BC, and has over eighty retail locations across the country that sell irresistible chocolate creations wrapped in royal-purple packaging. After teaching Purdys' top forty managers across the country the principles of developing personal accountability, I followed up with them a month later to hear what changes they had made. This is one of the many inspiring (and mouth-watering) stories I heard.

Purdys was experiencing recurring problems in the production of their decadent, hand-crafted creations. When processing the centers that go into various types of chocolates, such as caramel or ganache, operators must pour the centers onto a "slabbing table." Then they run a "plow" to flatten the center and create an even layer. The operator needs to move the plow in such a way that it produces an even distribution and the correct thickness and weight. It is a manual, labor-intensive process that tends to create unacceptable variances. When variances occurred, operators were often blamed and told to be more careful. However, the blaming and warning solution wasn't working, and the problems kept recurring.

After noticing these repeated production problems, Rachel, who is Purdys master chocolatier, decided to observe the production process firsthand. When she investigated, Rachel noticed several factors within the process that were contributing to the errors:

Problem 1: Faulty equipment. The slabbing table wasn't perfectly level, which made it difficult for operators to achieve an even distribution.

Problem 2: Improper tool. When ingredients such as nut pastes sit, the solids begin to settle in its container and the nut oil separates from the mass. Before they are used in production, they need to be remixed to ensure a uniform consistency. If the ingredients are not mixed well, the recipe will be inconsistent. Operators typically used a spatula to stir the ingredients, but this was like using a spatula to mix cement—not very effective. Obviously, a more powerful tool, a hand-mixer, would be more effective.

Problem 3: No standard operating procedure. Rachel asked each operator how they performed the plowing process. She discovered that each person had his or her own nuanced way of plowing. Some operators even stated that they had been trained the "proper way" and that they felt others were doing it incorrectly. However, the correct way couldn't be verified because there was no written process. Nobody knew for sure what the proper way was.

Solution: Rachel organized a meeting with about ten production employees and five office support staff and invited each operator to share one thing about the production process that bothered them the most. All the items were recorded on a spreadsheet that everyone could view. Each week, this continuous improvement team met to review the production issues and the status of their resolution.

By involving the production team in diagnosing the problems, they were able to find sustainable solutions. This resulted in the employees' personal buy-in to the solutions they came up with together. Establishing a weekly meeting created a communication vehicle to share best practices and clarify the process. It also created an accountability mechanism to ensure issues were followed through to solutions.

Rachel followed the three habits of personal accountability by short-circuiting the blame game and instead looking at systems issues that may have been contributing to the problem. This included looking at things that management had done or not done to cause these production problems. By taking the focus off people's mistakes and redirecting it onto process issues, Rachel and her team released the pressure on the production employees' amygdalae (defensive emotions), thereby freeing up their frontal cortices (rational capacity) to think through possible solutions.

This example illustrates accountability in action—taking ownership of results and working to improve future results.

Imagine if you had a boss like Rachel who disciplined herself to follow the three habits of personal accountability and took the time to accurately diagnose problems instead of immediately blaming the people closest to the mess. Now imagine being that type of boss. It is totally within your ability to do so, but it will take some impulse control, looking at things from a different perspective, and constant practice.

The three habits of personal accountability are tremendously powerful because they are simple and easy to memorize and because applying them consistently produces better outcomes.

Recently, I received a phone call from Hank, the COO of a financial services company who attended an accountability presentation I made to his executive peer group. "The reason I'm calling you," Hank said, "is because I've followed the three habits of personal accountability, and they work!" Hank proceeded to tell me about a time when he used the three habits of personal accountability to diffuse a potentially negative situation.

Hank received a call from the CEO, who was fuming over a serious mistake she caught in a press release written by Jared, the company's new director of public affairs. Fortunately, the CEO caught the mistake before it was published. "Is this the kind of work we can expect from Jared?" the CEO asked Hank. Now, Hank knew that Jared was a smart guy, so this kind of mistake didn't make sense. Then a lightbulb switched on in Hank's mind as he remembered the personal accountability presentation he had attended recently. Instead of silently agreeing with the CEO, he thought, *Perhaps this is a process problem.*

After a quick look, Hank discovered there was no established process for publishing press releases. If there had been, it would certainly include a checklist of quality-control items, such as who to consult and which sources of information to reference to ensure the content of press releases is accurate. Because of Hank's discovery, Jared engineered the solution to create such a checklist to ensure this type of mistake is never repeated. Possibly just as important as creating a new process to improve future results, Hank said, "Once I pointed out to the CEO that this was a process problem, it changed the entire tone and direction of the conversation. Instead of discussing whether we had made a hiring mistake, the CEO was actually excited that we figured out how to make sure she didn't have to continue being the gatekeeper on press releases."

After sharing this story, Hank recounted another situation that occurred a few days later when Hank was inclined to blame one of his VPs for not doing something the VP should have done. Then, remembering the three habits of personal accountability, Hank decided instead to engineer the solution to make it next to impossible for the VP to forget to carry out this particular responsibility again.

Following the three habits of personal accountability will not only make you a better leader, it will also make you a better person. It is an easy-to-memorize mental checklist that will keep you on the moral high road regardless of the problems you face in life. I try to walk myself mentally through the three habits every time I encounter a problem. For instance, one time I was providing a series of leadership workshops for the management team of a construction company. I had explained to the CEO and the CFO that their attendance at these workshops was crucial, or it would give licence to everyone else to miss them.

At the beginning of the second workshop, I waited patiently for everyone to stroll in and find a seat. About three minutes before we were to begin,

I noticed the CEO hadn't arrived yet. I turned to the CFO to ask if he knew where the CEO was. "Oh," he said, "he had something come up and said he would swing by in the afternoon." A flash of rage must have shot out of my eyes because the CFO's expression changed in an instant to reveal that he knew I was angry.

I collapsed back down in my chair and began to stew over what I would say to the CEO the next time I saw him. Somehow, in the middle of formulating the rant I wanted to dish out to the CEO, I remembered the three habits of personal accountability. *Don't blame*, I told myself. *There may be external factors outside of his control that are forcing his behavior.* Not really convinced that was true, and no less angry, I moved onto the second habit and looked in the mirror to see if I had done anything to contribute to the situation. *Well, I spelled out to them in the project expectations document that their attendance was critical. What else could I have done?*

After a moment of deliberation, a thought crept into my head. *Wait a minute . . . did I spell that out in the project expectations document?* That's when it hit me. Since this was a relatively new workshop series, I hadn't yet incorporated my standard practice of reviewing mutually agreed upon expectations with the project sponsors (in this case, the CEO and the CFO). I may have mentioned to them that their attendance was critical, but I couldn't be sure because I failed to send them that expectation in writing. In that moment of realization, the anger left me. Now freed from the amygdala hijack I was experiencing, my brain quickly moved to habit three: Engineer the Solution. *I need to add the project expectations step to the process for this workshop series,* I thought.

In a matter of two minutes, I walked myself through the three steps of personal accountability and managed to talk myself down from an emotional ledge. Except for the glimpse of anger that the CFO saw flash across my face, I handled myself professionally and was able to deliver a great workshop that morning.

Just before the afternoon portion began, the CEO walked in the room as if nothing had happened. I asked him why he missed the morning session. It turned out there was an accident on a job site, and an employee was injured.

The CEO immediately altered his plans at the last minute and drove to the job site to demonstrate the high priority the company placed on safety. So, an external factor *had* mitigated his otherwise unacceptable behavior after all.

There is no doubt that I am a better person and a better leader when I demonstrate the three habits of personal accountability. I am a better husband and father too. Now I know not to blame my wife or my children when something goes wrong around the house. Instead, I try to focus on the flawed processes that are contributing to the less-than-desirable outcomes. There is a strong correlation between my effort to live the three habits of personal accountability and the peace we feel at home as well as the confidence my children have in themselves and their abilities. We are also getting better at achieving the right results of having a clean kitchen, getting out the door on time, and making time for important one-on-one and family conversations.

Following the three habits of personal accountability will not only help you discover better, more sustainable solutions to your problems, doing so will also have a tremendously positive impact on those around you. This is the essence of leadership.

Leadership is not a position; it's how we choose to influence others while striving to achieve results.

Leaders elevate others to achieve a common goal. While the nuances of leadership may seem like a mystical art, leadership is much simpler, yet far more difficult, than most people imagine. However, the character you will build, the lives you will touch, and the results you will achieve as you practice the three habits of personal accountability will be well worth the effort.

Before you attempt to lead others, lead yourself by developing the three habits of personal accountability: 1) don't blame, 2) look in the mirror, and 3) engineer the solution. Developing these habits will help you create a path to a happier and more productive life for you and for those you lead.

Resources

You may access a number of free supplemental resources for this book at AvailLeadership.com/inspire-accountability-resources

About Avail Leadership

avail [uh-veyl]
verb: to be of use or value; profit; advantage

There is ample evidence that organizations are not leveraging their single greatest performance enhancing tool: leadership. Avail Leadership is a leadership development consultancy dedicated to helping organizations create cultures that produce stronger leaders and better results.

To learn about how Avail Leadership can help your organization implement the principles in this book and other principles of accountability, check out the *Creating Accountability Workshop Series* at AvailLeadership.com/creating-accountability.

AVAIL
LEADERSHIP

Acknowledgements

Thank you to my wonderful clients who invited me into their organizations and who generously shared their stories with me. In particular, thank you to Jim Puffalt, Al Bromley, and Mike Russell from the City of Moose Jaw; Lyn Krutzfeldt and Stacey Schaffer from AdvantAGE Assist; Bilal Khan and Brianna Uribes from New World Medical; Darwin Bozek and Tamara Janzen from Alberta Pension Services; and Karen Flavelle, Lawrence Eade, Paul Taylor, Janet Lee, and Rachel McKinley from Purdys Chocolatier.

I truly appreciate the opportunity I've had to present my ideas to thousands of CEOs at MacKay CEO forums and TEC Canada. They have helped me vet and refine my ideas and delivery. I especially want to thank Pat Kaiser who gave me my first break as a speaker by suggesting that I may be a good speaker for her CEO group. You really helped me launch my consulting and speaking career, Pat. I also want to thank Larry Ohlhauser who cared about me enough to give me helpful (and sometimes painful) feedback every time I spoke to one of his groups.

Thank you very much to my editors Wendy Mackinlay and Kevin Miller. Wendy did the heavy lifting of reviewing my very rough drafts, challenging my conclusions, and sharpening my thoughts. Kevin was extremely helpful with putting the professional polish on my writing and helping me come up with a marketable title after we discovered time and again that every other title we had considered was already taken!

I also want to thank, once again, all the authors and researchers who provided the raw material from which I drew my ideas. In particular, thank you to Zenger Folkman and to the Gallup organization for the valuable research you so freely share with the world. You have truly shaped the way the world now understands leadership and the influence great leaders can have. Additionally, I owe a special thank you to Colin Powell, Tasha Eurich, Atul Gawande, Chip Heath, and Dan Heath whose work I drew on repeatedly.

About the Author

Michael Timms has dedicated his career to making leadership easier and to helping leaders and organizations reach their potential. As a leadership consultant, author, and speaker, he has taught thousands of people in leadership positions how to harness the principles of accountability to transform virtually every aspect of their operations.

This is the first book in his Creating Accountability series. His previous publications include *Succession Planning That Works: The Critical Path of Leadership Development.*

Michael lives in British Columbia's Okanagan Valley with his wife and three daughters.

Endnotes

Chapter 1

1   Carolos Cândido & Sérgio Santos. "Strategy implementation: What is the failure rate?" *Journal of Management & Organization* 21 (2015): 237-262.

2   *Bridges: 20-Year Results From Surveying Strategy Implementation*, accessed Jan. 6, 2021, http://www.bridgesconsultancy.com/wp-content/uploads/2016/10/20-Years-of-Strategy-Implementation-Research-2.pdf.

3   Donald Sull et al. "Why Strategy Execution Unravels—and What to Do About It," *Harvard Business Review* (Sept. 7, 2017), accessed Jan. 6, 2021, https://hbr.org/2015/03/why-strategy-execution-unravelsand-what-to-do-about-it?referral=00060.

4   Kotter, "Failed Strategy Execution Due to Oversight by Corporate Boards?" *Forbes* (Oct. 24, 2012), accessed Jan. 6, 2021, https://www.forbes.com/sites/johnkotter/2012/10/24/failed-strategy-execution-oversight-by-corporate-boards/?sh=77803f7e3917.

5   Susan Sorenson, "How Employee Engagement Drives Growth," *Gallup* (June 20, 2013), accessed Jan. 6, 2021, https://www.gallup.com/workplace/236927/employee-engagement-drives-growth.aspx.

Chapter 2

1   Although not a direct quote, the wisdom contained in this sentence came from Dieter F. Uchtdorf in his address entitled "God Will Do Something Unimaginable," https://churchofjesuschrist.org/study/general-conference/2020/10/28uchtdorf?lang=eng.

2   Lisa Earle McLeod, "Why Millennials Keep Dumping You: An Open Letter to Management," *Forbes* (Oct. 1, 2015), accessed Jan. 6, 2021, https://www.forbes.com/sites/lisaearlemcleod/2015/10/01/why-millennials-keep-dumping-you-an-open-letter-to-management/?sh=4125833060b1.

3   "The Peter Principle Isn't Just Real, It's Costly," *NBER* (May 2018), accessed Jan. 6, 2021, https://www.nber.org/digest/may18/peter-principle-isnt-just-real-its-costly.

4   Corinne Purtill, "Your hotshot coworker would be a terrible boss, and research proves it," *Quartz at Work* (Feb. 23, 2018), accessed Jan. 6, 2021, https://qz.com/work/1212556/your-hotshot-coworker-would-be-a-terrible-boss-and-research-proves-it/.

5   Dave Sheinin, "Billy Beane is witnessing Moneyball's endgame: 'We're all valuing the same things,'" *Washington Post* (Feb. 16, 2018), accessed Jan. 6, 2021, https://www.washingtonpost.com/news/sports/wp/2018/02/16/billy-beane-is-witnessing-moneyballs-endgame-were-all-valuing-the-same-things/.

6   "Everybody, Somebody, Anybody and Nobody," *Smart Jokes*, accessed Jan. 6, 2021, https://www.smart-jokes.org/everybody-somebody-anybody-and-nobody.html.

7   Atul Gawande, *The Checklist Manifesto* (London: Picador, 2010), 103.

8   Kim Bellware, "Wells Fargo CEO Blames Multimillion-Dollar Fraud On The Lowest-Level Employees," *HuffPost US* (Sept. 14, 2016), accessed Jan. 12, 2021, https://www.huffingtonpost.ca/entry/john-stumpf-wells-fargo_n_57d87d54e4b0fbd4b7bc4c85.

9   Chris Arnold, "Former Wells Fargo Employees Describe Toxic Sales Culture, Even At HQ," *NPR*, (Oct. 4, 2016), accessed Jan. 12, 2021, https://www.npr.org/2016/10/04/496508361/former-wells-fargo-employees-describe-toxic-sales-culture-even-at-hq.

10   Chris Arnold, "Workers Say Wells Fargo Unfairly Scarred Their Careers," *NPR*, (21 Oct. 2016), accessed Jan. 12, 2021, https://www.npr.org/2016/10/21/498804659/former-wells-fargo-employees-join-class-action-lawsuit.

11   Randall Smith, "Copying Wells Fargo, Banks Try Hard Sell," *The Wall Street Journal*, (Feb. 28, 2011), accessed on Jan. 12, 2021, https://www.wsj.com/articles/SB10001424052748704430304576170702480420980.

12   E. Scott Reckard, "Wells Fargo's pressure-cooker sales culture comes at a cost," *The Los Angeles Times*, (Dec. 21, 2013), accessed Jan. 12, 2021, https://www.latimes.com/business/la-fi-wells-fargo-sale-pressure-20131222-story.html.

13   "Attorney General Shapiro Announces $575 Million 50-State Settlement with Wells Fargo Bank for Opening Unauthorized Accounts and Charging Consumers for Unnecessary Auto Insurance, Mortgage Fees." (Dec. 28, 2018), accessed Jan. 12, 2021, https://www.attorneygeneral.gov/taking-action/press-releases/

attorney-general-shapiro-announces-575-million-50-state-settlement-with-wells-fargo-bank-for-opening-unauthorized-accounts-and-charging-consumers-for-unnecessary-auto-insurance-mortgage-fees/.

14   Laura Keller, "Wells Fargo Plans to Close More Than 400 Branches Through 2018." *Bloomberg* (Jan. 13, 2017), accessed Jan. 12, 2021 https://www.bloomberg.com/news/articles/2017-01-13/wells-fargo-plans-to-close-more-than-400-branches-through-2018.

15   Matt Egon, "US government fines Wells Fargo $3 billion for its 'staggering' fake-accounts scandal," *CNN*, (Feb. 22, 2020), accessed Jan. 12, 2021, https://www.cnn.com/2020/02/21/business/wells-fargo-settlement-doj-sec/index.html.

16   "SEC Charges Former Wells Fargo Executives for Misleading Investors About Key Performance Metric," (Nov. 13, 2020), accessed Jan. 12, 2021, https://www.sec.gov/news/press-release/2020-281.

Chapter 3

1   Peter Senge, *The Fifth Discipline: The Art and Practice of the Learning Organization* (New York: Crown Business, 2006), 70.

2   Zachary Keck, "Nuclear Weapon Stockpiles: Past and Present," *The Diplomat* (Sept. 2, 2013), accessed Jan. 6, 2021, https://thediplomat.com/2013/09/nuclear-weapon-stockpiles-past-and-present/.

3   James Rogers, "This is how many nukes it would take to destroy society," *Washington Post* (June 15, 2018), accessed Jan. 6, 2021, https://nypost.com/2018/06/15/it-would-only-take-100-nuclear-weapons-to-destroy-society/.

4   "Donella Meadows," *Wikiquote,* accessed Jan. 6, 2021, https://en.wikiquote.org/w/index.php?title=Donella_Meadows&oldid=2792774.

5   Senge, 91.

6   "W. Edwards Deming," *Wikipedia,* accessed Jan. 6, 2021, from https://en.wikipedia.org/w/index.php?title=W._Edwards_Deming&oldid=984996830.

7   Editorial Inc. Staff, "Total Quality Management (TQM)," *Inc.*, accessed Jan. 6, 2021, https://www.inc.com/encyclopedia/total-quality-management-tqm.html.

8   "Appreciation for a System," *The Deming Institute* (Oct. 26, 2012), accessed Jan. 6, 2021, https://deming.org/appreciation-for-a-system/.

Chapter 4

1   Fred Kofman, *The Meaning Revolution* (Redfern, Australia: Currency, 2018).

2   My definition of leadership was inspired in part by the following quote by Ken Blanchard in his book, *The Secret*: "In reality, there are two tests of a leader. Do they get results? And do they have followers?"

3   Stephen R. Covey, *The 7 Habits of Highly Effective People: Powerful Lessons in Personal Change* (Salt Lake City: Franklin Covey, 2020).

4   Maya Angelou, "Dr. Maya Angelou Interview: Angelou on Dr. Martin Luther King Jr.'s Legacy," *Scholastic*, accessed Jan. 6, 2021, https://www.scholastic.com/teachers/videos/teaching-content/dr-maya-angelou-interview-angelou-dr-martin-luther-king-jrs-legacy/.

5   "Maya Angelou and Martin Luther King, Jr.," *Maya Angelou* (Jan. 16, 2017), accessed Jan. 6, 2021, https://www.mayaangelou.com/2017/01/16/maya-angelou-and-martin-luther-king-jr/.

6   Doris Kearns Goodwin, *Team of Rivals* (New York: Simon & Schuster, 2006).

Chapter 5

1   See "The Overuse of the 'Human Error' Explanation" for references.

2   Linda T. Kohn et al., *To Err is Human: Building a Safer Health System* (Washington, DC: National Academies Press: 2000).

3   Amy Edmondson, "Learning from Mistakes Is Easier Said Than Done: Group and Organizational Influences on the Detection and Correction of Human Error," *The Journal of Applied Behavioral Science* (1996), accessed Jan 6, 2021, https://www.researchgate.net/publication/250959492.

4   Peggy Hewitt, "Nurses' Perceptions of the Causes of Medication Errors: An Integrative Literature Review," *Libres.uncg.edu* (2010), accessed Jan. 6, 2021, https://libres.uncg.edu/ir/uncg/f/P_Hewitt_Nurses_2010.pdf.

5   Amy Arnsten et al., "Everyday Stress Can Shut Down the Brain's Chief Command Center," *Scientific American* (April 2012), accessed Jan. 6, 2021, https://www.scientificamerican.com/article/this-is-your-brain-in-meltdown/.

6   Laura Delizonna, "High-Performing Teams Need Psychological Safety. Here's How to Create It," *Harvard Business*

Review (Aug. 24, 2017), accessed Jan. 6, 2021, https://hbr.org/2017/08/high-performing-teams-need-psychological-safety-heres-how-to-create-it.

7   David Rock et al., "Kill your performance ratings," *Strategy + Business* (Aug. 8, 2014), accessed Jan. 6, 2021, https://www.strategy-business.com/article/00275?gko=c442b.

8   Amy Arnsten et al., "This is your brain in meltdown," *Scientific American*, 306(4) (Apr. 2012): 48-53, accessed Jan. 6, 2021, https://doi.org/10.1038/scientificamerican0412-48.

9   Simon Sinek, *Leaders Eat Last*. (New York: Portfolio, 2017).

Chapter 6

1   Ingrid Nembhard & Amy Edmondson, "Making It Safe: The Effects of Leader Inclusiveness and Professional Status on Psychological Safety and Improvement Efforts in Health Care Teams," *Journal of Organizational Behavior* 27 (Nov. 2006): 941-966.

2   Teresa Amabile & Steven Kramer, *The Progress Principle* (Cambridge, MA: Harvard Business Review Press, 2011).

Chapter 7

1   Brene Brown, *The power of vulnerability,* TEDxHouston (June 2010), video, https://www.ted.com/talks/brene_brown_the_power_of_vulnerability?language=en.

2   Susan Krauss Whitbourne, "5 Reasons We Play the Blame Game," *Psychology Today* (Sept. 19, 2015), accessed Jan. 6, 2021, https://www.psychologytoday.com/ca/blog/fulfillment-any-age/201509/5-reasons-we-play-the-blame-game.

3   James Reason "Human error: models and management," *BMJ* (March 18, 2000): 768–770, accessed Jan. 6, 2021, https://doi.org/10.1136/bmj.320.7237.768.

4   Richard J. Holden, "People or systems? To blame is human," *Professional Safety* 54 (12) (Dec. 2009): 34-41.

5   Sidney Dekker "The re-invention of human error," School of Aviation, Lund University (2002), accessed Jan. 6, 2021, https://citeseerx.ist.psu.edu/viewdoc/download?doi=10.1.1.522.4705&rep=rep1&type=pdf.

6   Holden, 34–41.

7   Mary R. Kwaan et al., "Incidence, patterns, and prevention of wrong-site surgery," *Arch Surg.* 141 (4) (April 2006): 353-357.

8   "Santiago de Compostela derailment," *Wikipedia*, accessed Jan. 6, 2021, https://en.wikipedia.org/w/index.php?title=Santiago_de_Compostela_derailment&oldid=986037419.

9   Steven Shorrock, "*The Use and Abuse of 'Human Error*,'" *Safetydifferently.com* (Oct. 11, 2013), accessed Jan. 6, 2021, https://safetydifferently.com/the-use-and-abuse-of-human-error/.

10   Curt Devin & Drew Griffin, "Boeing relied on single sensor for 737 Max that had been flagged 216 times to FAA," *CNN* (April 30, 2019), accessed Jan. 6, 2021, https://www.cnn.com/2019/04/30/politics/boeing-sensor-737-max-faa/index.html.

11   Mike Baker & Dominic Gates, "Lack of redundancies on Boeing 737 MAX system baffles some involved in developing the jet," *Seattle Times* (March 26, 2019), accessed Jan. 6, 2021, https://www.seattletimes.com/business/boeing-aerospace/a-lack-of-redundancies-on-737-max-system-has-baffled-even-those-who-worked-on-the-jet/.

12   Peter Robison, "Former Boeing Engineers Say Relentless Cost-Cutting Sacrificed Safety," *Bloomberg* (May 8, 2019), accessed Jan. 6, 2021, https://www.bloomberg.com/news/features/2019-05-09/former-boeing-engineers-say-relentless-cost-cutting-sacrificed-safety.

13   Ibid.

14   Ian Duncan, "Boeing 737 Max crashes were 'horrific culmination' of errors, investigators say," *Washington Post* (Sept. 16, 2020), accessed Jan. 6, 2021, https://www.washingtonpost.com/local/trafficandcommuting/boeing-737-max-crashes-were-horrific-culmination-of-errors-investigators-say/2020/09/16/72e5d226-f761-11ea-89e3-4b9efa36dc64_story.html.

15   Baker & Gates.

16   Dominic Gates, "Flawed analysis, failed oversight: How Boeing, FAA certified the suspect 737 MAX flight control system," *Seattle Times* (March 17, 2019), accessed Jan. 6, 2021, https://www.seattletimes.com/business/boeing-aerospace/failed-certification-faa-missed-safety-issues-in-the-737-max-system-implicated-in-the-lion-air-crash/.

17   For another example of how pressure from those in authority can compel employees to take safety shortcuts that lead to disaster, check out the docuseries *Challenger: The Final Flight*, released in 2020 on Netflix.

18   Dominic Gates, "How much was pilot error a factor in the Boeing 737 MAX crashes?" *Seattle Times* (May 15, 2019), accessed Jan. 6, 2021, https://www.seattletimes.com/business/boeing-aerospace/how-much-was-pilot-error-a-factor-in-the-boeing-737-max-crashes/.

Chapter 8

1   Holden, 34-41.

2   E. E. Jones & V. A. Harris, "The attribution of attitudes," *Journal of Experimental Social Psychology*, 3 (1) (1967): 1-24.

3   Holden, 34–41.

4   Dekker.

5   M. D. Alicke, "Culpable control and the psychology of blame," *Psychological Bulletin* 126 (4) (July 2000): 556-574. 6

6   Hilary Brueck, "How Human Brains Are Wired to Blame," *Fortune* (Dec. 4, 2015), accessed Jan. 6, 2021, https://fortune.com/2015/12/04/brain-wired-praise-blame/.

7   Lawrence Ngo et al. "Two Distinct Moral Mechanisms for Ascribing and Denying Intentionality," *Scientific Reports* 5 (2015), accessed Jan. 6, 2021, https://doi.org/10.1038/srep17390.

8   Anthony Wright, "Chapter 6: Limbic System: Amygdala," *Neuroscience Online* (Oct. 10, 2020), accessed Jan. 6, 2021, https://nba.uth.tmc.edu/neuroscience/m/s4/chapter06.html.

Chapter 9

1   Ben Popken, "Former Equifax CEO Blames One IT Guy for Massive Hack," *NBC News* (Oct. 5, 2017), accessed Jan. 6, 2021, https://www.nbcnews.com/business/consumer/former-equifax-ceo-blames-one-it-guy-massive-hack-n807956.

2   Christopher Zara, "The Dizzying Number Of CFPB Complaints Against Equifax Since 2012 Should Infuriate You," *Fast Company* (Sept. 18, 2017), accessed Jan. 6, 2021, https://www.fastcompany.com/40469235/the-dizzying-number-of-cfpb-complaints-against-equifax-since-2012-should-infuriate-you.

3   Krauss.

4   Colin Powell, *It Worked for Me*. (New York: Harper Perennial, 2014).

5   Edmondson, 1996.

6   Amabile & Kramer.

Chapter 10

1   "Historical mortality rates of puerperal fever," *Wikipedia*, accessed Jan. 6, 2021, from https://en.wikipedia.org/w/index.php?title=Historical_mortality_rates_of_puerperal_fever&oldid=979929160.

2   Max Roser and Hannah Ritchie, "Maternal Mortality," *Our World in Data*, accessed Jan. 6, 2021, https://ourworldindata.org/maternal-mortality.

3   Rebecca Davis, "The Doctor Who Championed Hand-Washing And Briefly Saved Lives" (Jan. 12, 2015), accessed Jan. 6, 2021, https://www.npr.org/sections/health-shots/2015/01/12/375663920/the-doctor-who-championed-hand-washing-and-saved-women-s-lives.

4   "Ignaz Semmelweis," *Wikipedia*, accessed Jan. 6, 2021, from https://en.wikipedia.org/w/index.php?title=Ignaz_Semmelweis&oldid=986797834.

5   Jason Headley, *It's Not About The Nail* (May 22, 2013), YouTube, https://www.youtube.com/watch?v=-4EDhdAHrOg.

6   Stephen Covey, *The 8th Habit* (New York: Free Press, 2005).

7   Bob Chapman and Rajendra Sisodia, *Everybody Matters* (New York: Portfolio, 2015), 39-40.

8   Ibid., 152.

9   Confidence is the belief in one's ability to accomplish a certain task. We generally gain confidence from repeatedly accomplishing a certain task successfully. Overconfidence, on the other hand, is having an unfounded or inflated belief in one's ability to accomplish a certain task. Overconfidence is usually detrimental to performance because an inaccurate view of our abilities will surely lead us to make unwise decisions.

10   Hank Rothgerber & Katie Wolsiefer, "A naturalistic study of stereotype threat in young female chess players," *Group Processes & Intergroup Relations* 17 (1) (June 25, 2013): 79-90.

11   Kate Hays et al., "Sources and Types of Confidence Identified by World Class Sport Performers," *Journal of Applied Sport Psychology* 19 (4) (2007): 434-456.

12   Ad de Jong et al., "Linking Employee Confidence to Performance: A Study of Self-Managing Service Teams," *Journal of The Academy of Marketing Science* (Oct. 1, 2006): 576-587.

13   Albert Bandura & Forest J. Jourden, "Self-Regulatory Mechanisms Governing the Impact of Social Comparison on Complex Decision Making," *Journal of Personality and Social Psychology* 60 (6) (1991): 941-951.

14   Robert M. Fulmer & J. Bernard Keys, "A conversation with Chris Argyris: the father of organizational learning," *Organizational Dynamics* 27, no. 2 (Autumn 1998): 21-32.

15   Chris Argyris, *"Skilled Incompetence," Harvard Business Review* (Sept. 1986), accessed Jan. 6, 2021, https://hbr.org/1986/09/skilled-incompetence.

16   Chris Argyris and D. Schon quoted by Peter Senge in *The Fifth Discipline*.

17   Chris Argyris, "Double Loop Learning in Organizations," *Harvard Business Review* (Sept. 1977), accessed Jan. 6, 2021, https://hbr.org/1977/09/double-loop-learning-in-organizations.

Chapter 11

1   Senge.

2   Errol Morris, "The Anosognosic's Dilemma: Something's Wrong but You'll Never Know What It Is (Part 1)," *New York Times* (June 20, 2010), accessed Jan. 6, 2021, https://opinionator.blogs.nytimes.com/2010/06/20/the-anosognosics-dilemma-1/.

3   The story of McArthur Wheeler and the connection to David Dunning's work was inspired by the talk "Lord, Is It I" by Dieter F. Uchtdorf (https://www.churchofjesuschrist.org/study/general-conference/2014/10/lord-is-it-i?lang=eng).

4   J. Kruger & D. Dunning, "Unskilled and Unaware of It: How Difficulties in Recognizing One's Own Incompetence Lead to Inflated Self-Assessments," *Journal of Personality and Social Psychology* 77, no. 6 (Dec. 1999): 1121-1134.

5   Oliver J. Sheldon et al., "Emotionally unskilled, unaware, and uninterested in learning more: Reactions to feedback about deficits in emotional intelligence." *Journal of Applied Psychology* 99, no. 1 (2014): 125-137.

6   Marshall Goldsmith and Mark Reiter, *What Got You Here Won't Get You There* (New York: Hachette Book Group, 2007).

7   Daniel H. Pink, *Drive* (New York: Riverhead Books, 2011).

8   Margarita Mayo, "The Gender Gap in Feedback and Self-Perception," *Harvard Business Review* (Aug. 31, 2016), accessed Jan. 6, 2021, https://hbr.org/2016/08/the-gender-gap-in-feedback-and-self-perception.

9   Tasha Eurich, "What Self-Awareness Really Is (and How to Cultivate It)," *Harvard Business Review* (Jan. 4, 2018), accessed Jan. 6, 2021, https://hbr.org/2018/01/what-self-awareness-really-is-and-how-to-cultivate-it.

10   Bill Benjamin, "Why Most People Lack Self-Awareness and What to Do About It," *Training* (March 18, 2019), accessed Jan. 6, 2021, https://trainingmag.com/why-most-people-lack-self-awareness-and-what-do-about-it/.

11   Thomas Gilovich, *How We Know What Isn't So* (New York: Free Press, 1993).

12   Philipp Alexander Freund and Nadine Kasten, "How Smart Do You Think You Are? A Meta-Analysis on the Validity of Self-Estimates of Cognitive Ability," *Psychological Bulletin* 138, no. 2 (2012): 296-321, accessed Jan. 6, 2021, https://doi.org/10.1037/a0026556.

13   David Dunning et al., "Why People Fail to Recognize Their Own Incompetence," *Current Directions in Psychological Science* 12, no. 3 (2003): 83-87.

14   Tomas Chamorro-Premuzic, "Why Do So Many Incompetent Men Become Leaders?" *Harvard Business Review* (Aug. 22, 2013), accessed Jan. 6, 2021, https://hbr.org/2013/08/why-do-so-many-incompetent-men. Referring to the article by Erin Stepp, "More Americans Willing to Ride in Fully Self-Driving Cars," *AAA NewsRoom* (Jan. 24, 2018), accessed Jan. 6, 2021, http://newsroom.aaa.com/2018/01/americans-willing-ride-fully-self-driving-cars.

15   Erich C. Dierdorff and Robert S. Rubin, "Research: We're Not Very Self-Aware, Especially at Work," *Harvard Business Review* (March 12, 2015), accessed Jan. 6, 2021, https://hbr.org/2015/03/research-were-not-very-self-aware-especially-at-work.

16   Tasha Eurich, *Insight* (Redfern, Australia: Redfern, 2018), 14.

17   Ibid., 145.

18   "John F. Kennedy Jr. plane crash," *Wikipedia*, accessed Jan. 6, 2021, from https://en.wikipedia.org/w/index.php?title=John_F._Kennedy_Jr._plane_crash&oldid=984529547.

19   Chamorro-Premuzic.

20   Robert Steven Kaplan, "What to Ask the Person in the Mirror," *Harvard Business Review* (Jan. 2007), accessed Jan. 6, 2012, https://hbr.org/2007/01/what-to-ask-the-person-in-the-mirror.

21   Travis Bradberry, "The Real Reason Your Boss Lacks Emotional Intelligence," *LinkedIn* (July 1, 2019), accessed Jan. 6, 2021, https://www.linkedin.com/pulse/real-reason-your-boss-lacks-emotional-intelligence-bradberry/.

22   Fabio Sala, "It's Lonely At The Top: Executives' Emotional Intelligence Self [Mis] Perceptions," *Consortium for Research on Emotional Intelligence in Organizations*, accessed Jan. 6, 2021, http://www.eiconsortium.org/pdf/executive_emotional_intelligence360.pdf.

23   Kaplan.

24   Dieter F. Uchtdorf, Dieter F., "Lord, Is It I?" accessed Jan. 6, 2021, https://www.churchofjesuschrist.org/study/general-conference/2014/10/lord-is-it-i?lang=eng.

Chapter 12

1   Joseph Folkman, "The Best Gift Leaders Can Give: Honest Feedback," *Forbes* (Dec. 19, 2013), accessed Jan. 6, 2021, https://www.forbes.com/sites/joefolkman/2013/12/19/the-best-gift-leaders-can-give-honest-feedback/#2da2dd674c2b.

2   Eurich, 172.

3   D. Druckman & R. A. Bjork (Eds.), *Learning, Remembering, Believing: Enhancing Human Performance* (Washington, BC: National Academy Press, 1994).

4   Kate Hays et. al., "Sources and Types of Confidence Identified by World Class Sport Performers," *Journal of Applied Sport Psychology* 19, no. 4 (Oct. 30, 2005): 434-456.

5   Ad de Jong et al.

6   Carol Dweck, "What Having a 'Growth Mindset' Actually Means," *Harvard Business Review* (Jan. 13, 2016, accessed Jan. 6, 2021, https://hbr.org/2016/01/what-having-a-growth-mindset-actually-means.

7   Don. Vandewalle et al., "The Influence of Goal Orientation and Self-Regulation Tactics on Sales Performance: A Longitudinal Field Test," *Journal of Applied Psychology* 84, no. 2 (April 1999): 249-259.

8   Jeni L. Burnette et al., "A Growth Mindset Intervention: Enhancing Students' Entrepreneurial Self-Efficacy and Career Development. Entrepreneurship Theory and Practice," *Entrepreneurship Theory and Practice* 44, no. 5 (Aug. 13, 2019): 878-908.

9   Carol Dweck, "The Power of Believing That You Can Improve," TED (Nov. 2014), accessed Jan. 6, 2021, https://www.ted.com/talks/carol_dweck_the_power_of_believing_that_you_can_improve?language=en#t-139022.

10   Druckman & Bjork.

11   Scott Berinato, "Negative Feedback Rarely Leads to Improvement," *Harvard Business Review* (January–February 2018), accessed Jan. 6, 2021, https://hbr.org/2018/01/negative-feedback-rarely-leads-to-improvement.

12   Bernard M. Bass, and Francis J. Yammarino, "Congruence of self and others' leadership ratings of naval officers for understanding successful performance," *Applied Psychology* 40, no. 4 (1991): 437-454.

13   Eurich, 168-169.

14   Marshall Goldsmith, "Ask This One Question And Become a Better Leader," *Inc.* (July 2014), accessed Jan. 6, 2021, https://www.inc.com/marshall-goldsmith/how-can-i-be-better.html.

15   Eurich, 210.

16   Randall Beck & Jim Harter, "Managers Account for 70% of Variance in Employee Engagement," *Gallup* (April 21, 2015), accessed Jan. 6, 2021, https://news.gallup.com/businessjournal/182792/managers-account-variance-employee-engagement.aspx.

17   Laszlo Bock, *Work Rules!* (New York: Twelve, 2015).

18   There are a number of good suggestions on how to get the most out of a multi-rater feedback tool in the following study: Frederick P. Morgeson et al., "Coming Full Circle: Using Research and Practice to Address 27 Questions About 360-Degree Feedback Programs," *Consulting Psychology Journal: Practice and Research*, 57, no. 3 (June 2005): 196-209.

19   Erich C. Dierdorff & Robert S. Rubin, "Research: We're Not Very Self-Aware, Especially at Work," *Harvard Business Review*

(March 12, 2015), accessed Jan. 6, 2021, https://hbr.org/2015/03/research-were-not-very-self-aware-especially-at-work.

20   Laurence Wood et al., "A literature review of multi-source feedback systems within and without health services, leading to 10 tips for their successful design," *Medical Teacher*, 28, no. 7 (Nov. 2008): 185-191.

21   Jack Zenger and Joe Folkman have a truckload of data on the effectiveness of multi-rater feedback and its impact on performance. Their webinar, "How Feedback Helps Us Succeed," provides a nice summary of their findings.

22   Jason M. Breslow, "Colin Powell: U.N. Speech '*Was a Great Intelligence Failure,*'" *Frontline* (May 17, 2016), accessed Jan. 6, 2021, https://www.pbs.org/wgbh/frontline/article/colin-powell-u-n-speech-was-a-great-intelligence-failure/.

23   Powell.

24   Simon Sinek, "Why good leaders make you feel safe," *TED* (March 2014), accessed Jan. 6, 2021, https://www.ted.com/talks/simon_sinek_why_good_leaders_make_you_feel_safe?language=ig.

25   Peter Bregman, "Why You Should Take the Blame," *Harvard Business Review* (April 8, 2013), accessed Jan. 6, 2021, https://hbr.org/2013/04/why-you-should-take-the-blame.html.

26   Valerie Jarrett, "Valerie Jarrett on Obama's upcoming book: 'I lived it and I still enjoyed reading,'" (Nov. 12, 2020), accessed Jan. 6, 2021, https://www.msnbc.com/andrea-mitchell-reports/watch/valerie-jarrett-on-obamas-upcoming-book-i-lived-it-and-i-still-enjoyed-reading-95798853669.

Chapter 13

1   Sabina Nawaz, "The Problem with Saying "Don't Bring Me Problems, Bring Me Solutions," *Harvard Business Review* (Sept. 1, 2017), accessed Jan. 6, 2021, https://hbr.org/2017/09/the-problem-with-saying-dont-bring-me-problems-bring-me-solutions.

2   Roger Connors, *How Did That Happen?* (New York: Portfolio, 2011), 195-196.

Chapter 14

1   Powell, 171-172.

Chapter 15

1   Michael Timms, *It's Not The Person, It's The System*, (December 2020), YouTube, https://www.youtube.com/watch?v=pb2OuHxZPC0.

2   "Stephen King," *Daily Routines,* accessed Jan. 6, 2021, https://dailyroutines.typepad.com/daily_routines/2009/01/stephen-king.html.

Chapter 16

1   There is a difference between leading indicators and lagging indicators which I will discuss in a future book. For the purposes of this book, we will focus on lagging indicators and call them "key performance measures." For more reading on the subject, see the book *The 4 Disciplines of Execution: Achieving Your Wildly Important Goals* by Chris McChesney, Sean Covey, and Jim Huling.

2   Laszlo.

3   Powell.

4   James D. Murphy, *Flawless Execution* (New York: HarperBusiness, 2006).

5   Gawande, 183-184.

6   Tom Agan, "The Secret to Lean Innovation Is Making Learning a Priority," *Harvard Business Review* (Jan. 23, 2014), accessed Jan. 6, 2021, https://hbr.org/2014/01/the-secret-to-lean-innovation-is-making-learning-a-priority.

Chapter 17

1   Murphy, 155.

2   If you want to get technical, a "process" is a high-level overview of the key steps to accomplish a task, a "procedure" breaks down an individual step of a process, and "work instructions" are an even more detailed breakdown of a procedure.

3   Gawande, 14.

4   Rene Marois & Jason Ivanoff, "Capacity limits of information processing in the brain, Trends Cognitive Sciences 9, no. 6 (June 2005): 296-305.

5   Benjamin C. Ampel et al., "Mental Work Requires Physical Energy: Self-Control Is Neither Exception nor Exceptional," *Frontiers in*

Psychology (July 5, 2018), accessed Jan. 6, 2021, https://www.frontiersin.org/articles/10.3389/fpsyg.2018.01005/full.

6   Clara Moskowitz, "Mind's Limit Found: 4 Things at Once," *LiveScience* (April 28, 2008), accessed Jan. 6, 2021, https://www.livescience.com/2493-mind-limit-4.html.

7   J. S. Saults & N. Cowan, "A central capacity limit to the simultaneous storage of visual and auditory arrays in working memory," *Journal of Experimental Psychology General*, 136, no. 4 (2007): 663-684, accessed Jan. 6, 2021, https://doi.org/10.1037/0096-3445.136.4.663.

8   People can increase their working memory capacity through focused practice, repetition, and applying mental tricks.

9   Study referenced in the book *Thinking, Fast and Slow* (p. 44) by Daniel Kahneman.

10   Julie Barzilay, "Doctors' Hand Hygiene Plummets Unless They Know They're Being Watched," *ABC News* (June 9, 2016), accessed Jan. 6, 2021, https://abcnews.go.com/Health/doctors-hand-hygiene-plummets-watched-study-finds/story?id=39737505.

11   Chip Heath & Dan Heath, *Switch* (New York: Crown, 2010), 91.

12   Ibid., 221-222.

13   "*Central Line-Associated Bloodstream Infections (CLABSI),*" *Johns Hopkins Medicine*, accessed Jan. 6, 2021, https://www.hopkinsmedicine.org/patient_safety/infection_prevention/.

14   Yazan Haddadin et al., "Central Line Associated Blood Stream Infections," *NCBI* (Dec. 14, 2020), accessed Jan. 6, 2020, https://www.ncbi.nlm.nih.gov/books/NBK430891/

15   Gawande.

16   "Boeing B-17 Flying Fortress," *Wikipedia,* accessed Jan. 6, 2021, https://en.wikipedia.org/w/index.php?title=Boeing_B-17_Flying_Fortress&oldid=987416799.

17   Ben Mulholland, "Human Error: How to Prevent Your Team From Self-Sabotaging," *Process.st* (May 25, 2018), accessed Jan. 6, 2021, https://www.process.st/human-error/.

18   Gawande, 33.

19   Ibid., 34.

20   Heath & Heath, 223.

21   Theodore Kinni, "The Critical Difference Between Complex and Complicated," *MITSloan* (June 21, 2017), accessed Jan. 6, 2021, https://sloanreview.mit.edu/article/the-critical-difference-between-complex-and-complicated/.

22   A. B. Haynes et al., "A Surgical Safety Checklist to Reduce Morbidity and Mortality in a Global Population," *New England Journal of Medicine* 360 (2009): 491-99.

23   Gawande, 80-81.

24   Murphy.

Chapter 18

1   Annamarie Mann & Ryan Darby, "Should Managers Focus on Performance or Engagement?" *Gallup* (Aug. 5, 2014), accessed Jan. 6, 2021, https://news.gallup.com/businessjournal/174197/managers-focus-performance-engagement.aspx.

2   a) Cândido & Santos, "Strategy implementation: What is the failure rate?" *Journal of Management & Organization* 21, no. 2 (Feb. 2015), 237-262; b) *Bridges: 20-Year Results From Surveying Strategy Implementation*, accessed Jan. 6, 2021, http://www.bridgesconsultancy.com/wp-content/uploads/2016/10/20-Years-of-Strategy-Implementation-Research-2.pdf; c) Donald Sull et al. "Why Strategy Execution Unravels-and What to Do About It," *Harvard Business Review* (March 2015), accessed Jan. 6, 2021, https://hbr.org/2015/03/why-strategy-execution-unravelsand-what-to-do-about-it?referral=00060 d) Kotter, "Failed Strategy Execution Due to Oversight by Corporate Boards?" *Forbes* (Oct. 24, 2012), accessed Jan. 6, 2021, https://www.forbes.com/sites/johnkotter/2012/10/24/failed-strategy-execution-oversight-by-corporate-boards/?sh=77803f7e3917.

3   Rich Horwath, *Deep Dive* (Austin: Greenleaf Book Group, 2009).

4   Laszlo.

Chapter 19

1   Medical Post staff, "Bigger plates and packaging lead to overeating, study finds," *Canadian Grocer* (Sept. 17, 2015), accessed Jan. 6, 2021, https://www.canadiangrocer.com/worth-reading/bigger-plates-and-packaging-lead-to-overeating-study-finds-57675.

2 Ibid.

3 G. J. Hollands et al., "Portion, package or tableware size for changing selection and consumption of food, alcohol and tobacco," *Cochrane Database of Systematic Reviews* (Sept. 14, 2015).

4 Brian Wansink, *Mindless Eating* (New York: Bantam, 2007).

5 Brian Wansink et al., "Ice cream illusions bowls, spoons, and self-served portion sizes," *American Journal of Preventive Medicine* 31, no. 3 (Sept. 2006): 240-243.

6 Wansink, 10.

7 Heath & Heath, 3.

8 This is a slightly modified version of a story told by Roger Connors and Tom Smith in their book *How Did That Happen?* (192-193).

9 This story was adapted from *Switch: How to Change Things When Change Is Hard* by Chip and Dan Heath.

10 "SawStop," *Wikipedia,* accessed Jan. 6, 2021, https://en.wikipedia.org/w/index.php?title=SawStop&oldid=986317023.

11 Heath & Heath.

Chapter 21

1 Jocko Willink, *Extreme Ownership,* (Oct. 16, 2018), TEDx University of Nevada, YouTube, https://www.youtube.com/watch?v=Qnr_VW-AuI4.

2 Jocko Willink & Leif Babin, *Extreme Ownership* (New York: St. Martin's Publishing Group, 2017), 27-28).

3 Jordan Fleguel, "Dr. Anthony Fauci wins $1 million Israeli prize for 'speaking truth to power'" National Post (Feb. 16, 2021), accessed Feb. 16, 2021, https://nationalpost.com/news/dr-anthony-fauci-wins-1-million-israeli-prize-for-speaking-truth-to-power.

Printed in Canada